Anticolonialism, Race and Violence in Basque Radical Nationalism (1892–1936)

Contemporary Hispanic and Lusophone Cultures

Series Editors
L. Elena Delgado, University of Illinois at Urbana-Champaign
Niamh Thornton, University of Liverpool

Series Editorial Board
Jo Labanyi, New York University
Chris Perriam, University of Manchester
Paul Julian Smith, CUNY Graduate Center

This series aims to provide a forum for new research on modern and contemporary hispanic and lusophone cultures and writing. The volumes published in Contemporary Hispanic and Lusophone Cultures reflect a wide variety of critical practices and theoretical approaches, in harmony with the intellectual, cultural and social developments that have taken place over the past few decades. All manifestations of contemporary hispanic and lusophone culture and expression are considered, including literature, cinema, popular culture, theory. The volumes in the series will participate in the wider debate on key aspects of contemporary culture.

20 Liz Harvey-Kattou, *Contested Identities in Costa Rica: Constructions of the Tico in Literature and Film*

21 Cecilia Enjuto-Rangel, Sebastiaan Faber, Pedro García-Caro, and Robert Patrick Newcomb, eds, *Transatlantic Studies: Latin America, Iberia, and Africa*

22 Ana Paula Ferreira, *Women Writing Portuguese Colonialism in Africa*

23 Esther Gimeno Ugalde, Marta Pacheco Pinto and Ângela Fernandes, eds, *Iberian and Translation Studies: Literary Contact Zones*

24 Ben Bollig, *Moving Voices: Poetry on Screen in Argentine Cinema*

25 Daniel F. Silva, *Empire Found: Racial Identities and Coloniality in Twenty-First-Century Portuguese Popular Cultures*

26 Dean Allbritton, *Feeling Sick: The Early Years of AIDS in Spain*

27 Ana Fernandez-Cebrian, *Fables of Development: Capitalism and Social Imaginaries in Spain (1950-1967)*

28 María Chouza-Calo, Esther Fernández and Jonathan Thacker, eds, *Daring Adaptations, Creative Failures and Experimental Performances in Iberian Theatre*

29 Anna Tybinko, Lamonte Aidoo and Daniel F. Silva, eds, *Migrant Frontiers: Race and Mobility in the Luso-Hispanic World*

30 Tess C. Rankin, *Feeling Strangely in Mid-Century Spanish and Latin American Women's Fiction: Gender and the Scientific Imaginary*

31 Robert Bayliss, *The Currency of Cultural Patrimony: The Spanish Golden Age*

32 Isabel M. Estrada, *Democrazy in Spain: Cinema and New Forms of Social Life (1968–2008)*

33 Ailsa Peate, *Subverting Sex, Gender, and Genre in Cuban and Mexican Detective Fiction*

Anticolonialism, Race and Violence in Basque Radical Nationalism (1892–1936)

MARIA REYES BAZTÁN

LIVERPOOL UNIVERSITY PRESS

First published 2026 by
Liverpool University Press
4 Cambridge Street
Liverpool
L69 7ZU

Copyright © 2026 Liverpool University Press

Maria Reyes Baztán has asserted her rights to be identified as the author of this book in accordance with the Copyright, Designs and Patents Act 1988.

All rights reserved. No part of this book may be reproduced, stored in a retrieval system, or transmitted, in any form or by any means, electronic, mechanical, photocopying, recording, or otherwise, without the prior written permission of the publisher.

The manufacturer's authorised representative in the EU for product safety is: Easy Access System Europe, Mustamäe tee 50, 10621 Tallinn, Estonia https://easproject.com (gpsr.requests@easproject.com)

British Library Cataloguing-in-Publication data
A British Library CIP record is available

ISBN 978-1-80596-619-7
eISBN 978-1-80596-620-3
ePub ISBN 978-1-80596-638-8

Typeset in Borges by
Carnegie Book Production, Lancaster

Contents

Acknowledgments ix

Abbreviations and Acronyms xi

Introduction 1

1. The Origins of Basque Anticolonialism: Colonial Defeat, Race and Otherness (1892–1903) 15

    The Life and Work of Sabino Arana y Goiri (1865–1903) 17

    Myths, Colonialism and Race in Sabino Arana's Thought: The Making of Basque Anticolonialism 24

    Anticolonialism or Hispanophobia? Contesting Sabino Arana's Anticolonial Claims 31

     Arana and Spain's Colonial Fronts before the '98 Disaster: The Rif, Cuba and the Philippines 33

     The Dying and Living Nations: Benevolent Colonialism after 1898 43

    Conclusion 50

2. Anticolonial Disengagement and British Exceptionalism (1903–1914) 51

    The Forging of Basque Moderates and Radicals 53

    Anticolonial Disengagement: The Conflict in Morocco and the *Semana Trágica* of 1909 57

    The Latin vs the Anglo-Saxon Races: Anti-Spanishness and British Exceptionalism 65

    Conclusion 74

3. The Re-Emergence of Anticolonialism and the Road to the Split of 1921 (1914–1921)   75
    The Triumph of Pragmatism: The CNV in the Mid-1910s   77
    'Good Colonialism' in the 'War of the Small Nationalities'   80
    The Easter Rising and the First Blow to the Theories of 'Good Colonialism'   88
    Wilsonian Fever: Euphoria, Crisis and the Re-Emergence of Basque Anticolonialism   93
    Conclusion   100

4. Towards a Global Insurrection System? International Networks, Brotherhood and Anticolonial Solidarity in the PNV-*Aberri* (1921–1923)   101
    The PNV-*Aberri*: Organisation, Composition and Rhetoric   102
    Gora Irlanda Azkatuta: Ireland's Anticolonial Example in Basque Radical Nationalism   108
    Same Oppression, Same Enemy: Basque Radical Nationalism and the Rif War   115
    The Triple Alliance of 1923: An International Insurrection System against Colonialism   124
    Conclusion   132

5. Insurgency, Radicalism and Internationalism during Miguel Primo de Rivera's Dictatorship (1923–1930)   135
    New Spaces, New Opportunities: Basque Radical Nationalism during Spain's First Dictatorship   136
    Enemies or Allies? The Struggle for International Recognition and the League of Nations   143
       Forging Direct Contacts: La Liga de las Naciones Oprimidas (1924)   143
       Seeking the Enemy's Help: Basque Appeals to the LN   149
    'To Arms!' Anticolonialism, Independence and Violence against Spanish 'Barbarism'   153
    Hispanismo vs Basqueness: Basque Radicalism and the Latin American Struggle for Independence   158
    Conclusion   163

6. 'Oppressed Peoples of the World, Unite!' Anticolonialism with a
   Purpose: Independence and Internationalism (1931–1936) 165

   Basque Nationalism during the Second Spanish Republic:
   Autonomy vs Independence 167

   'We Refuse to Talk with the Oppressor': Anticolonialism and
   Independence 171

   Euskadi: A Colony in the West 172

   Anticolonialism, Civil Disobedience and Violence 176

   Jagi-Jagi's Internationalism in a Period of Anticolonial
   Convergence: Direct Contacts and the Occupation
   of Abyssinia 180

   Racists or Anti-Racists? *Jagi-Jagi* and Its Two Approaches
   to Race 187

   Conclusion 192

Conclusion 193

Bibliography 199

Index 211

Acknowledgments

This book is for my parents, Luis and Teresa. Because the thought of being an academic, let alone writing a book and finishing it in the beautiful library of my Cambridge College, would have been unimaginable to me a few years ago. It still feels surreal, and it is thanks to the unconditional support and love my parents have given me over the years that I am here. I hope to dedicate many books to them.

This book is also for my uncle, Arturo José Chacón Cubel, who unfortunately won't be able to read it, but who has been in my thoughts ever since he left us. Now that it has been two years since he passed, I think about him with a big smile on my face, remembering the peace that his serene presence brought to us all.

There are many people who have contributed to making this book possible. First and foremost, I would like to thank my partner and best friend, Freya, who has been with me since the beginning of this project. This book could not have been written without her encouragement, reassurance and her proofreading of endless versions of the thesis and the manuscript. Thank you, Freya, for being the most loyal, supportive and selfless partner and friend one can imagine. I hope one day you will think as highly of yourself as you do of me.

Thank you to the Warwick History Department, for believing in this project and funding it between 2017 and 2021. Thank you to my supervisors, Rebecca Earle and Kirsty Hooper, whose advice has been invaluable in shaping this work. Kirsty: Thank you for all your help and guidance and for encouraging me to apply for the role of my dreams, which I now have at Girton College. Rebecca: I cannot thank you enough for your dedication and support over the years. I hope you know that your endless feedback (which scared me at the time!) continues to inspire my teaching practice today. Thank you to my external PhD examiner, Peter Anderson, for all his valuable comments and advice, which have greatly enriched this monograph.

I read somewhere on social media that the only good thing about being on a fixed-term contract is that you can cross paths with wonderful academics at different institutions. Whilst I do not seek to romanticise academic precarity in the slightest, I have been lucky enough to meet incredibly kind people at Warwick, Nottingham, Reading and Cambridge who have made my experience in each of those institutions worthwhile. I want to thank Par Kumaraswami and Tony Kapcia, for their endless warmth and kindness and for inspiring my passion for Cuban culture and history; to Ting Chang, for embodying the true spirit of solidarity and letting me stay in her house during my time in Nottingham; to Catriona McAllister, for her constant guidance and encouragement to get my book finally done (you are going to be so proud!) and to Stuart Davis, for not losing his patience despite me messaging him with constant questions, and for all the trust he has put in me. I am so lucky to have had you all as mentors and to be able to call you friends now. Thank you to all my colleagues and friends at Girton College, who have welcomed me with open arms since I joined in 2023.

To the rest of my academic friends who have made this project possible in one way or another: thank you! To Becky Hodgkinson, for her invaluable friendship and her immense help proofreading my book; to Liz Chant, for all the good times we have had since we met as I was leaving Warwick three years ago; to Alba Martínez Martínez, for those amazing two years in Oxford with her and Luis; to all my Warwick PhD friends, especially to Fabiola Creed, because she is simply brilliant and needs to know! Many thanks to Uxue Echanojauregui Ripa for her help in translating Basque sources, and to the rest of my students, who inspire me every day and confirm that I have chosen the right career.

To all my friends and family in València, Leamington Spa, Warwick, Oxford, Cambridge, and Madrid who have made this book possible: THANK YOU/GRÀCIES/GRACIAS! I hope you know who you are and how your support has helped me to give birth to this seven-year-old baby!

Maria Reyes Baztán,
Girton College, University of Cambridge
April 2025

Abbreviations and Acronyms

AC	Acció Catalana (Catalan Action)
ANV	Acción Nacionalista Vasca (Basque Nationalist Action)
CEN	Congress of European Nationalities
CNV	Comunión Nacionalista Vasca (Basque Nationalist Communion)
EAB	Emakume Abertzale Batza (Association of Nationalist Women)
EBB	Euzkadi Buru Batzar (PNV's executive committee)
EC	Estat Català (Catalan State)
ETA	Euskadi Ta Askatasuna (Basque Homeland and Freedom)
IRA	Irish Republican Army
JNB	Juventud Nacionalista de Bilbao (Bilbao's Nationalist Youth)
JVB	Juventud Vasca de Bilbao (Bilbao's Basque Youth)
LAI	League Against Imperialism
LN	League of Nations
LdNO	Liga de las Naciones Oprimidas (League of the Oppressed Nations)
PNV	Partido Nacionalista Vasco (Basque Nationalist Party)
TA	Triple Alianza (Triple Alliance)
UdN	Union des Nationalités (Union of the Nationalities)

Introduction

On 3 May 2018, the Basque armed pro-independence group Euskadi Ta Askatasuna (Basque Homeland and Freedom: henceforth ETA) announced its disbandment, putting an end to nearly 60 years of activity.[1] Since its emergence in 1959, anticolonialism made a fundamental impact on the imagination of ETA's young activists, who were not immune to the developments of 'Third-Worldism' and the decolonial struggles that followed the Second World War. Directly inspired by the wars of independence waged across the Global South, ETA initially framed its fight for Basque independence as an anticolonial struggle and believed that the only way to achieve independence was through a war of national liberation.[2] When fighting against colonialism, war became a necessity, or so ETA activists argued. This belief was key for ETA to sustain a long-lasting, violent campaign that claimed over 800 lives, as it provided a logical justification for violence. As Hannah Arendt recognised, violence 'stands in need of guidance and justification through the end it pursues'.[3]

This was not the first time anticolonial theories were applied to the Basque Country. As this book shows, since the late nineteenth century generations of Basque nationalists have regarded their fight as a struggle against colonialism. Basque nationalism emerged as Spain was about to lose its last overseas colonies. This parallel made the founder of Basque nationalism, Sabino Arana, claim that the situation of the Basques was akin to that of the Cubans and Filipinos, who were fighting against the Spanish

---

1 The organisation had announced the ending of its armed activity in 2011 and its definitive disarmament in 2017.
2 See Federico Krutwig (written under the pseudonym of Fernando Sarrailh de Ihartza), *Vasconia* (Buenos Aires: Norbait, 1963) and ETA, 'La insurrección en Euskadi', *Fondo Documental Euskal Herriko Komunistak* (1964), pp. 1–33. The latter text was written by one of ETA's founders, Julen Madariaga, and adopted by ETA in its Third Assembly (1964).
3 Hannah Arendt, *On Violence* (New York: Harcourt Brace Jovanovich, 1970), p. 17.

Empire to achieve emancipation. In other words, the Basque Country (or Euskadi) was also a colony of the Spanish Empire. However, whilst Cuba and the Philippines achieved their emancipation from Spain in 1898, Euskadi remained subjected to Spain. In the following decades, Basque nationalists developed Arana's theories and imagined Euskadi's national struggle as one against colonialism. The belief that Euskadi was involved in a global struggle against colonialism also encouraged Basques to defend the nationalist claims of other nations subjected to colonial rule.

This is the first in-depth study of the origins and development of anticolonial language and rhetoric within Basque nationalism. Instead of focusing on the period in which ETA was active (1959–2018), the monograph traces the waxing and waning of anticolonial ideas during the first few decades of the Basque nationalist movement (1892–1936). In particular, the book focuses on the use of anticolonial language by the radical, pro-independence branch of the Basque nationalist movement, although the moderate branch is a constant point of reference and comparison.[4] This is because the radical branch of the movement, of which ETA is the best-known representative, has been the main force behind the development of the Basque anticolonial corpus. As this book shows, in the period studied, anticolonialism was used by Basque radicals to legitimise their separatist and anti-collaborationist stance and to internationalise the movement.

Now, what is Basque anticolonialism? In this book, I use the term 'anticolonialism' to denote a discourse of rejection and opposition to both internal and international colonial or imperial practices.[5] Internally, Basque radical nationalists rejected the colonial situation they believed Euskadi had faced ever since the nineteenth century, which was when Arana posited that the Spanish invaded and put an end to Basque independence. The effects of

4 Whilst the radical branch rejected any form of collaboration with the Spanish state to achieve Basque nationalist goals, the moderates advocated for a more gradualist path and considered autonomy as a first step for Basque self-determination. The reason why the moderate branch is a point of comparison throughout is because the two branches of Basque nationalism coexisted within the same party (the PNV) in different periods covered by this book.

5 In the corpus analysed, Basque radical nationalists never established the difference between 'colonialism' and 'imperialism' and these were used interchangeably. However, a close reading of their texts suggests that Basque nationalists understood imperialism as the wider phenomenon and colonialism as the specific imperial practice to which they were subjected. In other words, Euskadi was portrayed as a victim of Spanish imperialism and as a colony within Spain as a result. In this book, I use the term 'anticolonialism' to refer to both colonial and imperial opposition. I have chosen this word over anti-imperialism to emphasise the Basque nationalist belief that Euskadi was a colony.

colonialism in Euskadi, Basque radicals believed, were multifaceted. Amongst these were the loss of political sovereignty, the racial contamination that Basques experienced, the progressive loss of Basque culture, language and traditions, and – at least for some nationalists – the arrival of capitalism. Therefore, one of the most important goals of Basque radical nationalism was to end this form of foreign dominion and consequently to 'restore' Basque independence. This belief made Basques align their struggle with that of other colonised nations and denounce international colonial practices. In fact, as we will see, Basque radical newsletters such as *Aberri* and *Jagi-Jagi* framed themselves as defenders of the oppressed nations and anticolonial champions.

My use of 'anticolonialism' does not mean that I believe that the situation of Euskadi was akin to that of former Spanish colonies or territories such as Morocco, Cuba or the Philippines. Instead, I use this term to argue that throughout the period studied, Basque radical nationalists imported and adapted a language originally developed in an external colonial setting to the Basque case. Thus, my book should not be thought of as a comparative study. Rather, it assesses the impact, development and different uses or functions of anticolonial ideas within the Basque nationalist movement.

Despite the obvious presence of anticolonial ideas in Basque nationalism, this has tended to be a secondary point of analysis and has been mentioned mostly in passing in existing scholarship. Furthermore, the few studies that have dealt with Basque anticolonialism have tended to focus either on the anticolonial writings of the founder of Basque nationalism, Sabino Arana, or on the period in which ETA operated.[6] This has left an important gap in the years that followed the death of Arana in 1903 and the birth of ETA in 1959. In particular, the years that this book studies (1892–1936) were crucial not only for the development of anticolonialism but for the making of Basque nationalism, as it was a period in which the two branches of the movement

---

6 See, amongst others: Jean-Claude Larronde, *El nacionalismo vasco: su origen y su ideología en la obra de Sabino Arana-Goiri* (San Sebastián: Txertoa, 1977); Gurutz Jáuregui Bereciartu, *Ideología y estrategia política de ETA: Análisis de su evolución entre 1959 y 1968* (Madrid: Siglo XXI, 1985); Javier Corcuera Atienza, *La patria de los vascos: Orígenes, ideología y organización del nacionalismo vasco (1876–1903)* (Madrid: Taurus, 2001); William A. Douglass, 'Sabino's Sin: Racism and the Founding of Basque Nationalism', in Daniele Conversi (ed.), *Ethnonationalism in the Contemporary World: Walker Connor and the Study of Nationalism* (London: Routledge, 2002), pp. 95–112; José Luis de la Granja, 'El *Antimaketismo*: La visión de Sabino Arana sobre España y los españoles', *Norba. Revista de Historia*, 19 (2006), pp. 191–203; Alexander Ugalde Zubiri, 'El primer nacionalismo vasco ante la independencia de Cuba', in Alexander Ugalde Zubiri, Cecilia Arrozarena, Félix Julio Alfonso López, Joseba Agirreazkuenaga (eds), *Patria y Libertad: Los vascos y las guerras de independencia de Cuba (1868–1898)* (Tafalla: Txalaparta, 2012), pp. 187–285.

(radicals and moderates) were formed and polarised according to the global and national events of the period.

The purpose of this book is not to fill a gap for its own sake. I argue that an in-depth analysis of Basque anticolonialism allows us to look at Basque nationalism with different eyes. In recent years, many different and valuable studies have highlighted the role of anticolonial actors in precipitating the end of colonial rule.[7] In contrast to the traditional studies that have focused on the role of western ideas and actors in ending colonialism, these studies have put their emphasis on the different individuals and organisations that challenged empire from both its centre and the peripheries. Unsurprisingly and understandingly, these studies have excluded the anticolonial ideas that Basque nationalists developed from their accounts. However, by focusing on these ideas and by tracing the influences that such movements had on the making of Basque anticolonialism, this book seeks to contribute to the growing field of global anticolonialism. Like existing scholarship in this growing field, this book does not focus on ideas that went from the west to the 'rest'. Instead, this book tells the story of how a group of western nationalists looked for inspiration beyond Europe to construct a powerful narrative that lives on today.

This study therefore draws on works about Basque nationalism that have challenged strictly local and national narratives and those that have explored the Basque nationalist movement through a global and transnational perspective.[8] In particular, the works of Xosé Manoel Núñez

---

7 See, amongst others, Erez Manela, *The Wilsonian Moment: Self-determination and the International Origins of Anticolonial Nationalism* (Oxford and New York: Oxford University Press, 2007); Vijay Prashad, *The Darker Nations: A People's History of the Third World* (New York: New Press, 2008); Michael Goebel, *Anti-Imperial Metropolis: Interwar Paris and the Seeds of Third-World Nationalism* (Cambridge: Cambridge University Press, 2015); Priyamvada Gopal, *Insurgent Empire: Anticolonial Resistance and British Dissent* (London and New York: Verso, 2019); Thomas K. Lindner, *A City Against Empire: Transnational Anti-Imperialism in Mexico City, 1920-30* (Liverpool: Liverpool University Press, 2023); Erez Manela and Heather Streets-Salter (eds), *The Anticolonial Transnational: Imaginaries, Mobilities, and Networks in the Struggle Against Empire* (Cambridge: Cambridge University Press, 2023).

8 See, amongst others: José María Lorenzo Espinosa, 'Influencia del nacionalismo irlandés en el nacionalismo vasco, 1916-1936', in XI Congreso de Estudios Vascos, *Nuevas formulaciones culturales: Euskal Herria y Europa* (Donostia: Eusko Ikaskuntza, 1992), pp. 239-47; Daniele Conversi, 'Domino Effect or International Developments? The Influences of International Events and Political Ideologies on Catalan and Basque Nationalism', *West European Politics*, 16 (1) (1993), pp. 245-70; Enric Ucelay-Da Cal, 'Cuba y el despertar de los nacionalismos en la España peninsular', *Biblid*, 15 (1997), pp. 151-92; Santiago de Pablo, '¡Grita Libertad! El nacionalismo vasco y la lucha por la independencia de las naciones africanas', *Memoria y civilización*, 15 (2012),

Seixas or Alexander Ugalde Zubiri have been a key source of inspiration for this project.[9] This book examines the development of Basque nationalism in parallel to that of key moments of global anticolonialism, including the ideas that emerged following the so-called Wilsonian moment, the connections and disconnections that anticolonial insurgents established with organisations such as the League of Nations (LN) and the solidarity campaigns that the Rif or the Abyssinian War generated across the world. It also traces the direct influences and connections that Basque radicals had with other anticolonial nationalist movements. This helps us to rethink Basque nationalism as a movement that sought to be part of the histories of global anticolonialism, and that evolved accordingly to contemporary global (and of course national) changes. As Erez Manela has pointed out, 'nationalism, as an ideology and as a form of political practice, evolved conceptionally and historically within an international context, and it cannot be fully understood outside that context'.[10] As this book shows, the case of Basque nationalism was not an exception to this rule.

By studying the tangible and symbolic connections that Basque nationalists established with other anticolonial movements, this book also stresses the limits of these networks. As Pau Dalmau has recently argued when examining the links between Riffians and Catalans during the Wilsonian movement, 'the epistemological benefits of finding connections in global history can

pp. 267-84; Niall Cullen, *Radical Basque Nationalist-Irish Republican Relations: A History* (Abingdon: Routledge, 2024).

9 Since the 1990s, Núñez Seixas has analysed the international dimension of sub-state nationalist movements within Spain during the inter-war period, explored the direct links between these movements and other similar ones emerging in the same period, and assessed the huge influence that they received from other nationalist movements like the Irish: See, for instance, Xosé Manoel Núñez Seixas, '¿Protodiplomacia exterior o ilusiones ópticas? El nacionalismo vasco, el contexto internacional y el Congreso de Nacionalidades Europeas (1914-1937)', *Vasconia. Cuadernos de Sección Historia-Geografía*, 23 (1995), pp. 243-75; Xosé Manoel Núñez Seixas, 'Ecos de Pascua, mitos rebeldes: El nacionalismo vasco e Irlanda (1890-1939)', *Historia Contemporánea*, 55 (2017), pp. 447-82; Xosé Manoel Núñez Seixas, *Patriotas transnacionales: Ensayos sobre nacionalismos y transferencias culturales en la Europa del siglo XX* (Madrid: Cátedra, 2019). See also the works of Alexander Ugalde Zubiri, including: Alexander Ugalde Zubiri, *La acción exterior del nacionalismo vasco, 1890-1939: historia, pensamiento y relaciones internacionales* (Bilbao: Instituto Vasco de Administración Pública, 1996); Alexander Ugalde Zubiri and Enric Ucelay-Da Cal, 'Una alianza en potencia en un contexto más amplio: la mirada distante de los movimientos nacionalistas vasco y catalán (1910-1936)', in Enric Ucelay-Da Cal, Xosé Manoel Núñez Seixas, Arnau Gonzàlez i Vilalta (eds), *Patrias diversas ¿misma lucha? Alianzas transnacionalistas en el mundo de entreguerras (1912-1939)* (Barcelona: Edicions Bellaterra, 2020), pp. 387-415.

10 Manela, *The Wilsonian Moment*, p. 8.

only be fully realised when global (dis)connections are also attended to'.[11] One of the main arguments of this book is that despite the undeniable presence of anticolonial ideas within the movement, Basque nationalists mixed anticolonial rhetoric with imperialist and sometimes Orientalist discourses. Since the movement first started, Basque nationalists reproduced and modified the racist logic of imperialist countries for which whiteness was a sign of superiority and therefore a legitimate reason to colonise other areas. This explains why, up until 1916, Basque anticolonialism was selective and targeted mostly against Spain: whilst Basques stressed Spain's alleged African nature to condemn its imperial activities, the colonial actions of Anglo-Saxon powers such as Britain or the US were explicitly praised. Although Basque radicals began to condemn all colonial powers following Ireland's Easter Rising in 1916 and the wave of anticolonial nationalism that followed Woodrow Wilson's Fourteen Points, imperialist and Orientalist dogmas never disappeared from the Basque radical corpus. This is particularly evident when looking at the Orientalist attitudes Basques developed toward the Riffians in northern Morocco, who were presented as childlike and different to Europeans. Indeed, Basque anticolonialism not only followed the developments of other contemporary anticolonial movements – from which Basques copied their rhetoric against empires – but also imported key ideas from imperial Europe.

By unpacking the set of complex and often contradictory ideas that existed in the Basque anticolonial corpus, this book offers a first glimpse into the complexities of European anticolonialism. I argue that the reason why these contradictory ideas existed within the same corpus is because Basque radicals were not necessarily driven by a genuine hatred of colonialism. Instead, one of the key findings of this book is that Basque anticolonialism was more strategic than heartfelt. I argue that, especially from the late 1910s and early 1920s when Basque anticolonialism was directed against all world empires, Basque anticolonialism served two important purposes: the legitimation of independence and the internationalisation of the movement. The book aims to inspire subsequent studies on the anticolonial (and pro-colonial) ideas that similar western nationalist movements developed, including the Irish nationalist movement and the Catalan and Galician movements, all of which are a continual source of reference in this book.

Assessing the evolution of Basque anticolonialism also invites the exploration of other crucial aspects of the Basque nationalist ideology,

---

11 Pol Dalmau, 'Catalans and Rifis during the Wilsonian Moment: The Quest for Self-Determination in the Post-Versailles World', *Contemporary European History*, 32 (2023), pp. 131–45 (p. 144).

such as race. This is because the Basque nationalist belief in being part of an anticolonial insurrection forced analogies between the Basques and other colonised nations. This proved slightly problematic for Basque nationalists, who developed strong claims against the Spaniards based on racial distinction. Indeed, one of the best-known features of early Basque nationalism is its racial claims: Sabino Arana famously stated that Basques were part of a pure, distinct and superior race, as opposed to the inferior and tainted Spanish race that invaded them in the nineteenth century.[12] This was repeated by generations of Basque nationalists, who used race as a point of identity and distinctness. This created a unique paradigm: in the Basque case, it was the colonised (the Basque) who was superior to the coloniser (the Spanish), and hence here colonialism lost its *raison d'être*. As such, the idea of two antagonistic races that had been forced to coexist in the same territory became a recurrent tool to justify Basque cries for independence.

This book also studies the development of Basque racial ideas and argues that they were not merely a Basque invention. Instead, as Chapter 1 proves, the idea of a distinct and unique Basque race had already been an element of obsession for nineteenth-century western anthropology, which was fixated on dividing the world into different races. Furthermore, the alleged racial inferiority of the Spanish, who were portrayed as inherently vicious, barbarian and lazy people, was nothing more than an extension of northern European stereotypes that had emerged following the decline of the Spanish Empire in the seventeenth century. These stereotypes, commonly known as the Black Legend, along with nineteenth-century pseudo-scientific theories that placed the Spaniards at the bottom of the European racial ladder, clearly had a profound effect on the imagination of Basque nationalists. Like their northern European neighbours, Basques perceived Spaniards as a sickly race that, unlike the so-called Anglo-Saxon races, was unable to sustain an empire.

12 The question of race has generated a great deal of literature, division and disagreement in studies of Basque nationalism. Most of these studies have been centred around the figure of Arana, accused by some of being a racist and defended by others as an anti-racist. Some scholars such as Conversi have argued that 'it is not certain how justly Arana can be accused of being a racist' as he maintains that Arana never formulated a biological theory of racial superiority and hierarchy. Others like Larronde have gone further and have said that Arana was explicitly anti-racist. Others such as William A. Douglass have placed themselves in the middle of the debate, arguing that Arana's racialist writings, 'while perhaps not constituting a clear biological theory of race, are myriad'. Daniele Conversi, *The Basques, the Catalans and Spain: Alternative Routes to Nationalist Mobilisation* (London: Hurst, 1997), p. 60; Larronde, *El nacionalismo vasco*, pp. 281–98; Douglass, 'Sabino's Sin', p. 106. Chapter 1 will engage directly with these debates.

Aside from tracing similarities between Basque and northern European discourses of race and empire, this book offers a new vision of how Basque nationalists perceived race by focusing on the interaction between race and anticolonialism. I argue that during this period Basque racial discourses were increasingly subordinated to Basque anticolonialism. First, racist claims were generally present when Basque nationalists wanted to stress the situation of national decadence Basques experienced due to having to mix their blood with the Spanish. These ideas were used as an anti-Spanish tool and to foster and promote independence ideas. Second, when talking about the international situation of the period, Basque nationalists denounced western racism and advocated the end of racial hierarchies. This served to establish symbolic links with other colonised nations and to internationalise the Basque cause. This was mostly the case from the 1920s onwards, when Basque radicals began to condemn the effects of global colonialism. Of course, this did not imply a complete eradication of racist beliefs in Basque nationalism. Attacking racism was just a way of situating the Basque struggle within a struggle against global colonialism, when many Global South movements were coming together to confront colonial structures. In other words, racist or anti-racist claims were strategically used according to the needs of the movement.

Their fervent desire to be part of the global moment of colonial insurgency that followed the so-called Wilsonian moment also prompted Basque radicals to consider different strategies used in colonial settings, including violence and civil disobedience. As we will see, from the early 1920s, Basque radicals developed provocative violent discourses against Spain that promoted the use of armed resistance to achieve freedom. This interpretation differed much from that of the Basque moderates, who advocated for the use of parliamentary methods and a gradualist strategy. Looking at multiple international examples, including that of Ireland, India or the Rif, Basque radicals believed that when parliamentary methods were exhausted, the use of force or civil disobedience tactics could be a solution to achieve full independence. On very limited occasions, these had a tangible effect, as demonstrated by the activity of Basque radicals in exile during the dictatorship of Primo de Rivera or by the civil disobedience practices led by *Jagi-Jagi* in the 1930s.

Although these early violent allusions have tended to be overlooked due to their alleged symbolic and purely verbal nature, they should not go unnoticed. Instead, the Basque radicals studied in this book advanced many discourses that their successors would adapt years later to develop a long-term, violent campaign. As Gurutz Jáuregui argued, ETA was a result of both Sabino Arana's nationalism (whose main premise was based on the notion that Euskadi was an occupied country) and Francoism, which made the occupation real.[13] Indeed, ETA was formed in 1959 by young activists frustrated with the Partido Nacionalista Vasco's (Basque Nationalist Party: henceforth PNV) inaction during the Francoist regime, which led them to take up arms. Whilst there are many differences – both theoretical and generational – between the Basque radicals that this book studies and the young activists who founded ETA in 1959, the latter had a clear predecessor to draw on.[14] First, ETA developed different tactics that had been seriously considered by its radical predecessors before – such as armed struggle – or that had actually been put into practice for the first time during the period studied in this book, including civil resistance methods such as hunger strikes. Second, ETA initially justified its violence by alluding to the colonial nature of Euskadi. This study thus elucidates some key reasons for ETA's long period of existence and its wide support within Basque society.

To carry out this study, this book draws on considerable archival work. Whilst it relies on a diverse range of primary sources, it primarily bases its analysis on nationalist newsletters. The monograph explores and analyses in depth the language deployed in Basque nationalist periodicals and publications issued between 1892 and 1936. It focuses on the publications that were issued in the Basque-Spanish region, mainly in Bilbao (Biscay), which was the cradle of early Basque nationalism. It also analyses periodicals published in exile from the period in which Basque nationalists were unable to publish at home due to the censorship imposed by Miguel Primo de Rivera's dictatorship (1923–1930).

Newsletters played a crucial role in Basque nation building and, as we will see, became one of the main pillars of the Basque nationalist movement alongside the PNV. For instance, in the first years, Basque nationalist ideas (which, as detailed in Chapter 1 had very few followers in the early years) were mainly promoted and popularised through newsletters by Sabino

---

13 Gurutz Jáuregui Bereciartu, 'Los orígenes ideológicos de ETA', in Antonio Elorza (ed.), *La historia de ETA* (Madrid: Temas de Hoy, 2000), pp. 171–85 (p. 171).

14 Many scholars have already located the roots of Basque violence in the period that precedes ETA. To name a few, see Jáuregui, *Ideología y estratégia polítca de ETA*; Joseba Zulaika, *Basque Violence: Metaphor and Sacrament* (Reno and Las Vegas: University of Nevada Press, 1988); Diego Muro, *Ethnicity and Violence: The Case of Radical Basque Nationalism* (London: Routledge, 2011); Cameron Watson, *Basque Nationalism and Political Violence: The Ideological and Intellectual Origins of* ETA (Reno: Center for Basque Studies, 2007); Gaizka Fernández Soldevilla, 'El simple arte de matar. Orígenes de la violencia terrorista en el País Vasco', *Historia y Política*, 32 (2014), pp. 271–98; Gaizka Fernández Soldevilla, *La voluntad del gudari. Génesis y metástasis de la violencia de* ETA (Madrid: Tecnos, 2016).

Arana. The same can be said about the period that followed Arana's death that this book studies: dozens of different newspapers were established, and every branch of nationalism had at least one periodical. Indeed, the role of newsletters in the making of the Basque nation was essential: weekly, or sometimes even daily, Basques read about local events and news; they learned about their shared history and the defining elements of their nationality; and they practised Basque grammar through weekly exercises that the publications offered. In sum, newspapers allowed Basques to imagine each other and to define national boundaries.

Apart from their role in nation-making, periodicals are an ideal source for this project because of the precision with which changes or continuities in the language used can be detected. For instance, in the last decade of the nineteenth century one can observe an extensive use of anticolonial language, addressed especially against Spain. This explicit anticolonial language, however, changed after the death of Arana, when we can observe a decline in anticolonial language in the first years of the twentieth century. The frequency of periodicals makes them extremely efficient in reflecting such changes, and in identifying their reasons, which as this book proves, obeyed both local and international factors.

Organised chronologically, the six chapters that form this book explore the untold story of how Basques appropriated and adapted anticolonialism to their language, including the contradictions that this entailed. Chapter 1 explores the life and work of the founder of Basque nationalism, Sabino Arana (1865–1903). The first part of the chapter examines how one man alone was able to launch one of the most powerful and influential nationalist movements in the western world. It also shows how his movement and national narrative relied on a compilation and reinterpretation of existing myths, historical events and pseudo-scientific theories of race. This narrative presented the Basques as a pure and ancient people who lived freely until the Spanish – racially, linguistically and culturally different – invaded them. Arana's narrative is the basis of this book, as it opened the door to a colonial reading of Euskadi's situation. The second part of the chapter focuses on the anticolonial element of Arana's narrative. By closely examining this rich corpus, I question the extent to which Arana should be viewed as an anticolonial champion and a defender of the oppressed. Not only did Arana famously praise the colonial practices of powers such as Britain and the US – suggesting that Arana regarded whiteness, represented by the Anglo-Saxon races, as a sign of superiority – but he also held patronising views of non-white insurgents.

Chapter 2 explores the period following Arana's death in 1903. Whilst Arana's anticolonialism has been the object of some studies, no attention has been paid to the development of Basque anticolonialism in the period that followed the untimely death of the founder of Basque nationalism. Instead, scholars have tended to focus on the ideological differences between the two branches of Basque nationalism that coexisted in the PNV: the radicals and moderates. Chapter 2 addresses this gap by exploring the course of anticolonial ideas in a period characterised by the enormous vacuum that Arana's death left within the movement. It argues that whilst both radicals and moderates regarded Arana as an unquestionable and almost messianic authority, from 1903 to 1914 they both left out an important aspect of Arana's doctrine: his anticolonialism. Unlike Arana, during this period both radicals and moderates rarely condemned colonialism or engaged in discussions about Spain and its imperial activities. Both radicals and moderates changed the interpretation of the Spanish invasion of Euskadi: whereas for Arana the Basque Country was a colony within the Spanish Empire, new generations of Basque nationalists tended to avoid comparisons with extra-European movements and erased most of the colonial connotations from their discourse. As we will see, Basque nationalists of this period developed pro-colonial arguments that resonated with ideas of British exceptionalism: whilst the 'Latin races' were placed at the bottom of the racial ladder, the British were at the top and their colonial activities were seen as benevolent.

Chapter 3 explores the global events that led to the polarisation of Basques radicals and moderates between 1914 and 1921. In 1921, after years of tensions, the most radical sections of the PNV were expelled from the party and formed their own political entity, the PNV-*Aberri*. This chapter focuses on how the issue of colonialism proved to be an important point of division for Basque moderates and radicals. Whilst the former continued advocating that certain nations or races (such as the British) could practise a benevolent form of colonialism, the latter began to deviate from this conception. The radical branch of nationalism was thus responsible for the re-emergence of Basque anticolonialism, which had been temporarily forgotten between 1903 and 1916. As we will see, events such as the Easter Rising of 1916 and the disappointment caused by Wilson's post-war order were used by the radicals to highlight the malevolence of all world empires, including the British. I claim that the differing view of colonialism that Basque radicals and moderates developed was not arbitrary but responded to the type of nationalism that both branches aimed to promote and achieve. The moderates advocated a form of parliamentary nationalism that sought the collaboration between the subjugated nation and the state that oppressed it. In contrast, the radicals rejected any form of collaboration with the oppressor and alluded to the imperialist and deceitful nature of the western powers, who had ignored petitions for self-determination from outside Europe following the First World War.

Chapter 4 assesses the brief but intense period that ran from the split of the Basque movement in 1921 until dictator Miguel Primo de Rivera's coup in 1923. Internationally, this was a period of global anticolonial upheaval in which Wilson's language of self-determination was appropriated and reinterpreted by nationalists in colonised territories to challenge imperialism. As this chapter demonstrates, Basque radicals or Aberrianos (as the members of the PNV-*Aberri* were commonly known, owing to the newsletter in which they published, *Aberri*, 'Homeland') were not immune to the developments of this period. The Aberrianos placed Euskadi in the wider context of colonial opposition and established tangible and symbolic networks with Irish, Catalans, Galician and Riffian nationalists. This chapter places the PNV-*Aberri*'s activity within the context of global anticolonial nationalism and analyses the ideas developed by Basque radicals during the early 1920s. It does this by focusing on three exemplary case studies, including the Basque views on the Irish struggle for independence (which made them consider the use of violence), the attitudes Basques developed towards the Rif War and the Riffians, and the formation of the Triple Alianza of 1923, which united Euskadi, Catalonia and Galicia against Spain. I show that although in this period Basque radicals condemned colonialism globally and compared Euskadi with extra-European nations such as the Rif, there were some important limits to this sympathy. Indeed, Basque radicals continued to maintain Orientalist and racist ideas towards non-white peoples, even with fellow Riffians. The coexistence of anticolonial and pro-colonial ideas within the same corpus is explained by the fact that anticolonialism was a mere rhetorical device used by Basque radicals to legitimise independence and to internationalise their movement.

Chapter 5 contributes to the scarce literature on Basque nationalism under Primo de Rivera's dictatorship (1923–1930) and argues that far from a period of immobilism, this was one of activity and dynamism for Basque radicals who managed to go into exile. By focusing on the activity and the newsletters that Basque radicals published from exile in the US and Mexico, the chapter demonstrates that during Primo's dictatorship, Basque radicals benefited from the ideas that emerged in their new homes, which were hubs of anticolonial thinking. They also experienced an intense period of radicalisation, the main manifestation of which was an increase in armed attempts against the dictatorship and in the publication of incendiary writings against Spain. Basque radical nationalists also sought to take advantage of this new moment and internationalise their movement. They did this in different ways, including forging networks with other groups (whose landmark was the creation of the anti-League of Nations organisation La Liga de las Naciones Oprimidas) or directly seeking the attention of the

LN. These ways of obtaining international attention, which at first glance might seem contradictory, were copied directly from other movements that had similar goals to the Basque nationalist movement. The last part of the chapter focuses on the rhetoric that the exiled Aberrianos used when talking about the Latin American struggles for independence – used against Primo's pro-Hispanic and pro-imperial discourses. These discourses put the Basques at the centre of Latin American Wars of Independence, showing once again that patronising discourses continued to be constant when talking about extra-European nations.

The last chapter of the book, Chapter 6, focuses on the rhetoric developed by one of the most representative organisations and newsletters of Basque radicalism, *Jagi-Jagi*. Published during the Spanish Second Republic, *Jagi-Jagi* stood out for its anticolonial rhetoric. As this chapter shows, Basque radical anticolonialism continued to have two important aims. On the one hand, framing Euskadi as a colony within the Spanish state was used by *Jagi-Jagi* to defend the necessary independence of the Basque Country against the moderate and pro-autonomy discourses of the main Basque nationalist party, whose main aim became the achievement of autonomy. The belief that Basques were involved in a struggle against colonialism led *Jagi-Jagi* to establish parallels with other colonised nations and to consider similar methods that had been applied in anticolonial struggles, namely civil disobedience and violence. On the other hand, condemning colonialism more globally served to internationalise the Basque cause and include it in a global context. The chapter studies some of the key moments in which *Jagi-Jagi* engaged in this global context, focusing on the Abyssinian War. The national and international anticolonial stance of *Jagi-Jagi* led the newsletter to have two differing conceptions of race: whilst racial claims were still present when condemning the degrading situation that Basques experienced owing to the Spanish invasion (with the intention of justifying independence), *Jagi-Jagi* adopted an explicit anti-racist posture when condemning global colonialism (as an attempt to internationalise the cause). Indeed, the different conceptions of race in *Jagi-Jagi* respond to the two well-defined strategies of Basque anticolonialism.

CHAPTER ONE

The Origins of Basque Anticolonialism: Colonial Defeat, Race and Otherness (1892–1903)

No account of Basque nationalism can start without addressing the life and work of its founder, Sabino Arana (1865–1903). During his short life, Arana was able to launch one of the most powerful and influential nationalist movements of the western world. As well as giving the Basque nation most of its national symbols and signs, he was responsible for developing an entire ideology calling for independence from Spain. He was able to justify this movement and mobilise the Basque community by constructing a national narrative in which independence seemed necessary. Whereas most nations have multiple organic nationalist intellectuals who are responsible for producing a nationalist rhetoric, the Basque nation owes most of its national work to only one man.[1]

Although Sabino Arana launched his movement in the last decade of the nineteenth century, it was not born in a vacuum. Before Arana, other intellectuals had developed a series of writings, myths and pseudo-scientific theories of race that stressed the uniqueness of the Basques. The young Arana compiled and reinterpreted those existing myths and theories in service of his movement's aims. As Diego Muro argues, 'Arana's political message appropriated pre-existing myths and memories of an idealised rural and Catholic past and combined it with a new anti-capitalist, racist discourse with a nationalist understanding of history'.[2] Arana's own understanding of

---

1 Amongst others Conversi has stressed the enormous legacy Arana left in the Basque movement, which owes most of its 'symbols and values' to him. Conversi, *The Basques, the Catalans and Spain*, p. 53. See also José Luis de la Granja, *Ángel o demonio: Sabino Arana. El patriarca del nacionalismo vasco* (Madrid: Tecnos, 2015), pp. 241–51.

2 Muro, *Ethnicity and Violence*, p. 58. Scholars agree that Arana reinterpreted Basque history to legitimise his political project. See, amongst many others, Santiago de Pablo and Ludger Mees, *El péndulo patriótico. Historia del Partido Nacionalista Vasco, 1895–2005* (Barcelona: Crítica, 2005), p. 14; Corcuera Atienza, *La patria de los vascos*, p. 364; de la Granja, 'El *Antimaketismo*', p. 196; de la Granja, *Ángel o demonio*, pp. 53–66; pp. 77–81 and pp. 131–76.

history – used to legitimise his political project (independence) – presented the Basques as a sacred and ancient people who lived freely until the Spanish – racially, linguistically and culturally different – invaded them in the nineteenth century. Indeed, Arana's narrative opened the door to a colonial reading of the Basque situation.

As William Douglass sustains, Arana was more a synthesiser of ideas than an original thinker, but there were ways in which he was a 'true visionary': 'in articulating his radical Basque nationalism (i.e. independentism), he underscored the Basques' shameful dilemma in being colonized by Spain.'[3] The idea that Euskadi's situation mirrored that of other colonies also made Arana sympathetic to other colonial insurgents around the world, especially those who – like the Basques, at least in his mind – were fighting against the Spanish Empire. Yet the extent to which this sympathy was in fact opportunistic has sparked debate.

I have identified two main interpretations among those that have addressed Arana's anticolonialism. On the one hand, some have labelled him as an opposer to all forms of colonial rule and as an anti-racist figure.[4] Others have questioned the intentions behind Arana's anticolonial claims and have delved into their contradictions, such as the fact that his anticolonialism

---

3 Douglass, 'Sabino's Sin', pp. 104–05.

4 See Larronde, *El nacionalismo vasco*, pp. 281–98. This vision has been confirmed in a recent documentary that Larronde filmed for the *Sabino Arana Fundazioa*: Jean-Claude Larronde, 'Sabino Arana y el colonialismo' (2020), https://www.youtube.com/watch?v=OprDTg-Jo_A&feature=youtu.be, and in a video-interview between Luis de Guezala (historian and archivist of the *Sabino Arana Fundazioa*) and Larronde: 'El anticolonialismo de Sabino Arana, fundador del nacionalismo vasco', *About Basque Country* (2021), https://www.youtube.com/watch?v=jzCVpz2k3oc&t=4s. In the first mini-documentary, released in 2020, Larronde begins giving examples of the demonstrations that protested at police brutality towards people of African descent, including the protests that followed the murder of African American George Floyd. It then proceeds to introduce the figure of Sabino Arana, suggesting that there are clear links between the anti-racist protests of 2020 and Arana's thought. In the video, Larronde states that Arana did not oppose only Spanish rule but all the problems generated by colonialism across the world at the end of the nineteenth century. He concludes the video by saying that those views, which were 'very progressive and advanced for the period', are still alive today. Larronde sustains this view in an interview in 2021, which sought to dismantle some of the myths surrounding Arana produced by 'the defenders of the Spanish state and by some sectors of the Basque nationalist left' and to present a new image of him. See also Corcuera, *La patria de los vascos*; Ugalde, *La acción exterior del nacionalismo vasco*, p. 85 and Ugalde, 'El primer nacionalismo vasco ante la independencia de Cuba', pp. 187–285. It is worth noting that whilst Larronde has eluded important aspects which contradict this view of Arana's thought, Corcuera and Ugalde have acknowledged these contradictions.

was not directed against colonial powers such as Britain and the US.[5] For instance, José Luis de la Granja has argued that Arana's anticolonialism was a product of his hatred of Spain.[6] Although it is true that on some limited occasions Arana condemned colonialism as a whole, this chapter agrees with the latter view and provides new evidence that emphasises the inherently imperialist nature of Arana's thought. In other words, I argue that Arana was not motivated by a genuine hatred of colonialism but by a profound hatred of Spain.

This extended chapter is an essential introduction to both the basis of Basque nationalism and the anticolonial claims that have formed part of its core since its origins. It begins by providing an account of the life and work of Sabino Arana, who will remain a key reference in this book. It then moves to consider the origins of Arana's particular vision of history, as well as the formation of one of Arana's most influential premises: the fact that the Basque Country had been colonised by the Spaniards in the nineteenth century. Once the basis of Arana's thought has been established, the chapter focuses on analysing his anticolonial thought. The last section is divided into two parts, which examine Arana's anticolonial thought both before and after the loss of the Spanish Empire in 1898. This overview of Arana's thought shows that although his political programme experienced abrupt changes, anticolonialism remained an essential part of his narrative. As this book demonstrates, the same can be said of most of his successors.

The Life and Work of Sabino Arana y Goiri (1865-1903)

Sabino Policarpo Arana y Goiri was born on 26 January 1865 into a comfortable family that specialised in shipping. He was born in Abando, a small locality of Biscay that in 1870 became a suburb of Bilbao owing to the rapid industrialisation the area was experiencing at the time. From a young age, Arana and his family were exposed to the effects of both the region's industrialisation and the Carlist Wars, which would be key to the development of Basque nationalism. On the one hand, alongside Gipuzkoa,

---

5 Jáuregui, *Ideología y estrategia política de ETA*, pp. 28-29; de la Granja, 'El Antimaketismo', pp. 191-203.

6 De la Granja, 'El *Antimaketismo*', p. 198. See also de la Granja, *Ángel o demonio*, p. 44 and pp. 97-98. Santiago de Pablo has also supported de la Granja's view on the anti-Spanish nature of Arana's anticolonialism. See de Pablo, '¡Grita Libertad!', pp. 269-70. In his monograph, de la Granja argues that despite the anti-Spanish nature of his anticolonialism, Arana did not show solidarity with Cuban and Filipino independentists. This chapter provides some nuance to these claims. See de la Granja, *Ángel o demonio*, pp. 97-98.

the Basque province of Biscay became one of the most important areas of industrialisation and modernisation within the Spanish state at the time. As a result of this, the population of the Basque Country in general, and of Arana's native Biscay in particular, grew rapidly, as many Spaniards from other parts of the peninsula settled there. In 1857, the population of Greater Bilbao was just over 40,000; by 1900 it had risen to nearly 168,000.[7] In addition, from the mid-nineteenth century Biscay's capital Bilbao became an international city thanks to its strong shipping industry. Despite the apparent opportunities that the rapid industrialisation of the area could have brought to a family in the shipping industry, the Aranas did not see the benefits of modern capitalism as they owned pre-industrial dockyards that had to be adapted to industrial needs.

The Arana family was also seriously affected by the Carlist War, which pitted Spanish liberals and absolutists against one another until 1876. The Carlist Wars started after the Spanish monarch Ferdinand VII died in 1833, and the country was divided over his succession. Whilst liberals defended the claims of Ferdinand's young daughter Isabella (known as Isabelinos), absolutists took the side of the late king's brother Carlos (known as Carlists). The Carlist Wars were, however, more than simple conflicts about succession.[8] The wars became a struggle between two conceptions of Spain. Whereas the Carlists advocated a Spain based on the values of absolutism, Catholicism, territorial autonomy and local privileges (such as Fueros); the Isabelinos had a more liberal and centralised conception of the state.[9] As a result, in the Basque Country, Carlism took the form of the defence of the Basque Fueros and privileges. This explains why the support for Carlism, whilst uneven across Spain, was stronger in Euskadi than elsewhere. As Daniele Conversi points out, the abolition of the Fueros in 1876 following the Carlist defeat 'was the key condition, though not the only one, for the subsequent appearance of Basque nationalism'.[10]

Arana's father was one of the many Basques who supported Carlism. In fact, he invested substantial amounts of money in arms for the Carlist army. Owing to his support for the Carlist cause, the Arana family had to go into exile in the French part of the Basque Country in 1873, where

---

7 Watson, *Basque Nationalism and Political Violence*, p. 50.

8 André Lecours, *Basque Nationalism and the Spanish State* (Reno: University of Nevada Press, 2007).

9 The territories that comprised the former Kingdom of Navarra were assimilated into Castile by Ferdinand II of Aragon in 1512 but managed to retain distinctive local codes which regulated the administration and the laws of the different Basque territories called *Foruak* or *Fueros*.

10 Conversi, *The Basques, the Catalans and Spain*, pp. 47–48.

they remained for three years. Arana's father, affected by the war and the decline of his business, died a few years later. Indeed, Sabino Arana's childhood and adolescence were stormy and troubled, marked by war, death and tragedy. During his early years, the young Arana inherited his father's ideas, declaring himself a Carlist, an anti-liberal, a devoted Catholic and an anti-Mason. The young Arana was, however, not anti-Spanish as he had not 'discovered' Basque nationalism just yet.[11] This was to change when Arana was only 17 when his older brother Luis Arana (1862–1951) convinced him that Biscay was not Spain.[12] Sabino himself remembered his 'conversion' from Carlism to nationalism, which took place in Easter 1882.[13]

As de la Granja argues, this 'conversion' did not imply a change of ideology but a change of homeland: Arana stopped considering Spain his *patria*, as for him, 'Biscay was not Spain'.[14] Owing to his personal experiences and beliefs, prior to 1882, Arana believed that liberalism was a major cause of the problems that his family and the Basques were facing. However, after that year Arana found a new enemy towards whom he harboured even greater antipathy: the Spanish. As Ludger Mees explains, Arana himself did not invent Basque ethnic identity; nevertheless, this 'was a new identity in one sense: it was exclusive and no longer compatible with Spanish identity'.[15] Indeed, the suffering that his family had experienced owing to his father's Carlist militancy and the transformation of the Basque territories caused by industrialisation and Spanish immigration convinced Arana that Biscay (and later Euskadi) would only achieve happiness once it became independent from Spain.[16]

Arana would articulate these ideas in what is unanimously considered the foundational work of Basque nationalism: *Bizkaya por su independencia*

---

11 José Luis de la Granja, 'La forja de un líder mesiánico: Sabino Arana (1865–1882)', *Sancho el Sabio: Revista de cultura e investigación vasca*, Extra 3 (2020), pp. 159–80 (p. 169).

12 In the early years of the Basque nationalist movement, Arana talked of Biscay rather than Euskadi. This changed around the mid-1890s, when he created the neologism 'Euskadi' to refer to all the Basque territories.

13 Since 1932, this day – known as Aberri Eguna (Day of the Homeland) – has been celebrated and commemorated by Basque nationalists annually.

14 De la Granja, 'El *Antimaketismo*', p. 193.

15 Ludger Mees, 'Ethnogenesis in the Pyrenees: The Contentious Making of a National Identity in the Basque Country (1643–2017)', *European History Quarterly*, 48.3 (2018), pp. 462–89 (p. 470). Although some of the Basque territories were under French jurisdiction, Arana mainly focused his hatred on the Spanish. Spain, as Mees recognises, was not France. Unlike France, nineteenth-century Spain was experiencing a period of deep imperial crisis, which culminated with the loss of its empire in 1898.

16 Juan José Solozábal Echavarría, *El primer nacionalismo vasco: industrialismo y conciencia nacional* (Madrid: Tucar, 1975), p. 331.

('Biscay for its independence', 1892). Arana's booklet recounted Biscay's 'four national glories' against the Spanish including the legendary Battles of Arrigorriaga (888), Gordejuela (1355), Ochandiano (1355) and Munguía (1470).[17] Although scholars have agreed that the book Arana wrote lacked any historical value, its political impact would be immense.[18] In *Bizkaya por su independencia*, his concept of independence was essentially formed: Arana was firmly convinced that Biscay, and with it the rest of the Basque territories, had been independent from Spain prior to the nineteenth century until they were forcibly subjugated.[19] In other words, Arana was then decisively convinced by the conversation he had with his brother in 1882: Biscay was not Spain.

Scholars such as de la Granja divide Arana's political life into three distinct phases.[20] His first political phase (the radical phase, 1893–1898) – characterised by fervent independentism (which as we will see, translated into anticolonialism), anti-Spanishness or anti-*maketismo* (hatred of *maketos*, a term widely used in nineteenth-century Bilbao to refer pejoratively to Spanish immigrants) – started following Arana's first public attempt to popularise his new movement. This took place in 1893, when Arana gave a speech (known as the *discurso de Larrazabal*, the Larrazábal vow) to the members of the Bilbao's pro-Fuero society, Euskalerria, in which he explained the ideas behind his booklet *Bizkaya por su independencia* and referred to Spain as a 'sickly and miserable nation'.[21] Arana's long speech concluded with

---

17 All translations in this book are mine unless specified. Unless indicated otherwise, the original is in Spanish. Sabino Arana, *Bizkaya por su independencia* (Bilbao: Edn Verdes, 1932), p. 12. These legendary battles were not Arana's invention but rather a modern version of a mixture of historical and legendary narratives that were compiled by the Basque Foralist literature in the second half of the nineteenth century.

18 Corcuera Atienza, *La patria de los vascos*, p. 209; Beltza, *El nacionalismo vasco, 1876–1936* (San Sebastián: Txertoa, 1976), p. 83.

19 See Pedro José Chacón Delgado, 'El concepto de independencia vasca en Sabino Arana Goiri', *Historia Contemporánea*, 50 (2014), pp. 75–103 (p. 85). For a complete vision on the uses of history in *Bizkaya por su independencia* to the benefit of Arana's ideology, see de la Granja, *Ángel o demonio*, pp. 53–63.

20 De la Granja's monograph on Sabino Arana offers a complete biography of the Basque leader, as well as a detailed analysis of the three stages of his political thought, which he divides into a radical (1893–1898), a moderate (1898–1902) and a pro-Spanish phase (1902–1903). See de la Granja, *Ángel o demonio*. This book follows this model.

21 Sabino Arana, 'El discurso de Larazabal', Begoña, 3 June 1893. Available online from http://www.sabinoaranagoiri.eus/PDF/PDF145.pdf. This book has benefited enormously from the online archive dedicated to the life and work of Sabino Arana, which I used to locate Arana's articles in various newsletters: https://

the words 'long live Biscayan independence!' and was received with a long silence and few signs of agreement.[22] Indeed, Arana's new movement had to compete with established and more popular movements such as Carlism and Fuerismo.[23] Despite the failure of Arana's first public propaganda effort, he did not give up. Only five days after his speech, Arana launched the first Basque nationalist newsletter, *Bizkaitarra* ('The Biscayan', 1893–1895), becoming its editor and virtually only contributor. *Bizkaitarra* managed to issue only around 1,500 copies (mostly distributed in Bilbao) during the two years in which it was issued.[24]

While *Bizkaitarra* was still being issued and Arana's ideas were being disseminated in Bilbao, he began to organise the movement politically. From *Bizkaitarra*, Arana announced his plans to establish a political organisation arguing that it was the right moment to do so.[25] Two months later, the society Euskeldun Batzokija, which is considered the first Basque nationalist organisation, was established.[26] The statutes of the new society evidenced the exclusionary nature of early Basque nationalism: members had to have Basque last names and anyone that practised an 'anti-Catholic or pro-Spanish' doctrine would be excluded from it.[27] Just one year after the establishment of Euskeldun Batzokija, another key pillar of Basque nationalism was established with the founding of the Bizkai Buru Batzar

www.sabinoaranagoiri.eus/archivo.php. When referencing Sabino Arana's articles in newspapers, I have used the pagination provided by the online archive.

22 Arana, 'El discurso de Larazabal'.

23 Whilst both Carlism and Fuerismo sought the restoration of the *Fueros*, this did not mean the same for both movements. Carlism was a reactionary movement strongly linked to the Ancient Regime which opposed liberalism's aims of achieving a centralised state. On the other hand, Fuerismo was largely a liberal movement that emerged among the urban middle and upper classes because of the (mostly economic) frustrations that followed the abolition of the *Fueros*. As Mees argues, the Fueristas did not question the unity of the state, but their main argument was that the state would only be strong again if regional (and national) particularities were respected and if the centre and the periphery agreed to continue living within the same framework. See Ludger Mees, *The Basque Contention: Ethnicity, Politics, Violence* (Abingdon and New York: Routledge, 2020), p. 39.

24 De Pablo and Mees, *El péndulo patriótico*, p. 9; de la Granja, *Ángel o demonio*, p. 68.

25 Arana was aware that the movements that could be attracted to Basque nationalism – including the reactionary and ultraconservative Carlists and the liberal members of Euskalerria – were experiencing internal tensions. Sabino Arana, 'Euskeldun Batzokija', *Bizkaitarra*, 24 May 1894, pp. 279–91 (p. 279).

26 *Batzoki* was a neologism invented by Arana that can be translated as 'meeting point', whereas *Euskeldun* means 'Basque-speaker'.

27 Arana, 'Euskeldun Batzokija', p. 281.

(Supreme Council of Biscay), generally considered the birth of the Basque Nationalist Party (henceforth PNV).

The incipient Basque movement did not have it easy, as its ideas were strongly opposed by the Spanish authorities. The Spanish state – which was involved in a period of generalised crisis internally and externally – did not take long to react against the internal threat that Basque nationalism posed and in 1895 the publication of *Bizkaitarra* was suspended and Euskeldun Batzokija was closed down. Significantly, Spanish authorities applied the same penal code that had been used in Cuba in response to Cuban separatism to shut down the Basque nationalist society.[28] Indeed, Spanish authorities equated the separatist tendencies that emerged both in the metropole and in the colonies. As we will see, so did Arana.

A year after launching a new Basque nationalist newsletter called *Baserritarra*, Arana's thought went through a period of moderation that lasted from 1898 to 1902.[29] The start of this period coincided with both the outbreak of the Spanish-American War and the end of the Spanish Empire, as well as the adhesion of the aforementioned Euskalerria society – whose members were known as Euskalerriacos – to the PNV in 1898. The incorporation of the moderate Euskalerriacos, led by the industrialist Ramón de la Sota and formed by sectors of local bourgeoisie, brought important victories to the movement: along with money and power, de la Sota's group brought a more moderate approach. As a result, the incipient Basque nationalist movement began to experience its first political triumphs.[30] As this book will show, however, this fusion was not the start of a story of victories, harmony and consensus. On the contrary, as the authors of *El péndulo patriótico* recognise, the ampliation of the social basis of the movement also sowed the seeds of a structural change that was to accompany Basque nationalism from then onwards: the confrontation of two well-differenced political and ideological projects that were articulated in the ideas of independentism and radicalism

---

28 Ugalde, 'El primer nacionalismo vasco ante la independencia de Cuba', p. 212.

29 The term *Baserritarra* refers to a person who lives in a *Baserri*, a traditional Basque farmhouse. *Baserritarra* managed to publish more issues than *Bizkaitarra* (around 3,000 issues), although it only had 265 subscribers. It also had a very short life, lasting only from May to August 1897. See Santiago de Pablo, Ludger Mees and José Antonio Rodríguez Ranz, *El péndulo patriótico. Historia del Partido Nacionalista Vasco: 1895–1936*, 2 vols (Barcelona: Crítica, 1999), I, p. 35.

30 Corcuera, *La patria de los vascos*, p. 500, and de Pablo and Mees, *El péndulo patriótico*, pp. 46–47. The arrival of the Euskalerriacos to the party also brought the so-called 'evolución industrialista' (industrialist evolution) as Arana began to accept Basque industrialisation.

(radicals) on the one hand, and autonomism and pragmatism (moderates) on the other.[31]

Despite the moderation of Arana's doctrine from 1898 onwards, the incipient Basque movement was not exempt from repression and censorship. For instance, in May 1902 Arana was imprisoned when he tried to send a telegram to the US president Theodore Roosevelt congratulating him for 'freeing' Cuba from Spanish rule.[32] Furthermore, a month later, 11 nationalist councillors of Bilbao were suspended after welcoming an Argentinian Navy vessel that made a stopover in the city. Different scholars believe that the strong repression that the movement experienced was the main cause for the abrupt shift that Arana's thought experienced at the end of his life, in which he seemed to replace independence for autonomy.[33] This phase, commonly referred to as *la evolución españolista* (the pro-Spanish evolution), began in 1902 when Arana wrote an article from prison that suggested a change of strategy. During this phase, Arana argued that the PNV should pursue 'a radical form of autonomy' (instead of independence) within the 'unity of the Spanish state' and publicly abandoned independence as the main objective of the nationalist movement.[34] He even suggested that to achieve this, the PNV would be replaced by a new party named the Liga de Vascos Españolistas (League of pro-Spanish Basques). As De la Granja argues, *la evolución españolista* meant the culmination of Arana's moderate phase, which had started in 1898: naturally, de la Sota's group seconded this strategy, whereas the Aranist faction (which included his brother Luis) disagreed but did not dare to challenge their leader.[35]

Despite Arana's public and abrupt shift towards regionalism, the founder of Basque nationalism never abandoned independence. Not only did he continue penning pro-separatist texts after 1902 but, as we will

31 De Pablo and Mees, *El péndulo patriótico*, p. 48.
32 Sabino Arana, 'Telegrama a Roosevelt', 27 May 1902, http://www.sag150.eu/archivo.php.
33 See, for instance, de Pablo and Mees, *El péndulo patriótico*, pp. 52–53; Beltza, *El nacionalismo vasco, 1876-1936*, p. 93. Solozábal has argued that whilst this change can be attributed to the intensification of the Spanish state's repression, this change took place in the context of a total crisis in Arana's thought, in which he began to reconsider the praxis of his ideas. He also considers that the start of this change of strategy began as early as 1897. Solozábal, *El primer nacionalismo vasco*, pp. 365–66. De la Granja situates the start of this evolution in 1898. José Luis de la Granja, *El nacionalismo vasco: (1876-1975)* (Madrid: Arco/Libros, 2000), pp. 32–33.
34 Sabino Arana, 'Interview', *La Patria*, 29 June 1902, pp. 2185–86 (p. 2186). See also Sabino Arana, 'Aclaraciones', *La Patria*, 6 July 1902, pp. 2180–84 (p. 2181), in which Arana proclaimed that the PNV abandoned the cause of independence.
35 De la Granja, 'El *Antimaketismo*', p. 199.

see, anticolonial texts against Spain remained constant throughout all his political periods (radical, moderate and *españolista*). Furthermore, two months before he died prematurely of the Addison's disease he suffered from, he named the radical nationalist Ángel Zabala his future successor. On 25 November 1903, the founder of Basque nationalism died aged 38, without having completed or developed the mysterious and contradictory *evolución españolista*. The debate over independence and autonomy was to condition the history of the PNV during the twentieth century. As Conversi argues, 'while the heirs of Arana remained in control of the party's ideology, the pragmatists (de la Sota and other former Euskalerriacos) controlled its political praxis'.[36]

Myths, Colonialism and Race in Sabino Arana's Thought: The Making of Basque Anticolonialism

As I have started arguing in this chapter, scholars unanimously agree that Arana was no inventor or original thinker. Instead, Arana's work, movement and narrative owed much to existing myths, theories and historical events. Arana used these to articulate a historical narrative that helped Basques gain a national consciousness and that presented Basque independence as necessary. As Sebastian Balfour has pointed out, 'the cultural components of this new nationalism [Basque] were an elaboration of narratives of national oppression in which there was much invention of the past and distortion of the present'.[37]

This does not make Basque nationalism exceptional: national communities and patriots rely on myths or on 'invented traditions' to legitimise their existence.[38] These myths rarely have historical validity, as they are an invention of organic nationalist intellectuals who modify or select historical events strategically to construct a glorious tale that justifies the existence of the 'oppressed nation' in question. These myths are addressed to the citizens of the nation and, as Walker Connor argues, although 'myths of unity have a capacity for engendering harmony they also have a capacity for accentuating

---

36 Conversi, *The Basques, the Catalans and Spain*, p. 68.
37 Sebastian Balfour, 'The Spanish Empire and its End: A Comparative View in Nineteenth and Twentieth Century Europe', in Alexei Miller and Alfred J. Rieber (eds), *Imperial Rule* (Budapest and New York: Central European University Press, 2004), pp. 151–60 (p. 158).
38 See Eric J. Hobsbawm and Terence Ranger, *The Invention of Tradition* (Cambridge: Cambridge University Press, 1983) or, for an ethno-symbolic approach of nationalism see Anthony D. Smith, *Myths and Memories of the Nation* (Oxford: Oxford University Press, 1999).

division'.³⁹ Perhaps unsurprisingly, the latter most often results. Furthermore, although the 'inventors' of these myths claim that these legendary tales are unique, most nationalist narratives follow a similar pattern. According to Matthew Levinger and Paula Franklin Lytle, all 'rhetoric of national mobilisation' has three elements in common: all nations claim to have a glorious past (when the original nation was free and pure); a degraded present (when the pure original nation finds itself in a state of decadence); and a utopian future (when the nation will free itself from oppression through collective action and will be as harmonious as it was during its glorious age).⁴⁰ This rhetoric is not confined to nationalist movements only but, as Levinger and Lytle argue, is highly effective in mobilising a community.⁴¹

As Gaizka Fernández Soldevilla has demonstrated, Arana elaborated the first model of the triadic structure of the Basque nationalist rhetoric, which was later amplified and refined by generations of Basque nationalists.⁴² According to Arana, Basques had lived freely and peacefully until the nineteenth century, when the Basque states were conquered by force, and subsequently lost their independence. Before that, Basques had fought for their independence against Spain throughout the centuries. This was the premise of Arana's first book *Bizkaya por su independencia*, in which Arana wrote about Biscay's alleged 'independence wars' and suggested that it was better to die than to live enslaved.⁴³ According to Arana, Basques had lost their millenary independence on 25 October 1839, 'a fatal day for the history of Biscay'.⁴⁴ This day marked the beginning of their 'slavery'.⁴⁵

Arana did not choose this date arbitrarily. Following the First Carlist War, a law issued on 25 October 1839 recognised and confirmed the Fueros

---

39 Walker Connor, *Ethnonationalism: The Quest for Understanding* (Princeton: Princeton University Press, 2018), p. 140.

40 Matthew Levinger and Paula Franklin Lytle, 'Myths and Mobilisation: The Triadic Structure of Nationalism', *Nations and Nationalism*, 7 (2) (2001), pp. 175-95 (p. 178).

41 Levinger and Franklin Lytle, 'Myths and Mobilisation', p. 178.

42 Gaizka Fernández Soldevilla, 'Mitos que matan. La narrativa del "conflicto vasco"', *Ayer*, 98 (2015), pp. 213-40 (p. 221). For a complete account of Arana's reading on Basque history see, for instance, de la Granja, *Ángel o demonio*, pp. 131-72 (pp. 150-57 more specifically).

43 Watson, *Basque Nationalism and Political Violence*, p. 59.

44 Sabino Arana, 'El 25 de Octubre de 1839', *Bizkaitarra*, 31 October 1894, pp. 381-84 (p. 381).

45 The word 'slavery' was used on multiple occasions by Arana to empathise the relationship that defined Spain and Euskadi. For instance, the nineteenth century was defined by Arana as a century of 'slavery'. See Sabino Arana, 'Efemérides infaustas', *Bizkaitarra*, 21 July 1894, pp. 314-21 (p. 318).

but enshrined that they would be 'subordinated' or 'subjected' to the Spanish constitution and the unity of the Spanish state. Arana, however, did not read this law as a recognition of the Fueros. Instead, according to him, this law meant the loss of Basque independence as, for him, Basque Fueros were incompatible with a Spanish liberal constitution.[46] With the law of 1839, Arana claimed, Alava, Gipuzkoa and Biscay – which had so far been 'independent and free'– 'became Spanish provinces'.[47] Indeed, Arana interpreted the Carlist Wars as national wars; something that had already been posited by a figure whom some have identified as Arana's predecessor: the early nineteenth-century French-Basque writer and intellectual Augustin Chaho.[48]

In sum, Arana believed that since 1839 Euskadi 'had been an occupied country'.[49] In order to stress the colonial nature of Euskadi, Arana compared the situation of Euskadi with that of other colonies. Alluding to the independence of many Latin American colonies that had themselves been freed from the Spanish Empire, Arana recognised the paradox of being colonised by a power which was itself disappearing. As he said in 1894:

> in this century, in which so many Spanish colonies were emancipated from their metropolis ... and you [Biscay] had to be subjected by this same nation, you, Biscay, you who never suffered foreign oppression, you who have always been a free nation![50]

Another article published in June 1899, when Spain had already lost its last colonies, confirmed Euskadi's colonial status:

---

46 De la Granja, *Ángel o demonio*, p. 182.

47 Sabino Arana, 'Fecha nefasta', *El Correo Vasco*, 21 July 1899, pp. 1723–26 (p. 1724).

48 Chaho had interpreted the First Carlist War as a conflict of national Basque liberation against Spain. See de Pablo and Mees, *El péndulo patriótico*, p. 5; Corcuera, *La patria de los vascos*, p. 44; Jon Juaristi, *El linaje de Aitor* (Madrid: Taurus, 2000), p. 77. For a good account of Chaho's ideas see Juaristi, *El linaje de Aitor*, pp. 76–107 and Xabier Zabaltza, *Augustin Chaho: Precursor incomprendido (1811–1858)* (Vitoria-Gasteiz: Servicio Central de Publicaciones del Gobierno Vasco, 2011).

49 Cameron Watson, *Modern Basque History: Eighteenth Century to the Present* (Reno: Center for Basque Studies, 2003), p. 183. In this quote, Watson uses the term Euskal Herria (the land of those who speak Basque), but I have decided to use Euskadi for consistency. Euskal Herria is a term that first appeared in the sixteenth-century and was used to refer the seven Basque territories: Biscay, Alava, Gipuzkoa and Navarra (which form Hegoalde or the Spanish Basque Country) and Soule, Lower Navarra and Labourd (which form Iparralde or the French Basque Country). Arana gave the Basque land a new term, Euzkadi (later popularised as Euskadi), 'the place of the Basque race'. This book will use the latter term.

50 Arana, 'El 25 de Octubre de 1839', p. 381.

Gipuzkoa and Alava and Biscay, which were independent states, became Spanish dominions and actual Spanish provinces like Cuba and the Philippines when the very same Spanish nation conquered them. It was only last year when, thanks to US protection, they [Cuba and the Philippines] emancipated from Spain.[51]

Arana continued making these comparisons until the last days of his life. Only a few months before his death, when commenting on a priest who during a Church service in Euskadi lamented the end of the Spanish Empire, Arana claimed: 'how can you tell us that Spain has lost its colonies ... when we have lost the same political life; when in 1839 our sovereignty to legislate and rule, that is, independence, was cancelled?'[52]

Arana seemed to believe that Euskadi suffered the same kind of oppression as Cuba and the Philippines. As this book shows, this proved to be a powerful narrative that was not forgotten by his successors. These timely comparisons were complemented by another powerful ingredient which was added to the nationalist narrative: not only had Euskadi lost its independence in a period in which other colonies achieved emancipation. Worse: the Basque territory had been colonised by what Arana perceived as an inferior race, which was to affect the alleged racial purity of the Basques. As Arana stated in 1899, 'there is nothing more logical than the current state of decline of the Basque nation, subjected every day to the corrupted influence of the immigration of the uncultured, brutish and effeminate [Spanish] peoples'.[53]

Like all the other elements of his narrative, Arana's calls for racial purity and his constant assertions of racial difference between Spaniards and Basques were not new. Before Arana, different intellectuals had stressed the uniqueness of Basque people in racial terms in keeping with the popularity

---

51 Sabino Arana, 'Las cuotas concertadas', *El Correo Vasco*, 23 June 1899, pp. 1689–92 (p. 1689).
52 Sabino Arana, '¿Ignorancia?', *La Patria*, 24 May 1903, pp. 2274–75 (p. 2275).
53 Sabino Arana, 'Extranjerización', *El Correo Vasco*, 10 August 1899, pp. 1760–61. The association between Spain and its people with femininity and inferiority in this highly gendered text makes it necessary to briefly explain Arana's misogyny. For him, Euskadi was an illustrative example of a virile nation and as a result, Basque women also had virile qualities that did not compromise their femininity. Despite this, he held strongly misogynist beliefs and excluded women from the movement in the early years. Arana's conception of women as inferior human beings led him to associate feminine qualities with the Spanish nation. See Nerea Aresti, 'De heroínas viriles a madres de la patria. Las mujeres y el nacionalismo vasco (1893-1937)', *Historia y política*, 31 (2014), pp. 281–308 (pp. 284–91). See also Mercedes Ugalde Solano, 'Dinámica de género y nacionalismo. La movilización de vascas y catalanas en el primer tercio de siglo', *Ayer*, 17 (1995), pp. 121–53.

of scientific racism in Europe in this period. The uniqueness of the Basques, which had already been stressed by intellectuals such as Wilhelm von Humboldt, 'fired the imagination of major figures in the emerging discipline of physical anthropology'.[54] For instance, craniometrists such as Swedish anatomist Anders Retzius and French anthropologist Paul Broca carried out pseudo-scientific studies of Basque anthropometry, legitimising the claimed existence of a Basque race. Retzius was the first to measure Basque skulls and concluded that Basques, Finns and Lapps were the only peoples able to survive the Aryan invasion of Europe.[55] In 1868, three years after Arana was born, Broca went further and concluded that, if the Basque language was the only one to have survived the 'Asiatic invasions', it was likely to suggest that this was because:

> this small mountainous region that the Basques still occupy today was never completely subjugated by the invaders, and that they yet conserve if not political sovereignty at least a numerical preponderance. It is therefore permissible to believe that their physical features have been less modified by their cross-breeding than that of other peoples of Western Europe.[56]

In contrast with western Europeans who were designated part of an Aryan race, the Basques were now presented as the only remnants of a pre-Indo-European-Aryan old Europe, becoming 'twice white and/or twice non-Oriental'.[57] Therefore, as Joseba Gabilondo suggests, the Basques began to be imagined as the only colonial subjects within Europe who were simultaneously classified as white.[58]

Anthropology at this time supported Arana's beliefs that the Basques were a unique race and that southern European races, like the Spaniards, were inferior.[59] Whereas some nineteenth-century thinkers like the French

---

54 See Douglass, 'Sabino's Sin', p. 102. Humboldt claimed that Euskera was the language that Iberians spoke before the Romans came to the Peninsula. With his writings, Humboldt continued and developed the long tradition of Basque-Iberian theories.

55 Joseba Zulaika, *Del cromañón al carnaval: los vascos como museo antropológico* (Donostia: Erein, 2000), p. 50.

56 Quoted from Paul Broca in Douglass, 'Sabino's Sin', p. 102.

57 Joseba Gabilondo, 'Imagining Basques: Dual Otherness from European Imperialism to American Globalization', *Rev. int. estud. vascos.*, 2 (2008), pp. 145–73 (p. 153).

58 Gabilondo, 'Imagining Basques', p. 153.

59 Western anthropologist discourses on racial purity and Basque uniqueness found opposition among some Spanish anthropologists and intellectuals. For

aristocrat Arthur de Gobineau divided the world into the so-called three great races (superior Caucasoids, intermediate Mongoloids and inferior Negroids), other European intellectuals began to debate the superiority or inferiority of certain 'races' or 'nationalities' within the Caucasian category.[60] From this debate emerged the notion that western and northern European 'races' or nationalities were superior to those of southern and central Europe. In the Spanish case, racial debates that placed Spain at the bottom of the hierarchy of European races were supported by common stereotypes that emphasised the cruel, backward and uncivilised nature of the country – stereotypes that had formed the core of the so-called Black Legend – and by the already established belief of an obvious Spanish decadence, which was confirmed with the end of the Spanish Empire in 1898. These debates had an essential impact on how Europeans (and Spaniards and Basques themselves) regarded Spain: as Michael Iarocci points out, 'Spain became a non-European Europe, a non-Western West ... Spain had become the image of everything modern Europe was not'.[61]

Naturally, the theories and cultural debates that stressed Spain's inferiority and barbarity and Basques' uniqueness were embraced and developed by Arana and his successors. By mixing myths and western anthropological discourses that suggested the existence of a distinct, unique and pure Basque race, Arana argued that the Basques were the first and earliest inhabitants of the peninsula and the oldest and purest race of Europe.[62] This

instance, theories of Aryan supremacy and purity were refuted by influential anthropologists such as Manuel Antón y Ferrándiz. See Joshua Goode, *Impurity of Blood: Defining Race in Spain, 1870–1930* (Baton Rouge: Louisiana State University Press, 2009), p. 86. Antón was part of a group of intellectuals for whom racial purity was not a sign of superiority and instead, they insisted on the benefits of racial mixing. Antón's disciple, Basque anthropologist Telesforo Aranzadi (cousin of the celebrated intellectual Miguel de Unamuno), argued in his doctoral thesis (published in 1889) that Basques were not racially pure but instead a hybrid of Iberian and Berber-related groups, Finns, Laplanders and Germanic peoples. However, some argue that he eventually abandoned his thesis of Basque hybridity to defend the purity and uniqueness of the Basque race (a theory obviously supported by Basque nationalists). See Susan Martin-Márquez, *Disorientations: Spanish Colonialism in Africa and the Performance of Identity* (New Haven, 2008), p. 45.

60 See Douglass, 'Sabino's Sin', p. 96.

61 Michael P. Iarocci, *Properties of Modernity: Romantic Spain, Modern Europe, and the Legacies of Empire* (Nashville: Vanderbilt University Press, 2006), p. 15.

62 The issue of whether Arana was a racist or not and the extent to which he was aware of western anthropology has divided scholars. Whether Arana had a biological conception of race or whether this was mostly based on cultural differences, I agree with Jeremy MacClancy that Arana was aware of the utility of these discourses to his movement. See Jeremy MacClancy, *Expressing Identities in the Basque Arena* (Suffolk:

contrasted with the mixed character of the Spanish race, which according to Arana was 'a product of all the invasions that have come to the peninsula for more than 40 centuries: Celt, Phoenician, Greek, Roman, German, Arab, the Latin element being predominant'.[63] In contrast, for Arana, the Basque race,

> is a very primordial race, which is not Celt, Phoenician, Greek, Latin, German or Arab, and it is not similar, apart from being human, to any of the races that inhabit the European, African, Asiatic or the American continents nor the Oceanic islands. It is so isolated in the universe that data has not been found to classify it amongst the rest of the races.[64]

Drawing on these theories, Arana imagined the Basque and Spanish struggle as one between opposing races, arguing that for the Basques to preserve their racial purity, independence was the only solution. As Douglass states, 'it was the Basques' shameful stain to be dominated by the central authority of such a pathetic state and colonized by what the wider European racialist discourse regarded to be inferior "Latin" racist stock'.[65] Thus, according to Arana, it was the coloniser (the Spaniard) and not the colonised (the Basque) who needed to be civilised.

Whilst this dogma was a rhetorical strategy to stress the inferior nature of the Spaniard and to ultimately mobilise the Basque population, it also served Arana to establish differences between the Basque (western and cultured) and the Spanish (non-western and blasphemous). In parallel with western Orientalism, Arana depicted the Basques in opposition to the Spanish other (in this case the coloniser, and not the colonised). This idea was present in many of his writings and, as this book will show, that of his successors. In an article titled 'Nos vamos civilizando' ('We are becoming civilised'), in a highly ironic tone, Arana criticised the fact that

> the same ones that are the cause of the loss of our peaceful and healthy habits [the Spaniards] have the audacity to tell us that they have civilised us, that we were in a state of barbarism until they came here, across the Ebro,

---

Boydell & Brewer, 2007), p. 114. Arana himself acknowledged this: 'ethnographically there is a substantial difference between the Spanish being and the Basque being, because the Euskaran [Basque] race is substantially distinct from the Spanish race, which is something we do not only ourselves say but all anthropologists as well.' Translated and quoted from Arana by MacClancy, *Expressing Identities in the Basque Arena*, p. 114. De la Granja has also linked Arana's discourses on race to the racist discourses of nineteenth-century Europe. See de la Granja, *Ángel o demonio*, pp. 76–78.

63 Sabino Arana, '¿Qué somos?', *Bizkaitarra*, 16 June 1895, pp. 606–08 (p. 607).
64 Arana, '¿Qué somos?', p. 607.
65 Douglass, 'Sabino's Sin', p. 105.

bringing with them bullfighting, flamenco dancing and singing, as well as the strikingly cultured language they have which tends to blaspheme and which contains dirty expressions, [and they have also brought] the knife and a whole host of [similarly] excellent civilising methods.[66]

In sum, Arana's nationalist rhetoric was based on the premise that Euskadi had been recently colonised by what he perceived as a barbaric and inferior race. Arana reached this conclusion by mixing and selectively compiling historical events, myths and racial discourses that supported his reading of history. These claims were particularly damaging at the time in which he was writing, which was one of anticolonial upheaval in the Spanish Empire. Arana used this circumstance to his advantage and denounced Spanish colonialism. The rest of this chapter explores the extent to which these solidarity claims were genuine or whether they reflected Arana's hatred of the deadly Spanish state and Empire.

Anticolonialism or Hispanophobia? Contesting Sabino Arana's Anticolonial Claims

Sabino Arana's thought and work has been the object of endless studies, some of which have attempted to deal with the anticolonial tone of his writings. Yet amongst other things, the racial element of his thought has prevented these authors from reaching a consensus. The contradictions of Arana's discourse are apparent: how could one condemn colonialism whilst using racist discourses against Spanish that emerged in imperial Europe?

Scholars have attempted to overcome the contradictions of Arana's discourse. Cameron Watson has argued that although Arana stressed the qualities of the Basque race over the Spaniards, 'he never envisaged a racial hierarchy in European society and, indeed … was quick to defend non-European (and non-Christian) peoples in their anticolonial struggles against European powers'.[67] As the previous section has demonstrated, other scholars have connected Arana's thought to the nineteenth-century trend of classifying humankind into different races. Yet some scholars like Javier Corcuera have argued that for Arana, the thesis of racial superiority did not affect the political rights of nations and he believed that all nations had the same right to independence.[68] Douglass, who has acknowledged the

---

66 Sabino Arana, 'Nos vamos civilizando', *El Correo Vasco*, 16 June 1899, pp. 1678–79 (p. 1679). Note 1: In the original, the use of adjectives and intensifiers (e.g. 'cultísima') is notoriously ironic and bitter.
67 Watson, *Modern Basque History*, p. 183.
68 Corcuera, *La patria de los vascos*, p. 445.

contradictions of Arana's thought and his racist views, has gone further and claimed that the founder of Basque nationalism sympathised with the colonised peoples of the world, and 'would most certainly have sympathised with the views of Frantz Fanon'.[69]

Although Douglass's claims are perhaps an overstatement, these arguments are not unreasonable. Like most of these authors recognise, Arana (although in my view, very sporadically) criticised the colonisation of different areas of the globe. Furthermore, especially prior to 1898, Arana (very) occasionally condemned the discourse of superiority that Europeans (usually referred as the 'white races') used as a pretext to dominate others. For instance, in an article published in 1893, Arana condemned the greed of the 'white race' who had invaded the American continent and now was attempting to do the same in north Africa, with the false excuse of being the carriers of civilisation.[70] In another article, which has been used by some scholars such as Ugalde to stress Arana's rejection of all types of colonialism, Arana argued that 'the white race' was 'the greatest vandal [race] of the world' but yet '[the Caucasians] still consider other races as inferior'.[71]

Whilst these examples should be acknowledged, they should not be used to claim that Arana generally held anti-racist views and that he condemned all forms of colonialism, as Larronde has argued.[72] Instead, as the rest of this chapter shows, Arana mixed these anticolonial statements with highly Orientalist and imperialist views of non-western people. For instance, in an article published in 1897, Arana condemned the invasion of

---

69 Douglass, 'Sabino's Sin', p. 105.

70 Sabino Arana, 'Los seudo-civilizadores', *Bizkaitarra*, 17 December 1893, pp. 189–90 (p. 189). It is worth noting that although this text began condemning the European conquests generally, it was mainly directed against the Spanish.

71 Sabino Arana, '¡Magnífico!', *Baserritarra*, 6 June 1897, p. 1303. See Ugalde, 'El primer nacionalismo vasco ante la independencia de Cuba', pp. 219–20. It is interesting that Arana publicly condemned racial hierarchies when he used the same argument to criticise the Spanish invasion of the Basques as the takeover of a superior race by an inferior one. Arana's belief in racial hierarchy and advocacy for the freedom of colonised peoples was not a contradiction during his lifetime. In fact, during the late nineteenth century 'scientific racists' such as Herbert Spencer and William Graham Sumner opposed imperialism openly. See John M. Hobson, *The Eurocentric Conception of World Politics: Western International Theory, 1760–2010* (Cambridge and New York: Cambridge University Press, 2012), pp. 84–105 (p. 85).

72 Larronde, *El nacionalismo vasco*, pp. 281–98. Although Ugalde presents a more nuanced vision and recognises some contradictions within Arana's thought, he also argues that Arana condemned all types of colonialism, as well as the evilness of the white race. Ugalde, *La acción exterior del nacionalismo vasco*; Ugalde, 'El primer nacionalismo ante la independencia de Cuba'.

the Americas generally but recognised that some peoples, owing to a lack of virtue and their ineptitude to govern themselves, had to be subjected to a foreign power to reach this; henceforth suggesting that not all 'races' were equal and justifying colonialism on some occasions.[73] Furthermore, apart from the examples mentioned above, Arana's anticolonial claims were directed solely at Spain. Indeed, as de la Granja has pointed out, Arana's anticolonialism was rooted in his anti-Spanishness.[74] In other words, Arana used his anticolonialism to attack Spain and legitimise Basque independence claims more than to support the colonised.

Arana and Spain's Colonial Fronts before the '98 Disaster: The Rif, Cuba and the Philippines

The emergence of Arana's anticolonialism is closely linked to the period in which he lived. During the Age of Empire, most of the world outside Europe and the Americas was divided into arbitrary territories controlled from distant metropolises. This period also saw the development of racial discourses that justified colonial intervention on an unprecedented scale as the civilising mission of the west. But this period did not affect all western powers equally: whilst powers such as Britain and France cemented their dominance and new colonial powers such as the US and Germany gained influence, Spain faced a major colonial crisis during Arana's lifetime. The traditional and pre-industrial Spanish Empire, which had experienced major losses in the first quarter of the nineteenth century, was about to lose its remaining territories with the emancipation of Cuba and the Philippines in 1898. As well as the wars of independence in the Caribbean and the Pacific, Spain faced a colonial crisis in north Africa in 1893 with the outbreak of the Melilla War.

Arana followed these events closely. As Watson has suggested, Spain's growing colonial problems – as well as other factors related with Spain's state-building – 'would provide opportunities for the dissemination of Arana's nationalist ideas'.[75] Whilst Riffian, Cuban and Philippine nationalists rose up violently against Spain, Arana challenged the stability of the metropole

---

73 Sabino Arana, 'Efectos de la invasión', *Baserritarra*, 11 July 1897, pp. 1326–37 (p. 1328).

74 De la Granja, 'El *Antimaketismo*', p. 198. Scholars such as Izaskun Álvarez have also stressed the opportunism of Arana's anticolonialism and have argued that he used the Cuban War of Independence and the pro-independence aspirations of Cubans as an opportunity to attack Spain. Izaskun Álvarez Cuartero, 'Lecturas de la independencia de Cuba en el discurso nacionalista de Sabino Arana', in Antonio Gutiérrez Escudero and María Luisa Laviana Cuetos (eds), *España y las Antillas: el 98 y más* (Sevilla: Diputación Provincial de Sevilla, 1999), pp. 199–214 (p. 201).

75 Watson, *Basque Nationalism and Political Violence*, p. 60.

by denouncing and questioning Spain's colonial practices. These claims probably had a great impact on the incipient Basque nationalist readership, as Arana portrayed Euskadi as an equal victim of Spanish imperialism.

The first opportunity Arana had to question the actions of the Spanish Empire was during the so-called Melilla War of 1893 in northern Morocco. This was the consequence of Spain's desire to establish a growing influence over Morocco and to legitimise its presence against other European powers that were already present in northern Africa, such as France. Spain's increasing interests in Morocco had already provoked a war there between 1859 and 1860. In 1893, the conflict was reactivated when Spanish workers who were constructing a military fort near a Mosque and a Muslim cemetery were attacked by Riffian Kabyles after the Spanish ignored the petitions of local leaders.[76] Although on a much smaller scale than in the previous war that Spain had declared on Morocco in 1859, during the Melilla War Spain reactivated its patriotic discourse against the Riffians through a repertoire of acts aimed at mobilising the Spanish public, including street demonstrations, hymns, subscriptions and fundraising.[77] During this time of imperial crisis, the Spanish establishment was desperately trying to bolster the country's patriotic mood by imagining a fast and glorious defeat. Amid this patriotic mobilisation and crusade against the 'Moors', Spanish socialists and anarchists – who believed that the conflict was detrimental to the Spanish working classes – and Arana were the only internal voices that dared to challenge Spanish imperialism.

In December 1893, *Bizkaitarra* published an issue that contained many articles written by Arana condemning Spain's intervention in Africa. An article titled '¿Somos españoles?' ('Are we Spanish?') reproduced a (probably invented) conversation between a French man and a Basque man about the origins of the Basques. The French man started this conversation by arguing that he was very surprised that the Basques wished Spaniards bad luck in Melilla. The Basque man responded arguing that 'Biscayans [Basques] are not Spanish by race, language, laws or history'.[78] This same opinion was expressed in another article in the same issue in which Arana mocked the fact that Spain had asked Biscay for men, money and weapons.[79]

---

76 Carlos Ferrera Cuesta, 'Explicaciones de una política exterior: la crisis de Melilla de 1893–1894', *Ayer*, 54 (2004), pp. 305-26 (p. 310).

77 Alfonso Iglesias Amorín, 'The Hispano-Moroccan Wars (1859-1927) and the (De)nationalization of the Spanish People', *European History Quarterly*, 50.2 (2020), pp. 290-310 (p. 297).

78 Sabino Arana, '¿Somos españoles?', *Bizkaitarra*, 17 December 1893, pp. 181-86 (p. 181).

79 Sabino Arana, 'Triunvirato Bizkaino', *Bizkaitarra*, 17 December 1893, pp. 190-92.

Other articles were more explicit. For instance, '¿De parte de quién está el derecho?' ('On which side is the law?') sums up Arana's attitude towards the Melilla War. In this article, Arana questioned 'with which right do the Spanish occupy that territory that is very far from being Spain' and argued that 'the Spanish took things that were not theirs ... and the Riffians are trying to recover what they lost four centuries ago'.[80] Arana continued his article stating that 'this was not the first time that Spain had provoked an unfair war against the Moors', referring to the war against Morocco in 1859.[81] Arana concluded with a clear critique of colonialism, arguing that 'it is well known that in international affairs the only law that has triumphed is the law of strength'.[82]

To support the Riffians and delegitimise Spain's colonial claims, Arana stressed the moral, military, physical and intellectual inferiority of the coloniser in comparison with the colonised. For instance, Arana attacked and mocked the alleged heroism, strength and bravery of the Spaniard in the colonial contest. According to Arana, although Spain initially underestimated the Riffian – seen as a cowardly sheep in opposition to the Spanish lion – they had soon realised that to 'reject those "little sheep" from the Riff, Spain had to spend 60 million pesetas'.[83] Arana denounced the Spanish press for disseminating fake rumours about the enemy and for manipulating the number of Riffian insurrectionists and of Spanish soldiers sent to the battle – strategically exaggerating the figures of the former and under-reporting those of the latter.[84] According to Arana, the Spaniards were the cowards who constantly had to retreat from the battle, not the Riffians.

Arana used Spain's colonial decline and the existing western stereotypes of southern Europe to project a vision of Spain as a backward, vicious and corrupt nation. He had started advancing this image in the first issue of *Bizkaitarra*, when he argued that whereas in the past 'Spain was the most powerful nation in the world', in the late nineteenth century it was 'the most rickety and feeble [nation]'.[85] The Riffian conflict offered Arana an opportunity to expand this vision of Spain, while inverting the colonial hierarchy that Spain – and the rest of empires – had long relied

---

80 Sabino Arana, '¿De parte de quién está el derecho?', *Bizkaitarra*, 17 December 1893, pp. 186–88 (p. 187).

81 Arana, '¿De parte de quién está el derecho?', p. 187.

82 Arana, '¿De parte de quién está el derecho?', p. 188.

83 Sabino Arana, 'El león español', *Bizkaitarra*, 17 December 1893, pp. 193–94 (p. 194).

84 See Arana, 'El león español'; Sabino Arana, 'Criterios', *Bizkaitarra*, 17 December 1893, p. 195.

85 Sabino Arana, 'Bizkaya en 1893', *Bizkaitarra*, 8 June 1893, pp. 168–70 (pp. 168–69).

on to legitimise its rule. According to Arana, it was not Spain's colonial subjects who needed guidance to develop and make progress, but Spain itself. Arana questioned 'what kind of culture the Spanish could bring to the Rif' and affirmed that 'so far, the Riffians are the ones who can give lessons to Spaniards'.[86]

Much to Arana's benefit, the peace in northern Morocco in 1894 was not the end of the problems of the Spanish Empire but the beginning of its disintegration. A year after the start of the ultimate War of Cuban Independence (1895–1898), Spain had to face a new anticolonial front with the outbreak of the Philippine Revolution in 1896. Against Spanish predictions, both rebellions would culminate in the loss of Spain's overseas territories in 1898. Despite their geographical distance from one another, we cannot understand the Cuban and the Philippine rebellions separately.[87] As John Blanco notes, the national heroes of Cuba and the Philippines, José Martí and José Rizal respectively, 'shared a series of ghostly parallels' that made their histories and that of their nations entangled.[88] Both were subjects and witnesses of the last colonies that Spain held, which led them to write anticolonial texts that would influence generations of Cubans and Filipinos. Furthermore, they both died as national martyrs only one year apart, with Martí's death occurring in 1895 during the ultimate War of Independence and Rizal's in 1896 when he was executed by the Spanish for his alleged connection to the violent Philippine Revolution. In fact, whilst Martí and Rizal never wrote about each other's struggles, the Spanish government was aware of their connections. As Benedict Anderson suggests, Madrid's decision to execute Rizal must be understood in the context of global anticolonial uprising, as it was also intended to have an impact in Cuba.[89]

Arana was very aware of the parallel development of these anticolonial rebellions against Spanish rule. As Larronde points out, the parallel

---

86 Arana, 'Los seudo-civilizadores', p. 189.

87 Many scholars have acknowledged the relationship between the national leaders of the Philippines and Cuba, José Rizal and José Martí respectively. See amongst others, Benedict Anderson, *Under Three Flags: Anarchism and the Anti-Colonial Imagination* (London and New York: Verso, 2005); John D. Blanco, 'Bastards of the Unfinished Revolution: Bolívar's Ismael and Rizal's Martí at the Turn of the Twentieth Century', *Radical History Review*, 89 (2004), pp. 92–114; Koichi Hagimoto, *Between Empires: Martí, Rizal, and the Intercolonial Alliance* (Basingstoke: Palgrave Macmillan, 2013). Some like Larronde have established links between Rizal, Martí and Arana. See Larronde, *El nacionalismo vasco*, pp. 282–84. See also, Larronde and Guezala, 'El anticolonialismo de Sabino Arana, fundador del nacionalismo vasco'.

88 Blanco, 'Bastards of the Unfinished Revolution', p. 93.

89 Anderson, *Under Three Flags*, p. 167.

between the nationalist movements of Cuba and Philippines and those in the peninsula reflect the crisis of the structure of the Spanish state and the end of a united, imperial Spain: the cracks (of the crisis) were heard both inside and outside the peninsula.[90] Indeed, like the Melilla War, both the Cuban and the Filipino rebellions provided an opportunity for Arana to strengthen his anti-Spanish campaign. Thus, in a very similar manner to the Riffian conflict, Arana delegitimised Spanish colonialism in both Cuba and the Philippines by stressing the military and physical inferiority of the Spaniards, as well as their 'uncivilised' customs. For instance, Arana refuted and mocked patriotic news stories which praised the superiority of the Spanish military over its colonies, and assured his readers that Spain was about to be defeated.[91] He also rejoiced that Spain was about to be beaten in the Caribbean.[92] In a section of an article published in the summer of 1895 titled 'La "Débacle" Española' (the Spanish debacle), Arana concluded with the same tone: 'We almost feel sorry for Spain. First Cuba for the Cubans or the Yankees...then Puerto Rico for the latter too and Philippines for the Japanese. Spain will have nothing else than Gibraltar.'[93]

Whilst so far, evidence seems to agree with the scholars that stress Arana's sympathy for other colonial subjects, we must question the extent to which Arana's anticolonialism was sincere or if it was mostly a product of his strong anti-Spanishness. Indeed, Arana was aware that the destruction of the Spanish Empire could imply a turning point in history. In 1894, after he made a balance of the situation in the west (Cuba), east (Philippines), south (Morocco) and north ('Catalonia, Galicia and other regions'), he claimed:

Without treasure, without patriotism in its leaders, without faith in its subjects, without morality, discipline, sources of wealth, hard work, culture and civilisation, decadent Spain is the most backwards nation of Europe: the laughing stock of the world.[94]

As this sentence shows, Arana was more interested in the debacle of Spain than in the freedom of its colonial subjects. The attitude Arana developed towards Cuba evidences this vision. Significantly, Arana did not support Cuban insurgents until he knew the loss of Cuba would have a real,

90 Larronde, *El nacionalismo vasco*, p. 282.
91 See for instance, Sabino Arana, 'España (ramillete escogido)', *Bizkaitarra*, 31 March 1895, pp. 551–54; Sabino Arana, 'Revista de la prensa: El Nervión', *Bizkaitarra*, 30 June 1895, pp. 629–30.
92 Arana, 'España (ramillete escogido)', p. 554.
93 Arana, 'La "Débacle" española', *Bizkaitarra*, 16 June 1895, pp. 619–20 (p. 620).
94 Arana, 'Efemérides infaustas', p. 317.

detrimental impact on Spain. Before Cubans rose up with weapons against the Spanish Empire, Arana even condemned Cuban insurgents. In late 1893, when talking about Cuban separatists, Arana classified this movement as an 'aberration' as its members 'lived in a territory which is not theirs and [who] are descendants of both Spanish and Africans'.[95] A year later, Arana confirmed this idea, arguing that Cuban separatist tendencies were less reasonable amongst its Spanish and *mestizo* inhabitants, 'intruders and invaders', than if they were held by its natural indigenous people.[96] 'As long as there are indigenous families in the archipelago and in the large territories of the American continent', the article continued, 'it is the native and not the European (who has snatched these poor people) who belongs in these territories.'[97] In the same article, Arana gave another crucial reason why he was not as sympathetic to the Cuban cause:

> We can only look at Cuba's separatism as a foreign question which ... does not affect our homeland at all and we don't care at all if they [Cubans] triumph. It will only affect us insofar as it can influence the internal situation of Spain, which is Biscay's oppressor ... as our triumph will be closer once Spain becomes more prostrated and ruined ... What economic consequences could the loss of Cuba have for Spain? Perhaps it is not a loss but an improvement of its [Spanish] treasure as it seems like its colonial expenses are higher than its income.[98]

This statement indicates that Arana was aware of the delicate economic situation in Cuba. Since the eighteenth century, Cuba had turned into one of the most prosperous and rich sugar colonies of the world. Nevertheless, the different internal and international conflicts that Spain had to face in the nineteenth century produced an economic deficit that the Spanish tried to solve with higher taxes. Aside from Arana's awareness of this issue, this text also confirms the anti-Spanish intention of his anticolonialism. Arana stressed this idea again in the same text:

> If, once Biscay finds enough strength to confront the foreign ruler through the union of its sons and its intimate alliance with other Basque states, there was an armed conflict [for Cuba's independence] between

---

95 Arana, 'Los seudo-civilizadores', p. 189.
96 Sabino Arana, 'El separatismo', *Bizkaitarra*, 31 December 1894, pp. 422–23 (p. 423).
97 Arana, 'El separatismo', p. 423.
98 Arana, 'El separatismo', pp. 422–23.

Cuba and its metropolis ... then the question will be different. But the peaceful separation of Cuba can't bring any good to Biscay.[99]

As Arana makes clear here, he seemed to believe that Spain would only be affected if Cuban separatists rebelled against Spain through a violent insurrection. It was only when Cuban rebels took arms against Spain for the third time that he penned some incendiary texts against Spain.[100] Arana did not even allude to or reference the aspiration of the Cubans or the ideas of José Martí, as their discourses (especially those on race, but also on the growing US influence in Latin America, as we will see) were mostly opposed.[101]

On top of the opportunism of Arana's professed anticolonialism, one must dwell on the sources of his political thought to determine the sincerity of his sympathy towards colonial insurgents. We only need to observe the patronising language that Arana deployed when talking about Spain and other areas Orientalised by the west, and how it resembled imperial discourses across Europe at that time. As I demonstrate, despite Arana's words of support towards anticolonial insurgents, Arana's anti-Spanish discourse relied on stereotypes that northern European empires used to establish differences between what they were and what they were not.[102] These discourses, in which Spain was equated with other Orientalised territories by the west as a means of discrediting it, reveal an Orientalist and negative vision of non-western territories.

To understand this, we need to go back to the discourses mentioned above, which denied Spain its European or modern status. Stephanie Lang observes that, 'in the "Orientalising" Europe which reaffirms itself through the colonised "other", Spain occupies a middle ground'.[103] This is because unlike other European and imperial powers, Spain was imagined by European intellectuals as a hybrid between civilisation and barbarism, between Europe and Africa. As Susan Martin-Márquez claims, 'the post-Enlightenment

99 Arana, 'El separatismo', p. 423.
100 Despite this verbal support, he declared his opposition to sending Basque patriots to fight alongside Cubans, as they were needed at home. See Sabino Arana, 'Rumores', *Bizkaitarra*, 30 June 1895, pp. 632–33 (p. 632).
101 Álvarez Cuartero, 'Lecturas de la independencia de Cuba', p. 213.
102 As Edward Said has famously established, the western world has constructed its image or identity by creating and stressing differences with the (colonised) 'other' to support claims to western superiority. Edward Said, *Orientalism* (London: Penguin, 2003).
103 Stephanie Lang, 'Más allá del Ebro, ¿Los salvajes? La "España Africana" como impulso del regeneracionismo catalán hacia 1900', in Christian von Tschilschke and Jan-Henrik Witthaus (eds), *El otro colonialismo: España y África, entre imaginación e historia* (Frankfurt am Main: Iberoamericana - Vervuert, 2017), pp. 105–30 (p. 108).

"re-discovery" of the Andalusian past led Spaniards and foreigners alike to Orientalize the Iberian nation', making Spain a nation that is at once both 'Orientalized and Orientalizing', 'self and other'.[104] Notably, in Spain, the proximity with Africa was used by some Africanistas (Africanists) to defend Spain's colonial claims in Morocco. Whereas some defenders of colonialism claimed that Spain was far superior to the 'savage' north African, other advocates of empire asserted that Spain's colonialism in Morocco would be far more successful than that of other European powers given the Spaniard's hybrid nature between civilisation and barbarism.[105] This idea of Spain's hybrid nature was also very much present in (both foreign and domestic) cultural representations of Spain: as Victor Hugo famously observed in his *Les Orientales* (1829), 'Spain is still the Orient; Spain is half African'.[106]

Arana engaged with these ideas, asserting the close links between Spain and Africa and with other Orientalised areas by the west.[107] He suggested in his articles that Spain was not half but entirely African. Reviving a French saying which allegedly originated in the nineteenth century, Arana claimed in 1895 that Spain continuously proved the saying 'Africa begins

---

104 Martín-Márquez, *Disorientations*, pp. 8–9.
105 Martín-Márquez, *Disorientations*, p. 52.
106 In French in the original. Victor Hugo, *Les Orientales: Les Feuilles d'Automne* (Paris: Librairie Hachette, 1872), p. 8.
107 Arana was not the only figure in Spain who engaged with the idea of the Spanish as uncivilised and inferior. Contemporary Catalan nationalists used this idea to distinguish themselves from the Spanish and to portray themselves as an extension not of Spain but of the 'civilised' France. After Spain lost its Empire in 1898, Catalan nationalists used this famous distinction between Europe and Spain to demand a new imperial project in which the imperial agenda would be transferred to Catalonia, whose more civilised and modern nature could allow them to continue, modernise and develop Spain's old imperial project. Whilst we can see some parallels in Basque and Catalan rhetoric about Spain being uncivilised, their aims were very different. Catalan nationalists used these ideas to proclaim themselves as the ideal candidates to take over the Spanish Empire, whereas Arana used them to attack Spain's imperial aims. For further analysis of the relationship between Catalan nationalism and empire see Lang, 'Más allá del Ebro', pp. 110–16 and Enric Ucelay-Da Cal, *El imperialismo catalán: Prat de la Riba, Cambó, d'Órs y la conquista moral de España* (Barcelona: Edhasa, 2003). See also Enric Ucelay-Da Cal, 'Els enemics dels meus enemics. Les simpaties del nacionalisme català pels «moros»: 1900–1936', *L'Avenç*, 28 (1980), pp. 29–40 (pp. 30–32) and Eloy Martín Corrales, 'Catalunya i el Marroc: un segle i mig de relació', *L'Avenç*, 256 (2001), pp. 18–26 (pp. 20–21). Corcuera has also compared the differences between Arana's attitude towards colonialism and those of Catalan nationalist leaders such as Prat de la Riba. See Corcuera, *La patria de los vascos*, pp. 444 and 448.

in the Pyrenees'.[108] 'Culture and civilisation', continued Arana, 'damages Spain's eyes.'[109] In another article that talked about a family in Madrid that was caught eating human flesh, Arana claimed: 'In Europe there are also cannibals. Spain is only united to Europe by a natural accident.'[110]

Indeed, comparing Spanish traditions, religious practices and customs with those of other areas generally Orientalised in the west offered a way of discrediting Spain. For instance, Arana constantly held that the Spanish practised an immoral and violent form of Christianity, different to that of the Basques and resembling how other Orientalised religions practised theirs. In an article that criticised Spain's methods of spreading religion, Arana argued that to 'disseminate religion through violence may be typical of Mohammed's religion but it is a path banned by Christ's religion'.[111] In another article, he commented that 'no matter how uncivilised or savage a country is they do not blaspheme the name of God the way the Spaniard does' and compared Spanish religious practices and their supposed tendency to blaspheme with that practised by Muslims and Buddhists, concluding that the way the Spanish practised religion was iniquitous.[112] These examples illustrate Arana's Orientalising view of other religions such as Islam, associating them with violence and backwardness.

Similarly, Arana compared Spain with Turkey, then considered the epitome of degeneration by the west, stressing both countries' lack of civilisation: 'in the west of Europe there are forty or so provinces of *maketos*, like in the east, where there is a Turkish kingdom. How we need other barbarians like those from the fifth century to civilise these poor people, who are far

---

108 Sabino Arana, 'Opresión', *Bizkaitarra*, 16 June 1895, pp. 618-22 (p. 619). Note: The sentence 'África empieza en los Pirineos' ('Africa begins in the Pyrenees'), widely used in the nineteenth century, was a derogatory French saying aimed at Spain that placed the country outside industrialised modernity. Its origins - which were first attributed to Alexandre Dumas *père* - are still unclear. See Teresa M. Vilarós and Michael Ugarte, 'Cuando África empieza en los Pirineos', *Journal of Spanish Cultural Studies*, 7.3 (2006), pp. 199-205.
109 Arana, 'Opresión', p. 619.
110 Arana, 'España (ramillete escogido)', p. 552.
111 Sabino Arana, 'La escuela en Bizcaya', *Bizkaitarra*, 24 April 1895, pp. 566-69 (p. 569). In this same article Arana protested the Spanish desire to impose their culture and language through Biscay's schools. He also condemned the Spanish colonisation of the Americas and argued that Spain only brought to the Americas 'immorality, misery and death', subjecting 'free nations, steal[ing] their resources and cause[ing] a deep abhorrence of the criminal conquistador' religion'.
112 Sabino Arana, 'Un pueblo caracterizado', *El Correo Vasco*, 18 June 1899, pp. 1681-82 (p. 1681).

away from the hand of God.'[113] This same Orientalist vein was present all throughout Arana's political thought, evidencing a tendency to 'other' Spain by conceptualising it as part of the 'Orient'.[114]

These assertions suggest that for Arana, being 'non-western' was necessarily linked with being uncivilised, barbaric and inferior. Furthermore, contrary to some Spanish Africanists, associations with Africa were not used to defend Spain's imperial claims in north Africa against other powers such as Britain or France, but to dismantle them. It was Spain's nature (not western, like other colonial powers) that invalidated its civilisation mission. As Arana claimed, 'the Spaniard does not pursue anything, does not dare to do anything and is worth nothing (just examine the state of its colonies)'.[115] Through this argument, Arana alleged that 'every now and then the Spaniard needs a foreign invasion that helps him to become civilised'.[116] This indicates that whilst sympathising with colonial insurgents, Arana also reproduced imperialist discourses that associated the colonised 'other' with an inferiority that the coloniser should not possess. From 1898 onwards, these beliefs led him to develop a selective view of colonialism that welcomed it when practised by what he perceived as superior and strictly western nations.

---

113 Sabino Arana, 'La prensa local. El Basco', *Bizkaitarra*, 24 February 1895, pp. 502–22 (p. 511).

114 For instance, in 1899, Arana commented on an anti-clerical riot that took place across three days in Zaragoza, during which rebels attempted to burn a Jesuit convent. When the rioters attempted to enter and loot the convent, the religious order allegedly raised an English flag. According to the article, Spanish nationalists and newspapers protested the raising of a foreign flag and accused the Jesuits of a lack of patriotism. Arana's reaction was, of course, very different. He argued that 'in countries where civilisation has not yet arrived, or has arrived to a lesser extent, like Turkey, Persia, China and others', religious orders were under the protection of a 'civilised nation and, in order to escape the effects of fanatism' they would fly the flag of their 'protective nation'. He claimed that Spain was in the same condition as those countries that had not yet achieved civilisation and therefore the Jesuits were perfectly entitled to raise the English flag. See Sabino Arana, 'Para remachar el clavo', *El Correo Vasco*, 29 June 1899, p. 1698.

115 Sabino Arana, '¿Qué somos?' (continued), *Bizkaitarra*, 30 June 1895, pp. 625–28 (p. 627).

116 Arana, 'Qué somos?' (continued), p. 627. Arana repeated this point in *Baserritarra*, when he claimed that civilisation was not needed in America where colonisation took the form of 'murder and theft'. Instead, 'the southern part of Europe' (Spain) was the region that 'could not civilise itself through even missionaries and needed a foreign invasion'. See Arana, 'Efectos de la invasión', p. 1328.

The Dying and Living Nations: Benevolent Colonialism after 1898

In April 1898, after over three years of colonial warfare in Cuba and nearly two in the Philippines, Spain found itself involved in another war with the US for the control of these territories. Although significantly shorter, the Spanish-American War was no less painful for Spain. After months of exacerbated patriotism fostered from above, Spain lost Cuba, the Philippines, Puerto Rico and the island of Guam to the US in a quick, humiliating defeat. Whilst for many this confirmed the alleged supremacy of the northern and Anglo-Saxon races over the Latin or southern, the loss of these colonies marked a turning point in the history of modern Spain, heralding the start of one of the most traumatic periods in its recent history. The wound that the loss of empire left within Spanish society explains why this episode has been commonly referred as the '98 Disaster.

Spain had lost most of its Latin American empire in the early nineteenth century. However, as Ismael Saz identifies, the loss of nearly all the Latin American colonies in the early nineteenth century did not provoke a national crisis like 1898 did.[117] Scholars have partly attributed this to the widespread notion that old colonial empires were disappearing in favour of a new 'informal' imperialism.[118] Balfour claims that the loss of overseas territories in the first half of the nineteenth century did not critically undermine the Spanish monarchical state because earlier in the century 'empire did not have the political significance it acquired later in the century when modernization and imperial competition created communities with national identities'.[119] In addition, whilst Spain had managed to retain its imperial status through its colonies of Cuba, Puerto Rico and the Philippines, in 1898 it completed a full transition from empire to nation state.

The end of the great empire on which the sun never set consolidated Spain's status as a second-class nation and seemed to confirm the ideas that had been circulating for two centuries about the decadence of the country. After 1898, the notion that Spain was a failed and backward nation, incompatible with modernity and alien to European culture, seemed more widespread than ever both within and outside the country.[120] As José Álvarez-Junco shows, the international rating of Spain as a power was at its lowest.[121] In May

---

117 Ismael Saz, 'Las herencias intelectuales de la pérdida del imperio americano', *Laboratorio di Storia*, 12 (2016), pp. 1–24 (p. 3).
118 Saz, 'Las herencias intelectuales de la pérdida del imperio americano', p. 3.
119 Balfour, 'The Spanish Empire and its End', p. 153.
120 Saz, 'Las herencias intelectuales de la pérdida del imperio americano', p. 3.
121 José Álvarez-Junco, *Spanish Identity in the Age of Nations* (Manchester and New York: Manchester University Press, 2011), p. 359.

44 *Anticolonialism, Race and Violence in Basque Radical Nationalism*

1898, as Spain was about to experience a colossal defeat by the US, British prime minister Lord Salisbury delivered a speech to parliament in which he established a clear division between 'great and living nations' and second-class or 'dying nations'. Although he did not mention Spain by name 'nobody doubted that, together with the Ottoman empire, it [Spain] was the most obvious example of a *dying nation*'.[122] In contrast, the living and great nations were those who could maintain empires, like Britain and the US.

Once again, Arana used the situation in Spain to his benefit. After 1898 Arana began to celebrate Spain's defeats and praised the American administration.[123] Most importantly, after the '98 Disaster, Arana engaged with the discourses that stressed the decline of Spain and developed Salisbury's distinction between living and dying nations: whilst the English-speaking countries were examples of superior nations, the Latin countries – mainly represented by Spain – were their opposite. As Iarocci sustains,

> This Manichean logic was integral to the rhetoric of modern colonialism: If Spain was barbaric, oppressive, fanatical, ignorant, bigoted, violent, and superstitious, modern European imperialism would imagine itself as civilized, liberating, tolerant, educated, fair-minded, peaceful, and rational.[124]

Like modern European imperialism, from 1898 Arana divided the world into these two binaries and nuanced his vision of colonialism. When colonialism was practised by a power like Spain, this was despicable and brought no benefits to the colonised, but when practised by Britain or the US, foreign domination could be advantageous. These assumptions, which echoed the negative characteristics of Spain and its empire grouped under the so-called Black Legend, resulted in a selective form of anticolonialism.

Following the '98 Disaster, Spanish intellectuals tried to find a cure for 'Spain's problem'.[125] For instance, some intellectuals became increasingly

---

122 Álvarez-Junco, *Spanish Identity in the Age of Nations*, p. 359. Salisbury's speech was delivered in the Royal Albert Hall (London) on 4 May 1898.
123 Watson explains how during the summer of 1898 Basque nationalist activity was limited to clandestine meetings where colonial defeats were celebrated. See Watson, *Basque Nationalism and Political Violence*, p. 86. Arana was aware that his admiration of Spain's enemy was painful for the wounded Spanish state. Three days after the outbreak of the Spanish-American War, a patriotic pro-war demonstration organised by a liberal society called El Sitio stoned Arana's house in Bilbao, pressuring Arana and his brother to leave the house and seek refuge.
124 Iarocci, *Properties of Modernity*, p. 15.
125 Whilst the idea of Spanish degeneration was nothing new, the '98 intellectuals offered different diagnoses and cures for Spain's 'sickness'. As Santos Juliá puts it, '98 intellectuals simply repeated, albeit more dramatically, what was already known in

concerned about Spain's legacy in Latin America and about the consequences of the growing US influence.[126] As a result, these intellectuals increasingly promoted and developed discourses based on the belief of 'a trans-Atlantic Hispanic family' united by the customs, lifestyle and traits that Spain brought to America (generally known as *Hispanismo*). Whilst compensating the loss of empire by stressing the 'benevolent' legacies of colonialism, these discourses confronted existing notions of Spanish brutality in Latin America. Unsurprisingly, Arana rejected these ideas. According to Arana, formerly colonised areas in Latin America and elsewhere did not owe anything to Spain. In a text that resembles the writings of one of the biggest exponents of the Black Legend, Fray Bartolomé de las Casas, Arana stated:

> It is fairly common to assert frequently and calmly that the Spanish domination in America was needed to Christianise those nations and there is nothing more incorrect than that: Columbus mobs stole lawlessly, they killed tribes that lived freely and calmly without mercy, they corrupted some other tribes and destroyed most of them, forcing those that were left alive to hate Christianism, instead of preaching with example.[127]

Like Las Casas in the sixteenth century, Arana criticised how Spaniards used religion to legitimise colonisation as well as the abuses of the Church against indigenous peoples. In another article published in 1902, Arana wrote:

> It seems that Christ's interest consists of Spain becoming big and powerful, even at the expense of the humiliation, slavery and misery of the nations that Spain has subjugated and exploited! It seems that the Church has to follow the orders of the State ... even to carry out acts as unlawful as the conquest and the enslavement of free nations![128]

---

the 1880s about the decadence of the [Spanish] race and the evilness of its politicians. What this generation of intellectuals added to the 'regeneration' discourse was that the Spanish problem was not caused by its politicians but instead by its corrupt political system (the so-called Restoration system and its corrupt practices, such as *caciquismo*). See Santos Juliá Díaz, 'Anomalía, dolor y fracaso de España', in *Conferencia Anual de la Society for Spanish and Portuguese Historical Studies* (Tucson, 1966), pp. 1–29.

126 Angel G. Loureiro, 'Spanish Nationalism and the Ghost of Empire', *Journal of Spanish Cultural Studies*, 4.1 (2003), pp. 65–76 (p. 67).

127 Arana, 'Efectos de la invasión', p. 1328. This article did not only condemn Spanish colonialism in the Americas, but also attacked the conquest of the 'three Americas from north to south'.

128 Sabino Arana, 'Los congresos católicos de España', *La Patria*, 27 July 1902, pp. 2198–200 (p. 2199).

According to Arana, Spain was an inherently evil expansionist and colonising nation. 'The foreign enemy [Spain]', Arana argued in 1899, 'has always had an unhealthy passion for dominating other nations.'[129] Thus, for Arana, the crisis that Spain was experiencing after 1898 was well deserved. Elsewhere Arana mocked a piece from a Madrid newspaper that lamented the dark times which Spain was experiencing. Arana wrote that this crisis was the product of 'pain provoked by themselves ... punishment for past crimes'.[130] According to Arana, Spain's misery and pain were 'the fatal consequence of centuries of bribery, selfishness and evil ... the twilight of an era of ignorance and detachment'.[131]

If Spanish colonialism was barbaric and evil, Arana saw British and US colonialism as benevolent. Arana did not hide the admiration he felt towards Britain and the US, and he famously sent two telegrams to both US president Theodore Roosevelt and British Prime Minister Salisbury congratulating them for their actions in Cuba and South Africa respectively. These telegrams marked the beginning of a long history of seeking international support and recognition for the Basque cause.[132]

Arana sent his telegram to Salisbury on 10 June 1902 at the end of the Second Boer War (1899–1902), a conflict between the British and the Boers, descendants of the Dutch settlers of South Africa, who had coexisted until diamonds and gold were discovered in the Boer states.[133] Arana's telegram, reproduced in *La Patria*, expressed his wish that the South Africans would find 'advantages

---

129 Sabino Arana, 'Causas del mal', *El Correo Vasco*, 27 July 1899, pp. 1729–31 (pp. 1729–30).
130 Sabino Arana, '¿Castigo o resurrección?', *El Correo Vasco*, 28 June 1899, pp. 1694–95 (p. 1695).
131 Arana, '¿Castigo o resurrección?', p. 1695.
132 Arana himself saw the international recognition of the movement as the main objective of the Roosevelt telegram. Whilst in prison, he wrote a letter to the American vice-consul in Bilbao begging him to send the letter to Roosevelt, and another to his wife explaining that with the telegram 'I only wanted the US and England to be aware that the Basques want independence'. Quoted in de la Granja, 'Cronología', p. 295. Arana sent his telegram to Roosevelt before the one he sent to Salisbury but for the purposes of this chapter, I discuss Salisbury's telegram first.
133 Prior to sending the telegram, Arana's attitude towards Britain in the war had been slightly more ambivalent. In 1901 he wrote one of his most famous anticolonial articles condemning colonialism globally and denouncing the oppression that people of colour experienced at the hands of white people. Nevertheless, in the same article Arana defended the British against multiple criticisms from western circles who took a pro-Boer stance, asking: 'Have the Boers even respected the blacks, as they want to be respected by the British? ... is the Boer's right over these lands superior to the right that the British had to preserve their life?' Arana argued that these pro-Boer claims were rooted in 'Anglophobic rage' and stated that 'the disgrace that the Boer is experiencing is as big as the one that they have caused to

under the gentle yoke [of] Great Britain', and hoped that 'British sovereignty mean[t]s protection rather than domination'.[134] According to Arana, powers such as Britain practised a 'gentle' and benevolent form of colonialism, which could bring enormous benefits to the colonised. Euskadi, Arana believed, could also benefit from this protection. He expressed this in June 1902 when, writing from prison, he argued that he aimed for 'the independence of Euskadi, under the protection of England'.[135] This strong Anglophilia is an example of the theories of 'good colonialism' that Arana's successors later developed.[136] In fact, as Ugalde argues, this telegram was used by Arana's successors to demonstrate the adoration that Arana felt for Britain.[137]

A month before, Arana had sent a very similar telegram to US president Theodore Roosevelt that never reached its recipient's hands as it was intercepted by the Spanish authorities and led to his imprisonment. This controversial text congratulated the US for freeing Cuba from 'slavery' and argued that the US was an example of greatness, justice and freedom, something beyond the

the black indigenous people'. See Sabino Arana, 'Pasatiempos mentales. Sobre la Guerra Sudafricana', *Euzkadi*, March 1901, pp. 1970–74 (pp. 1971 and 1972).

134 Original reproduced in 'Otro cablegrama de felicitación', *La Patria*, 15 June 1902, p. 2. Note: This view was clearly shared by many in *La Patria* as the article that commented the telegram mentioned that Arana's telegram to Salisbury praised '[England's] colonisation system and moderate imperial domination' and described England as a 'generous' power. 'Otro cablegrama de felicitación', p. 2.

135 Translated from de la Granja, 'Cronología de Sabino Arana (1865–1903)', *Sancho el Sabio*, 31 (2009), pp. 285–98 (p. 296).

136 This marked Anglophilia, manifested explicitly only after 1898, is probably related to the incorporation of the Euskalerriacos into the PNV during that year. This moderate group was formed by local members of the bourgeoisie, with strong links to shipbuilding and therefore, to Britain. Such connections should not be ignored: Bilbao's role as an international port city depended on Britain to a great extent. Jesús Mª Valdaliso argues that Spanish shipbuilders had to rely on Britain, which provided them with technology, capital and new patterns of organisation and finance. Jesús Mª Valdaliso, 'Spanish Shipowners in the British Mirror: Patterns of Investment, Ownership and Finance in the Bilbao Shipping Industry, 1879–1913', *International Journal of Maritime History*, 5.2 (1993), pp. 1–30 (p. 1). The fact that the leader of the Euskalerriacos, de la Sota y Llano, was himself one of the most celebrated local shipowners of the time and had strong commercial links with Britain helps to explain the proliferation of these pro-British texts after 1898.

137 Ugalde, *La acción exterior del nacionalismo vasco*, p. 135.

capacity of European, and particularly Latin, powers.[138] It also suggested that if Europe imitated the US, the Basque nation would be free again.[139]

Some scholars such as Ugalde have justified this telegram by arguing that Arana, like many contemporaries, believed that in 1902 Cuba would achieve full independence.[140] This view has been evidenced by the fact that when Arana was asked to clarify what he meant by Cuba being freed from slavery during his trial in 1902, he claimed that he wanted to 'manifest his joy for the freedom of the *Grande Antilla* from the slavery it had been subjected to, and had since suffered'.[141] He also acknowledged that the US was imposing a form of slavery, adding that 'according to history, Cuba has suffered two forms of slavery: firstly that by Spain and that of America [the US] later on'.[142]

However, whether Arana genuinely sympathised with Cuba's cries for independence or not, it is evident that he did not consider Spanish dominion to be the same as North American control. Furthermore, the telegram was not an isolated event. Arana's pro-US prose appeared very frequently in the newspaper *El Correo Vasco* (1899). One of his most recurrent ways to praise the 'virtuous' US administration was to compare it to not-so-bright Spain. For instance, Arana used Cervantes's *Don Quixote* and its protagonists Sancho Panza and Don Quixote to compare Spain to the US. Arana claimed that whereas a nation would be happy if 'like the US, had the head of Sancho ... and the heart of Quixote', a country would be hapless if it had Quixote's head and Panza's heart: 'Don Quixote's head is delusional ... Sancho's, however, enjoys perfect health.'[143] Arana believed that the main example of this kind of Quixotesque, unvirtuous and delusional country was Spain. Alluding to the Spanish-American War Arana claimed: 'can you see perhaps a country ... rushing into war against a giant that will welcome its attack with a smile? It's

138 Arana, 'Telegrama a Roosevelt'. The original reads: '[In] name of the Basque Nationalist Party [I] congratulate [the] extremely noble Federation that you preside for Cuban Independence, as it was able to free it [Cuba] from slavery. Your powerful States give an example [of] greatness and cult Justice and Freedom, unknown in History, and inimitable for European powers, particularly Latin [powers]. If Europe imitated [the US], the Basque nation, its most ancient nation, which enjoyed freedom for centuries [and] whose Constitution was praised by the States, would also be free'.
139 Arana, 'Telegrama a Roosevelt'.
140 Ugalde, 'El primer nacionalismo vasco ante la independencia de Cuba', p. 268.
141 Translated from Ugalde, 'El primer nacionalismo vasco ante la independencia de Cuba', p. 268.
142 Translated from Ugalde, 'El primer nacionalismo vasco ante la independencia de Cuba', p. 268.
143 Sabino Arana, 'Quijotismo y pancismo', *El Correo Vasco*, 29 June 1899, pp. 1696–97 (pp. 1696 and 1697).

because [Spain] dreams like Don Quixote.'[144] Another article mocked Spaniards who lamented the economic consequences that the war against 'one of the most powerful nations of the modern world' brought to Spain.[145]

Furthermore, unlike Spain, Arana seemed to believe that the virtue and civilisation of the US entitled it to colonise or 'intervene' in foreign countries, where 'anarchy' governed.[146] Like the Basque territories, the former colonies of Cuba and the Philippines 'were [Spanish provinces] ... until, last year [1898], thanks to the US protection, they emancipated from Spain'.[147] These articles, alongside the telegram sent to Roosevelt, show a highly paternalistic vision of the colonised – whose years of struggle against Spain were not acknowledged. For Arana, credit for independence went to North Americans, not to Cubans.

This same vision of the colonised as lacking any agency can be seen in another article, which argued that the practices carried out by the US's 'racial brothers' (the British) and the Spanish had long-lasting effects, as evidenced by the difference between North and South America:

> We don't know what certain races have in their blood that when they touch others they degenerate and corrupt them. This is exemplified by the history of the Romans and the history of all those nations who possess Latin blood. Whereas in the United States of America science accomplishes such a surprising degree of progress, Latin America closes the door to progress and opens it widely to every vice.[148]

The newly independent Latin American republics were not to blame for this degeneration. Instead, Spain was. As Arana argued, 'what has happened to all these nations that have been infected by the Latin(s) [races], is also happening to us now'.[149] Thus, under the protection and the sovereignty of Spain's antithesis – the US – new independent nations such as the Philippines and Cuba were to grow and progress.

144 Arana, 'Quijotismo y pancismo', p. 1697.
145 Sabino Arana, 'El que la hace', *El Correo Vasco*, 5 July 1899, pp. 1707–08 (p. 1708).
146 Arana used a very similar discourse to that seen in US war propaganda. See for instance, the famous image by Louis Dalrymple titled 'The duty of the hour; – to save her [Cuba, note the gendered language] not only from Spain, but from a worse fate' (1898). In this image, a hand is holding a pan (which has 'Spanish misrule' written on it) in which a woman representing Cuba is being cooked by the 'anarchy' of the island of Cuba.
147 Arana, 'Las cuotas concertadas', p. 1689.
148 Sabino Arana, 'Vocación de esclavos', *El Correo Vasco*, 25 August 1899, pp. 1178–79 (p. 1178).
149 Arana, 'Vocación de esclavos', p. 1778.

By perceiving the US as the saviour of Spain's former colonies, Arana seemed to ignore how, with the end of Spanish rule in both Cuba and the Philippines, a new form of indirect imperial rule had been established in the former colonies. In the Cuban case, the Platt Amendment (1901) confirmed Cuba's neocolonial status as it gave the US control of Cuba's trade and government, guaranteeing US intervention in Cuban affairs. In the Philippines, the American intervention in the archipelago led to the Philippine-American War (1899–1902), a brutal war that caused hundreds of thousands of Filipino deaths and which confirmed the US sovereignty of the archipelago. However, as proven in this chapter, Arana was not particularly interested in the effects that the US rule was to have in Latin America or in the Pacific as long as it damaged Spain's international and national reputation. Arana's anticolonialism, therefore, was more strategic than sincere.

Conclusion

In the last decade of the nineteenth century Sabino Arana was able to create and formulate what would become a highly influential nationalist movement in the following century. Nevertheless, as this chapter has shown, the movement was not born in a vacuum. Rather, Arana compiled and reinterpreted existing myths, historical events and pseudo-scientific theories of race in service to his movement. This narrative presented the Basques as an ancient and superior race who lived peacefully until Spain occupied their territory in the nineteenth century. Euskadi was turned into a colony through conquest, at a time when the Spanish Empire was disintegrating.

Arana's reading of the Basque Country as a colonised nation prompted him to write numerous anticolonial texts against Spain. Nevertheless, his support for anticolonial insurgents was conditional on the damage they could cause to Spain. As this chapter has proven, Arana did not support anticolonial causes because he was a defender of the oppressed and colonised peoples of the world. Instead, he held imperialist attitudes towards non-western peoples and his anticolonialism needs to be framed as a part of his anti-Spanish discourse. This is further supported by the fact that his anti-Spanish ideas were rooted in European colonialism. As the rest of this book will show, the idea that Euskadi was a colony within Spain was picked up by Arana's successors, who considered Arana to be a messianic figure.

CHAPTER TWO

Anticolonial Disengagement and British Exceptionalism (1903-1914)

On 25 November 1903, the father of Basque nationalism died prematurely due to frail health, leaving an enormous vacuum in the movement. Immediately after Sabino Arana's death, he became the Basque martyr per excellence and his followers even compared him to Jesus Christ.[1] Arana was the undisputable leader of Basque nationalism, 'the greatest man that Euskadi had ever produced'.[2] It is hence hardly surprising that the PNV and the Basque nationalist movement experienced a period of confusion and uncertainty after his death. This was accentuated by the fact that Arana had died shortly after he proposed that the movement should pursue autonomy rather than independence. The confusion that the abrupt changes in Arana's political thought caused among his followers influenced the formation of two factions or groups that have had to coexist within the PNV ever since: the radicals (who developed Arana's radical thought and advocated independence) and the moderates (who developed his pro-autonomy claims).

The years that immediately followed Arana's premature death are a key period in the history of the Basque nationalist movement as, amongst other things, the political programme and strategy of the PNV was established. Yet as Mees noted in 1990, the period between 1903 and 1923 has usually received scarce attention from scholars.[3] Although various studies have since contributed to the study of key events that took place in this extended period, such as the First World War, there is still room for an in-depth

---

1 José Luis de la Granja, 'Sabino Arana', in Santiago de Pablo, José Luis de la Granja, Ludger Mees and Jesús Casquete (eds), *Diccionario ilustrado de símbolos del nacionalismo vasco* (Madrid: Tecnos, 2012), pp. 120-21. See also de la Granja, *Ángel o demonio*, pp. 254-57.

2 Be-Euzko, 'D. Sabino de Arana y Goiri', *Patria*, 29 November 1903, p. 3.

3 Ludger Mees, 'El nacionalismo vasco entre 1903 y 1923', *Vasconia: Cuadernos de historia – geografía*, 17 (1990), pp. 115-39 (p. 115). For a comprehensive and complete account of the period between 1903 and 1923 see also Ludger Mees, *Nacionalismo vasco, movimiento obrero y cuestión social (1903-1923)* (Bilbao: Fundación Sabino Arana, 1992).

analysis of the first ten years that followed Arana's death. In particular, except for Ugalde, scholars have ignored how Basque nationalists perceived international events and other nationalist movements around the globe in this decade.[4] As a result, it remains unknown whether Basque radicals or moderates continued elaborating Arana's anticolonial discourse in a decade of internal disagreements.

This chapter explores how the first Basque radicals and moderates engaged with moments of anticolonial insurgence and how they perceived colonialism. It shows how during these years there was a significant decrease in Arana's characteristic anticolonialism in the two branches of Basque nationalism. Unlike Arana, from 1903 to 1914 radicals and moderates rarely condemned colonialism, and they did not sympathise with colonial subjects or frame Euskadi as a colony within Spain.[5] Whilst comparing Euskadi to former Spanish colonies such as Cuba or the Philippines had been a characteristic rhetorical device for Arana, the new generations of Basque nationalists tended to avoid comparisons with extra-European movements and erased most of the colonial connotations from their vocabulary.[6] This is not entirely surprising considering that Arana himself had deployed highly problematic language in relation to non-western areas and that after the loss of the Spanish colonies, Morocco was the only point of comparison that Basques could use to stress their colonial nature. As Martin-Márquez puts it, 'by decrying internal colonialism, separatists risked equating their own avowed nations with other areas colonized by the Spanish government –

4 Ugalde, *La acción exterior del nacionalismo vasco*.
5 An interesting exception is the condemnations of imperialism during the Russo-Japanese War (1904–1905) expressed in *Patria*. During the war, *Patria* explicitly criticised the colonialism of both belligerents. This was one of the only occasions on which Basque nationalist newsletters of the period wrote explicitly about and against colonialism. In an article published on 14 February 1904, *Patria* stressed that the Basques had no sympathy for either Russia or Japan, as the former was 'a hardened tyrant of nations' and the latter was an emerging oppressor that had received from its teacher ('the great European states') 'the passion of extra-national tyranny'. See Nik, 'Rusia y Japón', *Patria*, 14 February 1904, p. 3. Another article published in *Patria* in the same month condemned the war, arguing that 'it is obvious that the cause of this current war is nothing other than expanding the lands of each of the belligerent powers; [as well as] the thirst to extend their political domination over foreign races that have a perfect right to be independent'. This military conflict confirmed that the fever of European imperialism had reached Asia: 'Japan, that was free from the stain of oppressing other nations, had now been intoxicated by imperialism'. See Iturain, 'Ante el conflicto', *Patria*, 28 February 1904, p. 2.
6 With some limited exceptions, including when newsletters commented on the nationalist movements of India or Egypt, Arana's immediate successors compared themselves primarily to the different European nationalist movements of the period.

namely, during this period, Africa'.[7] During this period, Basques preferred to avoid such comparisons and refused to engage in discussions about Spain and its imperial activities in northern Morocco.

This chapter starts by briefly examining the evolution of the movement in the years following Arana's death. It then presents two case studies that illustrate how Basque nationalists perceived colonial insurgents and colonialism generally. First, through the case study of Spain's campaign in Morocco in July 1909 and the revolt it originated in the peninsula – known as the Tragic Week – the chapter demonstrates Basque nationalists' lack of commitment to anticolonialism. Second, the chapter moves to analyse how Basque radicals and moderates further developed some of Arana's ideas, including the belief in Anglo-Saxon exceptionalism, which led them to believe that some forms of colonialism could bring benefits to the colonised.

The Forging of Basque Moderates and Radicals

'The Master', 'the apostle', 'the Messiah' or 'the Basque martyr' – as Arana was consistently referred to by his followers – could not have disappeared at a worse time. In 1902, Arana launched a new strategy for the Basque nationalist movement, commonly referred to as *la evolución españolista* or the 'pro-Spanish evolution', that he was unable to complete or elaborate before his early death. This new project proposed the formation of a new pro-Spanish party that rejected the separatist and pro-independence doctrines that Arana himself had launched years before, producing a deep fracture among the first generations of nationalists. As Luis Castells identifies, this strategy allowed Arana's message to be understood from different and even opposing perspectives: whilst some preferred the first radical Arana, others chose his more pragmatic and possibilist policies.[8] In other words, whilst some opted to defend his separatist programme (radicals), others advocated for a more gradual path that considered autonomy as an option (moderates).

As many historians of Basque nationalism have noted, the accentuated division between radicals and moderates – which was not unique to Basque nationalism, as it also affected other movements such as Irish nationalism – would shape the history of the PNV during the twentieth century. It is hardly surprising that the coexistence of these two branches within the PNV had such an impact on the evolution of the party. As Santiago de Pablo and Mees have suggested, after Arana died what was at stake was not only the

---

7 Martin-Márquez, *Disorientations*, p. 45.
8 Luis Castells, 'El nacionalismo vasco (1890–1923): ¿una ideología modernizadora?', *Ayer*, 28 (1997), pp. 127–62 (p. 144).

control of the party by either of the factions but two different conceptions of nationalism.[9]

The radicals attempted to forget Arana's 'pro-Spanish evolution' and advocated for the complete separation of Euskadi from Spain. Basque radicals usually belonged to the lower-middle classes of Basque society and, like Arana, were apprehensive about the rapid transformation that the Basque Country was experiencing. The radicals controlled different periodicals in the period including *Patria* (1903–1906), *Aberri* (1906–1908) and *Bizkaitarra* (1909–1913). In contrast, the moderates advocated for a legal programme and a gradualist path that welcomed autonomy. In other words, unlike the radicals, they 'favoured reform and compromise rather than transgression or revolution'.[10] The moderates' organ of expression was *Euskalduna* (1896–1909), which belonged to the former Euskalerriacos who had joined the PNV in 1898. The former Euskalerriacos were usually linked with the local and industrialist bourgeoisie and had the money and social prestige the radicals lacked. As a result, both factions were partly dependent on each other: the radicals depended on the reputation and the economic power of the moderates, and the latter relied on the closeness that the former had with Arana when he was alive.[11]

Keeping these antagonistic but mutually dependent groups united within the same party was not easy. This was the main task that Arana's successor, radical nationalist Ángel Zabala (alias Kondaño), had to face. After years of harsh criticism in *Euskalduna*, a solution was found with the drafting of a programme-manifesto for the PNV that did not mention the two disputed words: independence and autonomy. Instead, the 1906 programme was a highly ambiguous manifesto, which established that the maximum aspiration of the PNV was the abolition of the 25 October 1839 law. As de Pablo points out, this made the PNV's struggle completely legal, as its main goal was to repeal a Spanish law.[12] This ambiguous programme was not only a stepping stone towards the legalisation of the party. It also postponed the heated dispute over whether the ultimate goal of the Basque nationalist movement was independence or autonomy. Each Basque nationalist was now able to interpret what the programme really meant and what the future of Euskadi was. Furthermore, the programme also widened the support base

9 De Pablo and Mees, *El péndulo patriótico*, p. 61.
10 Muro, *Ethnicity and Violence*, p. 74.
11 De Pablo and Mees, *El péndulo patriótico*, pp. 61–62. For a more recent examination of the radicals and the moderates as well as their mutual dependence see Mees, *The Basque Contention*, p. 61.
12 Santiago de Pablo, 'El Nacionalismo vasco ante el estado español (1895–1937)', *Studia Historica. Historia Contemporánea*, 18 (2000), pp. 79–93 (p. 84).

for the movement: any Basque who defended the Fueros could join the party if they proved that one of their four last names was Basque and if they accepted the submission of nationalism to the Catholic Church. As it had been for Arana, for the PNV 'race' (in this case determined by one's last name) and religion continued to be essential elements of the Basque nation.

When Zabala fulfilled the difficult task of unifying the party through an ambiguous programme that left the goal of the movement open to interpretation, he resigned as leader of the PNV. Yet the party continued to be led by the radical faction: from 1908, Luis Arana – Sabino's oldest brother and one of the leading representatives of Basque radicalism – ran the PNV until his removal from the party in 1915. Despite the sustained dominance of the radicals within the party, in practice the PNV was evolving towards more possibilist and flexible interpretations of nationalism. In other words: the PNV was radical in theory but gradually more possibilist in practice, which allowed a certain truce between the two factions until the mid-1910s.

Once the 'reconciliation' between the factions was reached and the party was completely legalised in 1908, the movement was able to work on its expansion and consolidation.[13] As Mees argues, between 1903 and 1923 the PNV was able to overcome its initial status as a small clandestine circle and evolve towards a powerful mass movement.[14] This is partly due to the fact that during this period, the PNV experienced a process of political reorganisation and expanded its electoral and social basis. Significantly, in 1911, a Basque nationalist Catholic union was created under the name Solidaridad de Obreros Vascos (Basque Workers' Solidarity). This illustrates how the PNV was transitioning from a small bourgeoise party to an organisation that included all sectors of Basque society, aside from non-Basque migrants or *maketos*.

Another explanation for the growth of the PNV in this period was printed media, which acted as a nation-building tool. As Muro points out, 'the PNV understood the importance of having a homogeneous high culture' and as a result each Spanish-Basque province established its own newspaper.[15] *Gizpuzkoarra* was founded in Gipuzkoa (1907); then *Bizkaitarra* in Biscay (1909); *Napartarra* in Navarra (1911) and *Arabarra* in Alava (1912). In 1913 these merged into the party's daily newspaper *Euzkadi*, which was able to run in great part thanks to popular subscription. These publications became essential tools for spreading cultural and behavioural patterns that clearly

---

13 In 1908 the PNV incorporated a clause in its programme stating that the party was committed to respecting and acting within the established legal framework.
14 Mees, 'El nacionalismo vasco entre 1903 y 1923', p. 115.
15 Muro, *Ethnicity and Violence*, p. 71.

defined who belonged to the national community. Indeed, print capitalism allowed the residents of the Basque nation to imagine each other across the different Basque provinces and to establish what being Basque meant. In turn, this allowed Basque nationalism to reinforce its presence in other provinces aside from Biscay, although Bilbao continued to be the centre of the movement.

Furthermore, the movement began to permeate different social and cultural spheres. This was facilitated by the satellite organisations of the party, such as the *batzokis* (Basque Centres), which were established in different cities and towns across Euskadi. The role of the *batzokis* – which were not only social spaces where nationalists gathered but also centres in which political and cultural activities took place – was key for the spread of nationalism outside Bilbao. Furthermore, the Juventud Vasca de Bilbao (Basque Youth of Bilbao: henceforth JVB), founded in 1907, also became an important satellite organisation of the party that helped organise the movement politically and organised cultural and sporting events.[16] According to Nicolás Ruiz Descamps, in the mid-1910s the JVB became the most important political-cultural centre of Bilbao with over 1,000 members in 1914.[17]

Indeed, as Mees argues, '[Basque] nationalism was not about (party) politics, but about life in general': Basque nationalism needed 'full-time patriots' who worked for their nation even in their spare time.[18] Thus, in order to reinforce their presence in different areas of Basque society, the PNV and the JVB organised different cultural activities (including nationalist theatre, music or popular festivities) and promoted 'non-Spanish' sports such as football and more generally, outdoor sports such as hiking – which led to the creation of propagandist mountaineer associations named

---

16 This was not the first youth organisation of Basque nationalism. In 1901, Euzko Gaztedia (Basque Youth) was created and in 1904 was followed by the Sociedad de Juventud Vasca (Basque Youth Society). As Nicolás Ruiz Descamps comments, both organisations contributed actively to promote Basque nationalism through propaganda. For further reference, see the two key studies on the Basque Youth: Íñigo Camino and Luis de Guezala, *Juventud y nacionalismo vasco. Bilbao (1901–1937)* (Bilbao: Fundación Sabino Arana, 1991) and Nicolás Ruiz Descamps, *Historia de las organizaciones juveniles del nacionalismo vasco (1893–1923)* (Bizkaia: Universidad del País Vasco, 2018).

17 Nicolás Ruiz Descamps, 'Juventud vasca de Bilbao durante la Restauración (1902–1923)', *Bidebarrieta*, 24 (2013), pp. 53–62 (p. 55). JVB eventually became one of the most (if not the most) influential organisations within Basque nationalism. These years also saw the start of the expansion of different Basque Youth organisations outside Bilbao, including one in Buenos Aires.

18 Mees, *The Basque Contention*, p. 56.

mendigoxales (mountaineers) in the first decade of the twentieth century. As Ruiz Descamps argues, during these years popular explanations for the importance of sports centred on a belief in the superiority of Anglo-Saxons or Germanic races, partly rooted in their sporting traditions as something that reinforced their supposed warrior character.[19] In contrast, the Latin races focused their education on intellectual issues, something that provoked the mental and physical degradation of young generations.[20] Thus, if Basques wanted to regenerate their race – tainted by the Spanish influence – they needed to practise sports.

In sum, after overcoming a general period of crisis and uncertainty, the PNV took crucial steps that would allow it to become a party of the masses later in the century. The movement was able to integrate sectors of society that had not been attracted to Basque nationalism before and to expand its influence beyond Bilbao. This had all been facilitated by the period of truce between Basque moderates and radicals caused by the approval of the ambiguous 1906 manifesto. The commitment to the manifesto was not the only thing that would bring moderates and radicals closer in this period. Instead, as this chapter demonstrates, both branches held a similar attitude in moments of anticolonial upheaval and had an analogous conception of colonialism. Analysing these attitudes, as well as their continuities and divergences with Arana's thought, is key to understanding the future tensions that the PNV experienced in the years leading to its split in 1921.

Anticolonial Disengagement:
The Conflict in Morocco and the *Semana Trágica* of 1909

In 1893, when the Spanish Empire was about to crumble and was challenged by Riffian Kabyles in northern Morocco, Sabino Arana was one of the few who dared to support the colonial insurgents and condemn Spain's operation during a crusade of pro-Spanish patriotism. As Alfonso Iglesias Amorín points out, the rejection of the 1893 military campaign was a precedent in the popular opposition to Spain's colonial wars, which was solidified in 1898 and culminated with the great campaign of resistance to the war in Morocco of 1909.[21] But, whereas the conflict of 1893 had eventually been forgotten by the Spanish population, 1909 became a central topic of conversation amongst the

---

19 Nicolás Ruiz Descamps, 'La prensa nacionalista en Vizcaya durante la Restauración: el espejo de una comunidad en construcción', *El argonauta español* (online), 5 (2008), https://journals.openedition.org/argonauta/970.
20 Ruiz Descamps, 'La prensa nacionalista en Vizcaya durante la Restauración'.
21 Alfonso Iglesias Amorín, 'Los intelectuales españoles y la Guerra del Rif (1909–1927)', *Revista Universitaria De Historia Militar*, 3.5 (2015), pp. 59–77 (p. 62).

general Spanish population and its intellectuals. Surprisingly, unlike Arana, this time neither Basque moderates nor radicals joined the great campaign of opposition that generated the new colonial front in Morocco in July 1909 and led to a popular revolt in Catalonia known as the *Semana Trágica* (the Tragic Week). Indeed, whilst Arana had explicitly supported anti-Spanish insurgents, Basque moderates and radicals distanced themselves from Spain's colonial endeavours and even condemned acts of rebellion against the empire during the first decade of the century.

Since Spain had lost its last colonies in 1898 and had been harshly labelled as a dying nation, Morocco was seen as the last opportunity to recover Spain's 'national glory' and enhance its international prestige. Nevertheless, the Moroccan experience demonstrated Spain's inability to negotiate with the rest of European powers, which saw the country as a weak and inept coloniser nation but also as a helpful ally in containing the expansion of other powers.[22] As such, Spain's presence in Morocco was determined by the geopolitical interests of other powers such as Britain and France.[23] With the green light from Britain, Spain had no option but to accept the clauses of the treaty of 1904 that divided Morocco into two spheres of influence. Spain, which was in no position to negotiate, received a much smaller territory than what had been offered by France a couple of years before. However, it was not the size of the Moroccan territory – which comprised about 20 per cent of the Moroccan land – that troubled Spain for the next years, but the instability of the area, which was known for the multiple uprisings that the Sultanate faced by Berber tribes. Spain's area of influence in Morocco was confirmed at the Algeciras Conference (1906), attended by the representatives of 13 powers which were all granted equal commercial status in Morocco, with the agreement that the sovereignty of the Sultan should be respected.[24]

Whilst the Algeciras Conference recognised internationally Spain's interests in north Africa, the country's reputation did not necessarily

---

[22] For a good account on Spain's colonial policy in Morocco and international relations from 1898 to 1914 see Sebastian Balfour, 'Spain and the Great Powers in the Aftermath of the Disaster of 1898', in Sebastian Balfour and Paul Preston (eds), *Spain and the Great Powers in the Twentieth Century* (New York: Routledge, 1999), pp. 13–32.

[23] Pablo la Porte, 'Marruecos y la crisis de la Restauración 1917–1923', *Ayer*, 63 (2006), pp. 53–74 (p. 71).

[24] This sovereignty, however, was not to last as in 1912 the Protectorate of France and of Spain was established. Balfour, 'Spain and the Great Powers in the Aftermath of the Disaster of 1898', p. 26. María Rosa de Madariaga argues that representatives from 11 nations attended the conference, as it does not include Sweden and the Netherlands in the list. See María Rosa de Madariaga, *Marruecos, ese gran desconocido. Breve historia del protectorado español* (Madrid: Alianza Editorial, 2013), p. 66.

improve. Instead, the bad perception that some powers such as France already had about Spain was intensified in the following years. In particular, the events that took place in 1909 in Morocco and on the peninsula were decisive for the vision of Spain abroad. In July of that year, six Spanish workers who were constructing a railway near Melilla were killed by a group of Riff rebels.[25] Although Spanish president Antonio Maura was reluctant to send troops to Morocco, the threat of French intervention in the area led him to intervene. Yet once again, the Spanish state showed its weakness as it was incapable of mobilising a widely unmotivated population still traumatised by the '98 Disaster. The consequences of the new conflict were harsh for Spain and its ego, as the Spanish army experienced significant defeats against the Riffians such as the so-called Disaster of the Barranco del Lobo on July 27, which left more than 150 dead and nearly 600 injured.[26] After the new colonial disaster, France did not doubt Spain's incompetence as a coloniser.

In parallel to the demoralising defeat that Spain experienced in Morocco, the Spaniards also faced a critical situation at home. On 26 July a week of protests – which would be known as the Tragic Week – erupted in Barcelona against the recruitment of reserve troops to fight in the Moroccan War. But what had started as a popular protest at the unjust conscription system turned into a week of widespread violence across Catalonia. During the Tragic Week, around 60 religious buildings (including churches and convents) were burned down and many others were looted.[27] Thus, in 1909, anticolonialism and anti-clericalism became part of the same agenda. This would be key for the Basque nationalists' lack of engagement with the parallel events of Morocco.

Despite its short duration, the Tragic Week was particularly bloody: over 100 civilians were killed and many more were injured.[28] On top of that, around 3,000 people were arrested and 17 people faced the death penalty.[29] Of those who were sentenced to death, only five were executed and the others were instead given life sentences. The fierce repression led by Maura was the object of both internal and external opposition. In particular, the execution of anarchist pedagogue Francesc Ferrer i Guàrdia, who was not even in Barcelona during the Tragic Week, provoked a wave of demonstrations

---

25 De Madariaga, *Marruecos, ese gran desconocido*, p. 78.
26 De Madariaga, *Marruecos, ese gran desconocido*, p. 80.
27 José Luis Comellas, *Del 98 a la Semana Trágica, 1898–1909: Crisis de conciencia y renovación política* (Madrid: Biblioteca Nueva, 2002), p. 267.
28 Sebastian Balfour, *The End of the Spanish Empire, 1898–1923* (Oxford: Clarendon Press, 1997), p. 125.
29 Josep Pich Mitjana, 'La Revolución de Julio de 1909', *Hispania*, 75 (2015), pp. 173–206 (p. 193).

across Europe that 'helped to renew a traditional view abroad of Spain as a land of intolerance and obscurantism'.[30]

Basque nationalists failed to use the excellent opportunity that these events provided them with to contribute to and engage with the national and international discourses that painted Spain as a backwards, intolerant nation and an inept colonial power. Instead, in the Basque newsletters published from the start of the Moroccan campaign of July to the executions of the orchestrators of the Tragic Week in October 1909, we observe a significant retreat from Arana's characteristic anticolonialism. *Euskalduna* stands out for its stony silence on the Moroccan crisis. Informing readers about events and movements abroad was not rare for *Euskalduna*, which reported news from places like Ireland and India during this same period.[31] However, in the five issues published between the start of the campaign in Morocco following the attacks in early July to its last number on 12 August, there is barely any reference to the events taking place in Melilla. The campaign was only commented on when with a very cautious tone, *Euskalduna* mentioned that perhaps it would be convenient that the festivities of the Basque patron saint San Ignacio de Loyola, celebrated annually on 31 July, were suspended due to the 'very special current situation', alluding to the conflict in Morocco.[32]

The attitude to this colonial conflict adopted by the radical newsletter *Bizkaitarra* was like that of its moderate counterpart. Although the radical newsletter wrote about the conflict in Morocco more than *Euskalduna* (potentially because the latter published its last edition in August 1909), *Bizkaitarra* always wrote about Morocco from a cautious distance and, on occasions, with a highly ambiguous tone.[33] Like *Euskalduna*, *Bizkaitarra* did not comment on significant colonial defeats experienced by the Spanish troops

---

30 Balfour, *The End of the Spanish Empire*, p. 201.

31 See, for instance, Anon., 'Notas nacionalistas irlandesas. Jubileo del canónigo Power', *Euskalduna*, 15 July 1909, p. 2; Anon., 'Lo que desea la India. Entrevista con Surendranath Banerjee', *Euskalduna*, 29 July 1909, pp. 3–4.

32 Anon., 'Para el consejo regional', *Euskalduna*, 29 July 1909, p. 5. The issue of the Basque festivity is expanded on later. See also Anon., 'Coincidiendo', *Euskalduna*, 5 August 1909, pp. 2–3 and Anon., 'Una moción', *Euskalduna*, 5 August 1909, p. 5.

33 This applies to texts written in *Bizkaitarra* in Euskera from July to December 1909. I can only find a reference to Morocco from all the texts in Euskera. This article reproduces the (probably invented) conversation between a Basque nationalist and a Basque Carlist who is willingly going to fight in Morocco. The Basque nationalist encourages the Carlist to go to battle, as the soldiers 'will win for Spain what it lost in America and the Philippines'. Kirikiño, 'Izpar Bat', *Bizkaitarra*, 24 July 1909, p. 1. In Euskera in the original. Translated for the author by Uxue Echanojauregui Ripa.

such as El Barranco del Lobo.³⁴ On occasions, *Bizkaitarra* pointed out that the patriotism of some Spanish newspapers led them to exaggerate the news coming from the Rif.³⁵ The radical newsletter, however, never condemned the military actions of the Spanish in Morocco or the conscription system. Instead, *Bizkaitarra* adopted a neutral position when talking about the conflict. The furthest the newsletter went was to say that whereas they did not doubt that the Spanish cause in Melilla was fair, this did not imply that the Riffian cause was wrongful as, in a way, the Riffians were doing the same as the Spanish: defending their nation.³⁶

Furthermore, the only thing that seemed to worry *Bizkaitarra* was the impact that the Moroccan crisis had on Euskadi. The newsletter devoted several articles to the potential cancellation of the annual festival of the Basque patron saint San Ignacio de Loyola due to the conflict in Morocco. For instance, in an article published in *Bizkaitarra* on 31 July 1909, the author complained about Bilbao's council's proposal to cancel the annual festival. In a note, the newsletter stated that Basque nationalists would celebrate the day regardless of what was decided, as they believed that 'glorifying our Saint would not be an obstacle for the triumph of justice in the current conflict in Morocco, which is what we all wish'.³⁷ On top of this ambiguous remark, from August 1909 *Bizkaitarra* devoted weekly articles about the rumours of a Biscayan counter-guerrilla force that was planned to be sent to Melilla.³⁸ What

---

34 I have only found one direct mention of this in December 1909, when *Bizkaitarra* gave an update about the number of casualties in the battle of 27 July 1909. This small article argues that when they previously mentioned the number of causalities in the battle, *Bizkaitarra* received a suspension warning, illustrating the high levels of repression and censorship that the periodical faced. See 'Naskaldija. Cosas que se leen', *Bizkaitarra*, 24 December 1909, p. 4.

35 See, for instance, 'Diarios y Semanarios', *Bizkaitarra*, 11 September 1909, pp. 2–3 and the series titled 'Periodismo español', particularly Euzkindaka, 'Carta Quinta a José María de Salaberría en América', *Bizkaitarra*, 16 October 1909, p. 4 and Euzkindaka, 'Carta sexta y última', *Bizkaitarra*, 23 October 1909, pp. 2–3. On 14 August 1909, *Bizkaitarra* reproduced an article from a 'Catholic and pro-Spanish newspaper' (note the ambiguity), in words of *Bizkaitarra*, to inform its readers about the conflict in Morocco. This article, which was extremely patronising and condescending towards the Moroccans, presented the Spaniards as brave and the Riffians as cowards. Hence it is possible that *Bizkaitarra* used this article as an example of the extreme patriotism of the Spanish newspapers. See Mariano Urbano, 'La guerra de Marruecos', *Bizkaitarra*, 14 August 1909, p. 3.

36 See Anon., '¿Lapsus? ...', *Bizkaitarra*, 7 August 1909, p. 3.

37 Anon., 'La festividad de San Ignacio. En Bilbao', *Bizkaitarra*, 31 July 1909, pp. 1–2 (p. 1).

38 See, for instance, Juan Domingo de Legarda, 'Cosas del tiempo. Torrente de patriotismo', *Bizkaitarra*, 4 September 1909, pp. 1–2; Sidi-Musa, 'La contraguerrilla "du

seemed to concern *Bizkaitarra* was not that Biscayan men were going to fight in what Arana would have labelled as an unfair war, but the fact that this was to imply a substantial economic cost for the Basques. As a result, and perhaps unknowingly, Basques were engaging with similar discourses used by influential Spanish intellectuals who, instead of criticising colonialism, condemned issues such as the high cost of sustaining a war.[39]

As anticolonialism among Basque nationalists decreased, patronising attitudes towards Moroccans became the norm.[40] Like Arana, although more strongly and explicitly, his immediate successors associated and equated a lack of civilisation with Africa. The patronising and Orientalist view of Basque nationalists in the period is perhaps better reflected in a series of articles that *Bizkaitarra* published about Morocco from July 1909, aimed at helping readers understand the current conflict. These articles were attributed to Spanish intellectual and devout Catholic Modesto Hernández Villaescusa, who in 1893 wrote a book titled *La cuestión de Marruecos y el conflicto de Melilla* ('The Moroccan Question and the Conflict in Melilla'). In the first article of the series, Spain's enemies were described as 'untamed, savage, opposed to civilisation, determined in their hatred and enemies of all foreign influence'.[41] The patronising and racist attitudes expressed in these articles continued throughout the series. For instance, an article published in August which talked about the geography of the Moroccan Empire argued that:

> The fertility of this country [Morocco] is surprising. It is no exaggeration to declare that if an intelligent and diligent race was to populate the country, its cereals would supply the whole of Europe. There, all types

---

Marechal" León', *Bizkaitarra*, 11 September 1909, p. 3; and the mini articles (usually of sarcastic nature) published in the section 'Naskaldija' (p. 4) in *Bizkaitarra* on 21 August 1909, 28 August 1909, 4 September 1909, 11 September 1909, 18 September 1909, 25 September 1909, 2 October 1909, 9 October 1909, 16 October 1909, 4 December 1909. The counter-guerrilla was eventually not sent, but *Bizkaitarra* continued protesting with a mocking tone about it and about its leader Isidoro León until the end of the year.

39 For the discourses of Spanish intellectuals see Iglesias Amorín, 'Los intelectuales españoles y la Guerra del Rif', pp. 68–69.

40 As I have noted in Chapter 1, these ideas, which reinforced Orientalist imaginings of places in Asia, the Middle East and north Africa, were not rare in Spain and affected other peripheral nationalist movements within the peninsula. Catalan regionalism, which found many sympathisers in *Euskalduna*, held strong imperialist views. For instance, the official establishment of the Spanish Protectorate of Morocco in 1912 was well received amongst Catalan nationalist circles. Martín Corrales, 'Catalunya i el Marroc', pp. 20–21.

41 Modesto Hernández Villaescusa, 'De actualidad', *Bizkaitarra*, 31 July 1909, pp. 2–3 (p. 2).

of crops are unknown. Everything is rudimentary, backwards, basic and unable to help the mother earth on its admirable prodigality.[42]

Other articles in the series were about the five different 'races' that inhabited the Moroccan Empire, 'the Moors, the Arabs, the Blacks, the Jews and the Berbers'.[43] The section dedicated to 'the Moors' argued that whilst 'the Arab, is the only noble and generous race from those belonging to the Semitic family', the Moor, 'despite their immediate contact with Europeans ... is easily the more brute, stupid and corrupt of all the races inhabiting the Empire'.[44] Unsurprisingly, during this decade, Basque nationalists used the words 'Africa/n' and 'Riffian' as an insult and as a synonym for barbarism and savagery in the articles they published.[45]

Similar adjectives to those used to describe the local inhabitants of Morocco were deployed in *Euskalduna* and *Bizkaitarra* to condemn the events that took place in Catalonia during the Tragic Week of 1909. Indeed, whereas both newsletters stood out for their cautious approach to Spain's colonial conflict and for their patronising attitudes towards the Moroccans, the newsletters also concurred in their vision of the Tragic Week, which they both condemned harshly. For instance, *Euskalduna* referred to the events in Barcelona as 'an attack to the most basic principles of dignity and human rights'.[46] The protagonists of the Tragic Week, the newsletter argued, were 'enemies of the order and the law'.[47] *Bizkaitarra* agreed: the protagonists of the 'savagery' committed in Barcelona were a group of '"civilised" Kaffirs'.[48] In sum, the events of the last week of July were classed as 'unworthy, criminal'.[49]

The attitude that both newsletters adopted towards the events of the Tragic Week is hardly surprising. Considering that, as noted above, Basque

---

42 Modesto Hernández Villaescusa, 'Marruecos. Geografía del imperio', *Bizkaitarra*, 7 August 1909, p. 2.

43 See Modesto Hernández Villaescusa, 'Marruecos. Etnografía', *Bizkaitarra*, 14 August 1909, pp. 1-2 and Modesto Hernández Villaescusa, 'Marruecos. Etnografía', *Bizkaitarra*, 21 August 1909, p. 3.

44 Hernández Villaescusa, 'Marruecos. Etnografía', *Bizkaitarra*, 14 August 1909, pp. 1-2.

45 See for instance, C. de Astoreka, 'La gran semana', *Patria*, 4 September 1904, p. 3; Iturain, 'Nacionalismo y autonomismo (conclusión)', *Patria*, 5 June 1904, p. 1.

46 Anon., 'La historia se repite', *Euskalduna*, 5 August 1909, p. 1.

47 Anon., 'La historia se repite', p. 1.

48 Anon., 'Los farsantes de la democracia. Los anarquistas en acción. Para "El Liberal en Bilbao" y sus lectores', *Bizkaitarra*, 23 October 1909, p. 3. Note: 'Kaffir' or 'cafre' (from 'Cafrería') is a racial slur that was used to refer to black Africans in South Africa. 'Cafre' is still used in Spain as a pejorative word or insult meaning 'savage' or 'brute'.

49 K., 'Crónica obrera. Huelgas y motines', *Bizkaitarra*, 14 August 1909, p. 2.

nationalism was a strongly Catholic movement, it was to be expected that both radicals and moderates would condemn a rebellion that took on a symbolic and actual anti-clerical tone. The fact that the protagonists of the riots of 1909 were seen as enemies of Catholicism, just like the Riffians, was used to question their civilisation. Furthermore, the anti-socialist and reactionary views of Basque nationalists were not a secret and thus it is evident that they found it difficult to sympathise with the organisers of the riots in Catalonia, who were mostly socialists, anarchists and republicans. After all, as *Bizkaitarra* recognised in an article that condemned the events of 1909, socialism was a strictly atheist and anti-Catholic movement.[50] By 1909 the PNV was an anti-socialist party, opposed to anything connected with socialism and its aspirations, including the campaign to establish an eight-hour workday.[51] As *Bizkaitarra* stated, 'more Basqueness, implied less socialism, and more socialism, less Basqueness'.[52]

However, the reactionary attitudes of Basque nationalists are not enough to explain their retreat from anticolonialism, as they were silent and cautious about the Moroccan question even before the riots in Catalonia took place. Instead, a more satisfactory explanation can be found in both the patronising attitudes Basques held towards Moroccans and their fears of repression of the Basque movement by the Spanish government. As explored in the first section of the chapter, during this period the Basque nationalist movement aimed to put an end to its semi-clandestine past to become a party of the masses that respected the legality of the Spanish system entirely. Although Basque radicals would begin to support the use of violent actions in the following decades, during the first decade of the twentieth century they advocated for a legal and non-violent path that would allow Basque nationalism to flourish as a dominant political force.

This vision had been imposed by the moderates, who always defended a parliamentary and gradual change. In fact, *Euskalduna* – which was very wary of the repression that the Basque movement could experience – advised their readers to be sensible and respectful in times of national crisis. The newspaper expressed this explicitly when it argued that it would be convenient to suspend the celebrations of San Ignacio de Loyola of 1909, 'in order to avoid the highly likely event that the enemies of both nationalism and [public] order, would use those festivities as a pretext for

50 See K., 'Crónica obrera', p. 2.
51 See Anon., 'Tribuna libre. La jornada de ocho horas', *Bizkaitarra*, 30 March 1912, pp. 1–2.
52 Anon., 'En la llaga', *Bizkaitarra*, 31 July 1912, p. 2.

staging provocations and altering public peace'.[53] Another article, published after the events of the Tragic Week finished, agreed, and argued that the enemies of Basque nationalism would do anything to portray the movement as a 'rebel group, outside the law that needs to be pursued endlessly until it is exterminated'.[54] *Euskalduna* was not wrong: peripheral nationalist movements across Spain suffered strong repression by the state and fierce opposition from different sectors of society, which used every opportunity to attack them.[55] Adding this to the patronising attitudes that both moderates and radicals held towards Moroccans, who were considered as not worthy of comparison with the Basques, it is no surprise that neither publication applauded the actions of the Riffians and the insurgents of the Tragic Week who challenged Spain in 1909.

The Latin vs the Anglo-Saxon Races: Anti-Spanishness and British Exceptionalism

The fact that Basque radicals and moderates did not condemn Spain's imperial activities in north Africa does not mean that their anti-Spanishness had decreased. Instead, as Spanish intellectuals discussed how they could regenerate the state to address the anxieties related to the loss of empire, Basque nationalists responded to these discourses with a highly racialised and xenophobic rhetoric that denied the possibility of Spain being regenerated or 'cured'. Furthermore, developing Arana's thinking, Basque nationalists expanded on the distinction that Lord Salisbury had established between dying and living nations in 1898. Whilst Spain was the epitome of a dying nation – and hence its presence in Euskadi was the cause of all the problems and miseries of the nation – Britain was its opposite: a living and benevolent nation whose rule brought nothing but benefits to its territories. In sum, whilst Arana's immediate successors decided to retreat from his anticolonialism, they inherited and developed his anti-Spanishness and his problematic discourses on race.

Like Arana and many other western figures of the time, Basque nationalists classified the world into different races. An article published in *Bizkaitarra* in 1911 read: 'an eighteenth-century sophism wants to make us believe in the equality of the men and of races; but the truth is that every race has its

---

53 Anon., 'Para el consejo regional', p. 5.
54 Anon., 'Coincidiendo', p. 3.
55 In fact, during 1909 many Spanish periodicals falsely accused Catalan separatism of being behind the events of the Tragic Week. See Pich Mitjana, 'La revolución de julio de 1909', pp. 190–92.

particular mental constitution from which their institutions, thoughts and arts derive.'[56] There was no doubt that Spain, painted as the most uncultured, inhuman and incapable nation, was at the bottom of the racial ladder and hence its coexistence with the Basques was unfeasible. Like Arana, his successors believed that it was necessary to avoid the mixing of the Basque and the Spanish races. As *Patria* stated, the 'Basque of relatively pure blood ... is superior to the average Spanish immigrant' and to the 'mestizo or [the person] resulting from mixings in which sexual selection has not obeyed scientific criteria in conformity with moral [criteria]'.[57] In an article arguing against racial mixing published in 1908, *Aberri* argued that

> The alliances between Basque and Spanish families attack the race directly ... to watch over the purity of the race and its development is the most important mission of the Basque social action ... and because this [racial] development and survival is affected by the emigration that weakens it and the Latin immigration that taints it, we, the nationalists, need to pay special attention to these problems to resolve them according to the needs of the nation.[58]

56 Luis de Eleizalde, 'Tercera parte: Nación vasca', *Bizkaitarra*, 26 August 1911, pp. 1–2 (p. 1).
57 Abérkale, 'Sección amena. Caso de patología', *Patria*, 19 June 1904, pp. 2–3 (p. 2).
58 Kizkitza, 'Sobre reintegración foral', *Aberri*, 14 March 1908, pp. 1–2 (p. 2). There is enough evidence to assume that Basques were acquainted with contemporary arguments against racial mixing, developed across Europe by Eugenicists and shaping Nazi thought in Germany. In the same year that this article was published in *Aberri*, *Euskalduna* reproduced an article from *Politisch-Anthropologische Review*, a German monthly magazine that was deeply influenced by social Darwinist theories and had strong anti-Semitic undertones. This article, which examined the industrial transformation that Germany was undergoing at the time, argued that the current influx of immigration was affecting the country's ethnic composition and therefore its future as a nation. The transition from a pure national state to a multiracial one, this article argued, was to have long-term consequences in the future of the German Empire, as had been the case of the Roman Empire, which waned due to 'miscegenation'. Whereas 'the English have conquered a great part of the world and dominate it both in politics and in civilization thanks to their caste superiority and national consciousness' and whereas 'Japan's industry creates a place for their nation's race ... [the industry of the] German Empire destroys the races of its country and replaces them with a *mestizo* population, of less value'. The similarities between Germany and Euskadi were obvious to *Euskalduna*: both nations received a wide influx of immigrants owing to the strong industrialisation of both areas. The arrival of Spanish immigrants and the subsequent mixing with the 'purely raced' Basques was to have long-term consequences for the future of Euskadi, in *Euskalduna*'s view. See Von Saucken-Heinrichswalde, 'La desnacionalización de Alemania por la industria', *Politisch Anthropoligische Revue*, reproduced in Spanish in *Euskalduna*, 7 May 1908, p. 2.

Basque nationalists believed that the inferiority of the Spanish could be seen in day-to-day language, traditions and culture. For instance, the Spanish language was considered vulgar and blasphemous and as *Euskalduna* stated 'blasphemy is one of the greatest signs of lack of culture'.[59] Whereas 'the Spaniard is the most blasphemous man in the world' ... 'in Euskera blasphemy or improper words do not exist'.[60] The imposition of the Spanish language on Euskadi had perverted their villages and customs. If nationalists wanted the Basque race to survive, it was necessary to speak Euskera.

The intrinsic nature and behaviour of the Latin race was also distinguished from that of the Basques in many ways. Spaniards were depicted as greedy and violent, as the 'invasion' of Euskadi proved. Important proof of their violent nature was the high crime rate in the Spanish state which, an article in *Patria* claimed, was the highest in Europe.[61] In contrast, the article argued, the crime rate in Euskadi was very low, situating the Basques 'in the first place among the most cultured and humanitarian races'.[62] Contrary to the Spanish, the Basques were peaceful by nature. As *Euskalduna* stated, 'in this country, model of democracies, everyone's freedom has always been respected and continues to be respected today in the same way that our ancestors did'.[63] *Bizkaitarra* agreed, arguing that the spirit of the Basques was not perverted by 'hateful imperialism' as Basques did not go to the Americas 'with the aim of conquest, like many other nations'.[64]

Overall, Basque nationalists claimed that the customs and traditions of the Spanish, which were totally unlike theirs, determined their level of culture and civilisation. As for Arana, the ways in which Spain practised Catholicism were used to differentiate the Basques from the Spaniards and to exemplify the lack of culture and civilisation of the latter. For instance, Spanish priests smoked and drank, unlike Basque ones.[65] Furthermore, Basque nationalists used bullfighting as an example of the lack of civilisation among the Spanish.[66] Basque traditions were perverted

---

59 Maiz Tar Prantzesko, 'La blasfemia', *Euskalduna*, 17 March 1906, p. 6.
60 Maiz Tar Prantzesko, 'La blasfemia', p. 6.
61 See Jaizkibel, 'Contrastes entre las razas Española y Euzkeriana', *Patria*, 31 January 1904, p. 3.
62 Jaizkibel, 'Contrastes entre las razas Española y Euzkeriana', p. 3.
63 Anon., 'El peligro castellano', *Euskalduna*, 5 August 1905, pp. 1-2 (p. 1).
64 Juan Cruz de Espetxea de Larrínaga, 'A través de la historia', *Bizkaitarra*, 28 August 1909, pp. 1-2 (p. 1).
65 Alcoholism – which was believed to be an endemic danger imported by the Spanish – began to be criticised by Basque nationalists during this period. See, for instance, Anon., 'Solidaridad de Obreros Vascos', *Bizkaitarra*, 11 January 1913, p. 3 or Amén, 'El alcoholismo', *Bizkaitarra*, 19 August 1911, p. 2.
66 See, among others, Chaviri, 'De vital interés', *Euskalduna*, 12 May 1906, pp. 6-8.

by 'barbaric' festivities such as bullfighting – brought by the Spanish to Euskadi – 'unworthy of any civilised people' or, as another article recalled, 'worthy of being celebrated in Africa, where there is no sense, where "Zulism" rules'.[67] Other articles suggested that Spain's barbarism surpassed that allegedly found in Africa and encouraged missionaries to evangelise the former instead of the latter.[68] As *Patria* stated in 1904, Spain was nothing but 'an extension of the Rif' and 'really needs an English invasion in order to straighten out its brain and morality'.[69]

Indeed, whilst the Spaniards were considered to be at the bottom of the racial ladder alongside African peoples, the British were at the top. As shown in Chapter 1, this was not a belief held only by the Basque nationalists of the period. After the 1870s, 'it was common in Europe to think that the Latin nations or races were entrapped in a spiral of degeneration, which contrasted with the advancement of the Anglo-Saxon nations'.[70] Once the loss of the last Spanish colonies in 1898 confirmed the widespread notion of the progressive degeneration of the Latin races, Arana's successors continued stressing the idea of Anglo-Saxon superiority, which contrasted sharply with the inferiority of the 'mixed-race' Spanish.

What is more, according to Basque nationalists, the differences between Latins and Anglo-Saxons had a crucial effect on how both races governed their territories as the superiority of the latter allowed them to rule effectively and benevolently. This belief resulted in what I call the theories of 'good colonialism', according to which the imperialist actions of the Anglophone nations were justified by their benevolence towards their colonies, which needed their intervention and protection to grow and develop. This demonstrates that Basque nationalists believed that imperialism was not inherently evil but could be necessary when practised

---

See also Anon., 'Naskaldija', *Bizkaitarra*, 31 July 1909, p. 4; Anon., 'Naskaldija', *Bizkaitarra*, 31 July 1912, p. 4; Anon., 'Naskaldija', *Bizkaitarra*, 7 September 1912, p. 4.

67 Anon., 'Era de esperar', *Euskalduna*, 29 July 1909, p. 5 and C. de Astoreka, 'La gran semana', p. 3. Another significant example is an article in *Euskalduna* which observed that at the Algeciras Conference 'the civilised nations tried to steer the barbaric and backward Moroccan Empire towards reform and progress'. However, the labelling of Spain as a 'civilised nation' is used here sarcastically, as the article claims that in Spain more importance had been given to a bullfight event in honour of the King than to other transcendental events, such as the Algeciras Conference. Chaviri, 'De vital interés', pp. 6–7.

68 The reverse use of the 'civilisation' rhetoric always remained in Basque nationalist discourse. See Eletarja, 'La Religión en España', *Aberri*, 7 July 1906, pp. 7–8.

69 Iturain, 'Nacionalismo y autonomismo', p. 1.

70 Loureiro, 'Spanish Nationalism and the Ghost of Empire', p. 66.

by what they deemed as 'superior races'. Of course, if practised by Spain, it was automatically despicable.

An article published in *Euskalduna* in 1906 perfectly exemplifies how Basque newsletters promoted ideas of Anglo-Saxon superiority and how these echoed Arana's writings after 1898. The article, titled 'La independencia de Cuba' ('Cuba's independence'), commented on the situation in Spain's former colony and argued that 'Latin races, as a wise French writer said, do not have any political sense, and because of this they rule very badly. If we add to this their lack of common sense, they are in a worse condition to govern.'[71] This way of ruling differed from that of the 'Anglo-Saxon race'.[72] Hence, the article argued, even if this nation stopped existing as a completely free Hispano-American Republic, Cuba would not lose anything, as it would continue enjoying the freedom it has under the Yankee protection.[73] In a highly patronising tone, the article stated that 'losing bad habits and replacing a decadent spirit for a vigorous one is not something bad but the opposite. Cubans are still big kids and they need a Mentor that guides them.'[74]

This article is not an isolated example. As Nerea Aresti has established, many pre-war Basque nationalists considered Anglophone nations as the vanguard of progress and an example to follow by communities which, like the Basque, were still finding their own path.[75] In particular, in the first decade of the twentieth century, Basque nationalists built on Arana's telegram to British Prime Minister Salisbury and devoted many words of praise and admiration towards Britain.[76] During his time, Arana had used the

---

71 Anon., 'La independencia de Cuba', *Euskalduna*, 6 October 1906, pp. 3–4 (p. 3).

72 Anon., 'La independencia de Cuba', p. 4.

73 Anon., 'La independencia de Cuba', p. 4. It is worth noting some exceptions to this belief are found in an article on *Bizkaitarra* when talking about the situation that the Philippines experienced with its new oppressors, the United States. See Anon., 'Ecos Nacionalistas', 30 October 1909, *Bizkaitarra*, p. 2.

74 Anon., 'La independencia de Cuba', p. 4. The same article suggests similarities between the state of slavery experienced by Cubans under Spanish rule and that of the Basques today. However, the author argues that despite the deep 'Latinisation' they suffer, the Basques will still be able to regenerate themselves.

75 Nerea Aresti, 'El gentleman y el bárbaro. Masculinidad y civilización en el nacionalismo vasco (1893–1937)', *Cuadernos de Historia Contemporánea*, 39 (2017), pp. 83–103 (p. 87).

76 In the twentieth century, most of these theories of 'good colonialism' focused on Britain. As stated in the previous chapter, evidence suggests that Basque Anglophilia was related to the close commercial relationships between the Basques and the British. In particular, some influential moderates had important educational, cultural and commercial links with Britain. For instance, the leader of the former Euskalerriacos, de la Sota y Llano, merged his company with that of his cousin and associate partner Eduardo Aznar de la Sota to form a unique shipping company which had important links with Britain. The relationships between de la Sota y

Boer War as a pretext to praise the British actions; now it was the struggle for Irish Home Rule that shaped Basques' attitudes towards British colonialism.

During the 1800s and early 1910s, Ireland was involved in a long fight to achieve autonomy from the British Empire. This was the aim of the so-called Irish Home Rule movement, which had attempted to achieve self-government for Ireland since the First Home Rule Bill in 1886. After another failed attempt in 1893, the Third Home Rule Bill was finally introduced in 1912, giving hope to Irish nationalists, if only temporarily (the Bill was immediately suspended during the First World War). The movement was admired and emulated elsewhere in the British Empire and also reached the Basque Country.

Whilst Arana had written a limited number of articles about Irish nationalism, his immediate successors wrote constantly and admiringly about the Irish. For both radicals and moderates, the British willingness to grant autonomy to their dominions evidenced that imperialism was not inherently evil. In that period, the Irish nationalists seeking Home Rule were not necessarily opposed to the Empire either. Instead, Ireland's 'semi-colonial' nature, forged complex relationships with the British Empire. As Alvin Jackson notes, 'Home Rulers fought to break the Union, the link with the imperial motherland, but in many cases they were content that Ireland should participate fully within the structures of Empire'.[77]

Between 1903 and 1914, the Irish example became a mirror in which the Basque nationalists saw themselves reflected. Comparisons between the two movements were not difficult to make. Both movements had important internal divisions and, like the Irish, some Basque nationalists believed that they were an example of a race that had been deprived of its own state.[78] Both Ireland and Euskadi, Basque nationalists claimed, had been assimilated into Britain and Spain respectively in the same century: the Irish lost their freedom through the 1800 Act of Union and Euskadi in 1839.[79] Moreover, the

---

Llano with Britain were so close that King George V awarded him a knighthood of the Order of the British Empire, conferring on him the title Sir. Other influential moderate ideologues such as industrialist Eduardo de Landeta Aburto studied in Britain. As we will see in Chapter 3, the 1910s marked a new period of close commercial interaction between Britain and Euskadi given the new opportunities that the First World War provided.

77 Alvin Jackson, 'Ireland, the Union, and the Empire, 1800–1960', in Kevin Kenny (ed.), *Ireland and the British Empire* (Oxford and New York: Oxford University Press, 2004), pp. 123–53 (p. 137).

78 Núñez Seixas, 'Ecos de Pascua', p. 454 and Ugalde, *La acción exterior del nacionalismo vasco*, pp. 112–13.

79 See for instance Anon., 'La Irlanda y el Home-Rule', *Aberri*, 8 June 1907, pp. 1–2. This article stated that had the English not assaulted the Irish constitution a century

deep Catholic roots of Irish nationalism strengthened Basque connections with the Irish.[80] As an article in *Aberri* stated, 'there is no [Irish] Catholic who does not love the independence of their homeland and who does not use all available means for the vindication of their national rights'.[81]

Basque nationalists followed the Irish Home Rule movement with enthusiasm. Indeed, on this occasion, the moderates of *Euskalduna* imposed their vision of the Irish struggle: the gradualist parliamentary and pro-autonomy programme of the Irish moderates – as opposed to the revolutionary and radical Fenian movement – constituted an example that the incipient Basque movement could follow.[82] Convinced of the feasibility of the Irish example, *Euskalduna* reproduced speeches by Irish nationalist leaders which presented the Home Rule question as a movement that resolved 'a vital issue for the interests of Ireland' and provided the power to 'cut the chains and to free the youth of Ireland'.[83] Home Rule was seen as the perfect model of parliamentarianism and autonomy, a model that, according to an article in the Irish newsletter *Weekly Freeman* and reproduced by *Euskalduna*, would solve Ireland's national aspirations and would bring peace and happiness to the island.[84] Home Rule and the Irish Parliamentary Party constituted 'a vivid example for the Basques'.[85]

The Irish example also turned into an opportunity to highlight the intrinsic differences between their respective oppressors. As Niall Cullen has noted, 'for Basque nationalists, engagement with the Irish Question – enmeshed within the context of Britain and her Empire – also provided ample opportunity for the PNV to hold a mirror to Spain and its comparative

earlier (implicitly referring to the Act of Union), they would not be faced with the Irish nationalist problem.

80 Catholicism was also useful in establishing connections with Polish nationalists, who were also an important influence on the Basques.

81 Anon., 'La Irlanda y el Home-Rule', p. 1.

82 Núñez Seixas notes how after Arana's death the practical sense and the pro-autonomous strategy of the Euskalerriacos and its organ of expression *Euskalduna* was imposed when articulating the international vision of the PNV. Núñez Seixas, 'Ecos de Pascua', p. 454.

83 Anon., 'Los nacionalistas irlandeses', *Euskalduna*, 9 April 1908, p. 2.

84 Anon., 'La convención nacional irlandesa', *Weekly Freeman*, reproduced in Spanish in *Euskalduna*, 18 February 1909, pp. 2–3. Note: *The Weekly Freeman* was the weekend version of the *Freeman's Journal*, a nationalist newsletter that was published in Dublin from 1763 to 1924. The *Weekly Freeman* began to publish in 1871. This same argument was repeated in an article published in *Euskalduna* in 1905: P.C.G., 'Quince años de Home-Rule. Una Irlanda pacífica y próspera', *La Renaixença*, reproduced in Spanish in *Euskalduna*, 10 June 1905, pp. 2–3 (p. 3).

85 Anon., 'La convención nacional irlandesa', p. 3.

attitude towards the Basque Country'.[86] Thus, *Euskalduna* used the Irish example to paint England as an example of progress and development and Spain as an archaic and intransigent nation, the antithesis of Britain.[87] An article that *Euskalduna* reproduced from the Catalan regionalist newsletter *La Renaixença* (The Renaissance) stressed these differences:

> It is important to point out that England, in general, does not tend to send civil servants to Ireland as ignorant and depraved as Spain does in Catalan provinces … What would [John] Redmond [leader of the Irish Parliamentary Party] say if, instead of speaking about the representatives of a state as cultured and civilised as the British, had been referring to the Spanish governmnet?[88]

As these articles suggested, Ireland had every right to claim freedom and would benefit enormously from autonomy – yet its oppressors and colonisers were not immoral and malevolent like the Spanish but were, rather, the main

---

86 Cullen, *Radical Basque Nationalist-Irish Republican Relations*, p. 29. In his recent book, Cullen argues that the admiration of Ireland and the Anglophilia of the Basque movement was not necessarily contradictory. See Cullen, *Radical Basque Nationalist-Irish Republican Relations*, pp. 29–30.

87 See for instance Anon., 'Ejemplo que imitar', *Euskalduna*, 10 March 1906, p. 5; P.C.G., 'Quince años de Home Rule'; Anon., 'Como aquí', *Euskalduna*, 9 December 1905, pp. 5–6, or Z, 'La paja en el ojo ajeno', *Euskalduna*, 18 May 1907, pp. 2–3. Ugalde notes that despite the strong Anglophile leanings of *Euskalduna*, the newsletter paid attention to the Indian anticolonial struggle. See Ugalde, *La acción exterior del nacionalismo vasco*, pp. 174–75. It is worth noting that *Bizkaitarra* was far more neutral than *Euskalduna* in its praise of Britain and on occasions, the radical newsletter condemned the despotic actions of Britain in its colonies. See, for instance, Anon., 'Ecos nacionalistas. Unión de los indios', *Bizkaitarra*, 23 October 1909, p. 2; Arieta Tar Ander, 'Carta abierta a Ramiro G. de R', *Bizkaitarra*, 7 January 1911, pp. 3–4 (p. 3) and Utare, 'Ecos nacionalistas. Triunfo nacionalista irlandés', *Bizkaitarra*, 21 May 1910, p. 4. Yet this does not mean that *Bizkaitarra* did not occasionally praise Britain. For instance, in 1911 an article in *Bizkaitarra* that encouraged Basque nationalists to practise sports, used England and its passion for sports as an example and observed that the country was amongst the most prosperous nations. See Anon., 'De Gimnasia', *Bizkaitarra*, 28 January 1911, p. 2. Later that year, the radical newsletter reproduced an article from another Basque newspaper that talked about the formation of federal parliaments throughout Britain and acknowledged with pride the imperial character of Westminster. The article concluded that 'in the North, healthy winds that acknowledge the personality of small nationalities blow'. Anon., 'De colosal importancia', *Bizkaitarra*, 22 April 1911, p. 3. In 1912, shortly after Home Rule was approved in Ireland, *Bizkaitarra* commented with enthusiasm that 'what in Ireland is a living reality, is still for us [the Basques] a fervent desire'. X, '¿Home Rule Euzkadiano?', *Bizkaitarra*, 11 May 1912, p. 2.

88 P.C.G., 'Quince años de Home-Rule', p. 3.

representatives of European civilisation. If Ireland achieved its national dreams, this would be both because of the sacrifice and devotion of the Irish but also because of the generosity of their coloniser. In this way, Basque nationalists believed, on certain occasions a nation without a state could achieve its aspirations through the protection of its ruler.

Spaniards, Basques claimed, should imitate Britain. This idea was explicitly defended in an article named 'Ejemplo que imitar' ('An example to imitate'), which established comparisons between South Africa, Ireland and the Basque Country. The article argued that after the 'cruel war' of South Africa (the Second Boer War) and the years of Irish struggle for Home Rule, Britain had decided to fulfil the political aspirations of their enemies instead of repressing them. In Spain, as the article posited, things took a completely different turn as the country ignored and silenced the Basque petitions.[89] As the article concluded,

> the difference in methods taken towards very similar matters by the English and the Spanish state has no other explanation than the fact that England thinks and works in harmony with the aspirations of those it governs; and in Spain, immersed in its usual petty politics, issues are not thought through as the country acts always in the heat of the moment, always seeing dangers that do not actually exist. That's why England is great.[90]

Another article addressed the same issue, criticising Spain's reluctance to give autonomy: 'and then we say we want to become European! ... and then we say that we want to escape from this state of backwardness and stagnation in which the nation finds itself ...!'[91] In sum, England, unlike Spain, was great because it was going to grant the Irish what they had been fighting to achieve for years: Home Rule.

As the next chapter evidences, the vision of Britain as a benevolent colonial power dominated the PNV's newspaper *Euzkadi* in the following years. Only a few radicals led by the pro-independence leader Luis Arana would call the alleged generosity of Britain into question after the Easter Rising of 1916. This rebellion was essential for the shaping and polarisation

---

89 Anon., 'Ejemplo que imitar', p. 5. A previously mentioned article, which highlighted the 'Latin races'' lack of political ability and the superiority of the Anglo-Saxon races, had already attributed Spain's imperial demise to the reluctance of the Spaniards to grant their colonies' autonomy. See Anon., 'La independencia de Cuba', p. 3.
90 Anon., 'Ejemplo que imitar', p. 5.
91 Anon, 'Como aquí', p. 6.

of the two branches of Basque nationalism. Whereas for Basque radicals this confirmed that British benevolence was a myth, Basque moderates continued developing their theories of 'good colonialism'. These changing conceptions of colonialism accentuated the tensions between radicals and moderates, who eventually split in 1921.

Conclusion

The years between 1903 and 1914 saw a retreat from Arana's classic anticolonial rhetoric. Basque nationalism transitioned from a nationalist movement with anticolonial undertones (which was not exempt from contradictions) to a classic European form of nationalism with marked Orientalist tendencies. Despite having a great chance to contribute to the existing discourses on the ineptitude of Spain as a colonising power in north Africa, Basque nationalists opted to distance themselves from the topic. However, Basque nationalists fuelled other existing debates such as the differences between Latin and Anglo-Saxon races, as Arana had before them. These differences allowed them to distinguish between two forms of colonialism: a benevolent type – practised by superior races such as the Anglo-Saxon races – and a despicable one, carried by southern European races (most prominently Spain). The attitudes examined in this chapter were not going to be forgotten by certain groups within the movement. The theories of 'good colonialism' were widely promoted by Basque nationalists during the First World War, which they used opportunistically to legitimise the actions of the Allies in the global conflict. Furthermore, although anticolonialism re-emerged in the radical branch of Basque nationalism during the so-called Wilsonian moment, racist views would be a constant in the period studied in this monograph. The problematic views of empire that Basques held in the first half of the twentieth century responded both to the necessities of the movement and the international context. The basis for these views is found in the period explored in this book so far.

CHAPTER THREE

The Re-Emergence of Anticolonialism and the Road to the Split of 1921 (1914–1921)

Despite the significant disagreements between Basque moderates and radicals, the PNV Manifesto of 1906 managed to circumvent their differences by avoiding the loaded and disputed words of independence or autonomy. The solution reached in 1906 managed to keep both radicals and moderates content for a few years. Yet between 1914 and 1921 it became evident that the reconciliation between the branches was only temporary, as new divisions emerged within the movement. These unresolved tensions led to the split of the Basque movement into two in 1921, after radical sections of the movement were expelled from the PNV, which had changed its name to Comunión Nacionalista Vasca (Basque Nationalist Communion: henceforth CNV) in 1916.[1] This rupture had its origins in a 'badly cured wound' (Arana's 'pro-Spanish evolution') and the always present but unsolved debate over autonomy and independence.[2]

Whilst many scholars have explored the different internal and external factors that contributed to the polarisation and alienation of the two branches of Basque nationalism, they have tended to neglect an important point of division that pushed moderates and radicals apart: the issue of colonialism.[3] As demonstrated in Chapter 2, both Basque radicals and moderates abandoned Arana's anticolonialism despite their differences and,

---

1 This name had been adopted by the party informally from 1913. In this chapter, I use the new name that the party used in this period, the CNV.

2 De Pablo and Mees, *El péndulo patriótico*, p. 76.

3 To name a few: Ugalde, *La acción exterior del nacionalismo vasco*; de Pablo and Mees, *El péndulo patriótico*; Núñez Seixas, 'Ecos de Pascua'; Ruiz Descamps, *Historia de las organizaciones juveniles del nacionalismo vasco*; Alejandro Pulido Azpíroz, *Neutralidad en pie de guerra. El País Vasco y Navarra ante la Primera Guerra Mundial (1914–1918)* (Madrid: Sílex Universidad-Historia, 2021). Although scholars such as Núñez Seixas claims that the split of 1921 ultimately stemmed from endogenous causes, he has argued that the Irish question acted as a 'talismán' that defined the positions of each of the factions within the movement. Núñez Seixas, 'Ecos de Pascua', p. 462.

following the Irish example, believed that parliamentarism and dialogue were the paths that they should follow to achieve self-determination (whether this meant independence or autonomy). The belief that the Irish demands were met thanks to the benevolence of Britain also led moderates and radicals to posit that colonialism was not always evil.

These similarities disappeared in the years this chapter studies. The CNV adopted the moderates' strategy of gradualism and autonomy and continued to endorse the theories of 'good colonialism'. In contrast, from 1916 a small group of Basque radicals led by Sabino Arana's oldest brother, Luis Arana, began to condemn all forms of colonialism regardless of who was the coloniser and who was the colonised. This differing view of colonialism was not arbitrary. Instead, each branch made an argument about colonialism that supported their political goals in the context of the First World War. On the one hand, the CNV's vision of Britain and the rest of the Allies as protectors of the weak and small nations was used to defend its national programme, based on autonomy, collaboration and gradualism. On the other hand, the Basque radicals who dared to reject the official party's programme argued that all the powers involved in the Great War were equally imperialists, and that independence was the only way forward. In other words, the rejection or support of colonialism became a rhetorical device to promote autonomy or independence. As the rest of the book shows, the rejection of all forms of colonialism also allowed Basque radicals to equate their struggle with that of other anticolonial nationalists and to consider violence as a method of achieving freedom.

This chapter examines the differing visions of colonialism that Basque moderates and radicals held between 1914 and 1921, focusing on how they reacted to and interpreted key events and ideas of the period. After a brief introductory section explaining the evolution of the movement up to the split of 1921, the chapter explores how the official line of the CNV was Anglophile and pro-Allied during the First World War, and how this stance was justified using the theories of 'good colonialism'. I then examine how a section of Basque radicalism began to challenge these ideas for the first time during the Easter Rising of 1916, which allowed radicals to put into question the theories of a benevolent form of colonialism. The chapter concludes with an exploration of the period of extended radicalisation that followed the end of the Great War and the so-called Wilsonian moment. Understanding how radicals and moderates became increasingly divided over issues related to colonialism is key to comprehending the future evolution of Basque radicalism and its use of anticolonialism, which will be the focus of the rest of the book.

The Triumph of Pragmatism: The CNV in the Mid-1910s

Whilst the first decade of the twentieth century saw the dominance of the radical branch within the Basque nationalist party, from the mid-1910s the moderate project began to prevail in the CNV. This change began to gain ground after the expulsion of the radical and authoritarian leader of the party, Luis Arana, in late 1915. Luis Arana's presidency had seen a reinforcement of the radical faction. However, once he was out, the CNV was free to promote a more pragmatic and moderate plan of action, which distanced itself from Sabino and his brother Luis's radicalism. Because of this, Mees argues, Luis's expulsion from the CNV has usually been interpreted by historians as the culmination of the long fight for power within the party, which was won by the advocates of a bourgeois and pro-autonomy nationalist model.[4]

Once this shift in power began to take place, the CNV led some important victories that signalled the triumph of the party's efforts over the previous decade. Encouraged by the revival of the nationalities question during the First World War, Basque nationalism continued to expand its influence beyond Biscay, as demonstrated in the provincial elections in Gipuzkoa, where the first nationalist candidate was elected as provincial deputy in 1915 and a second in 1917. Furthermore, these years saw other key electoral victories, including a majority win in Bilbao's council, as well as the election of councillors in other areas of Biscay, Gipuzkoa and Navarra. But the victory of the CNV went beyond local elections. In February 1918, the CNV ran in the Spanish general elections, obtaining seven seats. As de Pablo and Mees point out, the CNV of 1918 had little in common with the early PNV, having successfully become a respectable political option for the affluent classes of society.[5] In addition to a solid electoral presence, the CNV also had a powerful daily newspaper, which reinforced and spread its ideas. *Euzkadi* – which dealt not only with politics but also with sport, culture, religion and international affairs – soon became one of the most read newspapers in the Basque Country and was a powerful instrument for the expansion of Basque nationalism.[6]

---

4 See Mees, 'El nacionalismo vasco entre 1903 y 1923', p. 126. As Mees notes, the reasons of Luis Arana's marginalisation within the party were more complex and involved other reasons, which will be considered later. See footnote 45 in this chapter for further details.

5 De Pablo and Mees, *El péndulo patriótico*, p. 65.

6 Mees, 'El nacionaliso vasco entre 1903 y 1923', p. 124; Javier Díaz Noci, 'Historia del periodismo vasco (1600–2010)', *Mediatika: Cuadernos de Medios de Comunicación*, 13 (2012), pp. 1–261 (p. 132).

During these years, the CNV also took some important steps towards the internationalisation of the movement. Since the start of the movement, Basque nationalists had followed the evolution of other nationalist movements around the world with interest, which sometimes acted as a point of reference for the Basques.[7] Before the Great War, Basque nationalists mostly established verbal and symbolic contacts with other nations, but the conflict provided a solid opportunity for the Basques to play a tangible part in the global clash between small and big nations. This shift from symbolic to tangible connections was marked by the CNV's participation in the III Conference of the Union des Nationalités (Union of the Nationalities: henceforth UdN) in June 1916. This was the third conference held by the UdN or the Office Central dés Nationalités (Central Office of the Nationalities), a transnational organisation founded in 1912 that advocated for the self-determination of stateless nations in Europe.[8] The Conference, which took place in Lausanne, was attended by 23 delegates representing 29 nations. Although most of the nations represented in the conference were European, Lausanne also saw the convergence of some African and Asian nations such as Egypt, Syria and Tunisia. The 1916 Conference marked an important turning point for the CNV: its three delegates presented its political programme and aspirations, based on the abolition of French and Spanish laws, to a group of nationalists from different parts of the world who became aware of Euskadi's claims, many of them for the first time. As *Euzkadi* stated, this congress put an end to the isolation of Basque nationalism.[9]

Beyond electoral victories and international exposure, the new direction of the party brought important changes to the party's rhetoric and practices. In 1916 the PNV officially changed its name to Comunión Nacionalista Vasca, which gave the party a 'more vague and less exclusive name' and

---

7 Whilst Sabino Arana had normally focused his attention on extra-European movements opposing the Spanish Empire, his immediate successors mostly shifted their attention to western movements. For instance, from 1910 CNV ideologue Luis de Eleizalde (who wrote under the pseudonym Axe) penned a series of articles named 'Países y razas', 'Countries and races' (first published as articles in *Euzkadi* and later as a monograph), which were designed to show Basque nationalists 'the paths that other European nationalities … had followed'. Quote translated from Ugalde, *La acción exterior del nacionalismo vasco*, p. 211. These articles focused exclusively on western movements, except for a section devoted to the Japanese case. See Luis de Eleizalde, *Países y razas. Las aspiraciones nacionalistas en diversos pueblos (1913–1914)* (Bilbao: Universidad del País Vasco, 1999).

8 The UdN grouped the demands of different European nationalities during the Great War. Ultimately, it had no influence in the peace negotiations, and disappeared in 1919.

9 Ugalde, *La acción exterior del nacionalismo vasco*, p. 253.

disassociated it from Arana's original nomenclature.¹⁰ Furthermore, some attempts to mitigate Sabino Arana's racism were made by influential CNV ideologues such as Luis Eleizalde, who argued that he did not seek to defend the untainted racial purity of the Basques and that all races and nations in Europe, like Euskadi, had foreign but assimilated elements in their nations.¹¹ But without a doubt the key manifestation of the CNV's pragmatic evolution was the pro-autonomy campaign that the party led between 1917 and 1919. During these years, the achievement of autonomy became the party's main goal. This also implied a rapprochement to the Catalan moderate movement, which backed up the CNV's pro-autonomy strategy. As Mees states, as a result, the old dream of the Euskalerriacos of a party of order that safeguarded the interests of the bourgeoisie dominated the nationalist strategy during the years of the war.¹²

The confirmation of a pragmatic strategy by the CNV did not come without opposition. Luis Arana and his followers, who regrouped under the Euskeldun Batzokija after his expulsion from the party, constantly criticised the posture of the CNV, which they considered a deviation from Sabino Arana's orthodoxy. These criticisms were articulated in the Euskeldun Batzokija's organ press, [the third] *Bizkaitarra*, which was born with the double objective of defending Luis Arana's interests and counteracting the influence of the CNV's newspaper, *Euzkadi*.¹³ Nevertheless, Luis Arana and his followers were a minority within the movement. In fact, the expulsion of Arana from the party in late 1915 was not only backed up by the 'moderate and bourgeois' faction of the party but also by all the nationalist organisations in Gipuzkoa, Alava and Navarra and the majority of those in Biscay, including the radical JVB.¹⁴

Other than from the Euskeldun Batzokija, the CNV did not suffer significant internal opposition during its golden years. This changed when the pro-autonomy campaign failed in 1919, plunging the CNV into a period

10 Watson, *Basque Nationalism and Political Violence*, p. 101. De la Granja argues that the change of name had a double meaning: it confirmed that the PNV encompassed a wide inter-class nationalist community and that its members were united by Catholicism as an essential element of its community or party. See Jose Luís de la Granja, 'El nacionalismo vasco en el tiempo de las Irmandades da Fala: Moderados, radicales y heterodoxos (1916–1923)', in Ramón Villares Paz, Xosé Manoel Núñez Seixas and Ramón Máiz Suárez (eds), *Irmandades da Fala no seu tempo: perspectivas cruzadas* (Santiago de Compostela: Consello da Cultura Galega, 2021), pp. 273–95 (p. 277).
11 Núñez Seixas, '¿Protodiplomacia exterior o ilusiones ópticas?', p. 254.
12 Mees, 'El nacionalismo vasco entre 1903 y 1923', p. 128.
13 De Pablo and Mees, *El péndulo patriótico*, p. 64.
14 Mees, 'El nacionalismo vasco entre 1903 y 1923', p. 128.

of deep crisis. Up until then, the CNV's pragmatism and its ambiguity had kept most radicals and moderates within the party happy. After all, the CNV had not publicly rejected independence as a possible further goal to be pursued after achieving autonomy, contributing to the support the campaign of autonomy enjoyed from across the party. However, the failure of the autonomy project produced frustration and eventually radicalisation within some sections of the Basque nationalist movement, particularly affecting the Basque Youth and its newsletter *Aberri*, which issued its first issue in late 1916.[15]

As Ruiz Descamps notes, from 1919 the radicals of JVB had clearly taken control of the periodical.[16] Ever since the radicals controlled the publication, *Aberri* began to proclaim itself as the defender of Sabino's orthodoxy, devoting multiple articles questioning the doctrine of the CNV and even beginning to consider violence as a plausible option. As a result, radicals and moderates confronted each other directly through the pages of *Aberri* and *Euzkadi* until 1921, when their coexistence within the same party became evidently unfeasible. In the rest of this chapter, I explore the polarisation of different sections of Basque nationalism, which would form two separate political parties after 1921: the moderate CNV and the radical PNV-*Aberri*. The latter was composed by the radicalised *Aberri* and some of the key dissidents of Euskeldun Batzokija.

'Good Colonialism' in the 'War of the Small Nationalities'

In summer 1914, as the hostilities of the Great War began, Spanish president Eduardo Dato declared Spain's official neutrality in the conflict. This decision was justified by reasons including the lack of infrastructure for modern war in Spain as well as its hope of obtaining a leading role in peace negotiations. However, this did not produce the outcome that the Spanish government had hoped for. Far from becoming a referee in international relations or a new imperial nation that left behind the '98 Disaster, the Spanish Restoration system nearly crumbled during the Great War.[17] Spain's neutrality in the

---

15 JVB was one of the most (if not the most) influential organisations within Basque nationalism at the time but there were many other Basque Youth organisations across Euskadi.

16 Ruiz Descamps, *Historia de las organizaciones juveniles del nacionalismo vasco*, p. 275.

17 As Maximiliano Fuentes Codera has explained, during the Great War intellectuals and politicians thought that the European conflict was a great opportunity to recover Spain's prestige as an imperial nation. As a result, the so-called 'Iberism', which sought to incorporate Portugal into Spain, found new momentum. These theses were also developed by Catalan regionalists. See Maximiliano Fuentes

war heralded an era of deep crisis, proving that the corrupt and archaic Spanish political system was incapable of responding to issues including the escalating Moroccan conflict, social agitation – intensified by the Russian Revolution – and nationalist demands. As Albert Balcells summarises, 'Spain did not go to war but the war came to Spain'.[18]

Despite the official neutrality of the country in the conflict, the Great War divided Spanish society and produced what many historians have classified as a 'civil war of words'. As Francisco Romero recounts, the First World War 'presented a verbal crash between two Spains that was a portent of the real civil war that still lay a generation in the future'.[19] The dispute between those who supported the Allies – who came to represent the values of democracy and freedom – and the Central Powers – who symbolised authority and order – was lived with such intensity that cinemas avoided giving news of the conflict to prevent fights.[20]

In particular, the Great War proved divisive for the Spanish urban intellectual and political elites. During the first weeks of the conflict, the official neutrality was only questioned by some influential figures from different political spectrums such as Republican Alejandro Lerroux and the leader of the Liberal Party, the Count of Romanones. Yet after the first Battle of the Marne in September 1914, Spain saw the emergence of a strong pro-Ally movement, comprised of different intellectuals and political organisations of all beliefs, including most of the Catalan nationalist movement (except for the Lliga Regionalista, the Regionalist League, which supported Dato's government neutrality). On the other hand, the Court, the aristocracy and the army – which hid their Germanophilia behind the defence of Spain's official neutrality – alongside other conservative circles such as the Catholic Church and the Carlists, sympathised with Germany in the Great War.[21] Unlike other Catholic and conservative parties in Spain and Euskadi, which considered the Central Powers as the protectors of conservative or

Codera, 'Imperialismos e iberismos en España: perspectivas regeneradoras frente a la Gran Guerra', *Historia y política: ideas, procesos y movimientos sociales*, 33 (2015), pp. 21–48.

18 In Catalan in the original. Albert Balcells, *El projecte d'autonomia de la Mancomunitat de Catalunya del 1919 i el seu context històric* (Barcelona: Parlament de Catalunya, 2010), p. 12.

19 Francisco Romero, 'Spain and the First World War', in Balfour and Preston (eds), *Spain and the Great Powers in the Twentieth Century*, pp. 42–63 (p. 44).

20 Romero, 'Spain and the First World War', p. 44.

21 As Fuentes Codera points out, Germanophilia and neutrality became synonyms. For a good summary and analysis of the differing attitudes adopted in Spain, see Maximiliano Fuentes Codera, 'Germanófilos y neutralistas: proyectos tradicionalistas y regeneracionistas para España (1914–1918)', *Ayer*, 91.3 (2013), pp. 63–95.

religious values, the CNV adopted a pro-Ally stance during the conflict. This attitude not only led to conflicts with other local newspapers such as the conservative, Catholic and pro-German daily *La Gaceta del Norte*, but it also created important tensions within the Basque nationalist movement itself, explored in further detail in the next section.

The international conflict dominated the contents of *Euzkadi*. *Euzkadi* reproduced up-to-the-minute news of the war – the majority of which came from London, Paris or Amsterdam – as well as detailed chronicles of the conflict. The newspaper even had its own collaborators who covered the war and wrote detailed chronicles. Manuel Aznar Zubigaray (who always wrote under the pseudonym Gudalgai (recruit) when writing about the war) wrote almost-daily war chronicles in Spanish.[22] This made him highly popular in both pro-Ally and Basque nationalist circles. Gudalgai was even invited by both French and British commanders to visit the front in 1916, from where he wrote several war chronicles. Apart from Gudalgai, *Euzkadi* also had another collaborator, Evaristo Bustinza (alias Kirikiño), who wrote about the war in Euskera.[23]

There are several reasons for the widespread support for the Allies within the CNV from the beginning of the conflict.[24] On the one hand, areas of the Spanish state including Euskadi and Catalonia experienced substantial economic growth during the war, whereas some agrarian regions of Spain went into deep economic depression. In Euskadi, the Basque shipping industry particularly grew immensely owing to the growing demands of the war, especially manufacturing for the British, which allowed the creation of new local banks. The strong commercial ties between Euskadi and Britain contributed to the continued praise of the British in *Euzkadi*. Britain was

---

22 For Aznar's journalistic career during the Great War see Javier Díaz Noci and Koldobika Meso Ayerdi, 'Manuel Aznar Zubigaray: los inicios de la prensa nacionalista vasca. De Imanol a Gudalgai (1913–1914)', *Obra Periodística*, 1 (2010); Díaz Noci, 'Historia del periodismo vasco (1600–2010)', pp. 133–34; Javier Díaz Noci, 'El recluta periodista: Manuel Aznar, cronista de la Guerra Mundial para el diario *Euzkadi*', in Xavier Pla and Francesc Montero (eds), *En el teatro de la guerra: cronistas hispánicos en la Primera Guerra Mundial* (Granada: Editorial Comares, 2020), pp. 351–56.

23 Whilst Gudalgai aimed to maintain some objectivity when reporting on the war, Kirikiño's chronicles were strongly anti-German and enthusiastically pro-Ally, more in line with *Euzkadi*. Iñaki Anasagasti and Josu Erkoreka, *Dos familias vascas: Areilza-Aznar* (Madrid: Foca, 2003), quoted in Ruiz Descamps, *Historia de las organizaciones juveniles del nacionalismo vasco*, p. 79. Both Gudaldai and Kirikiño belonged to the JVB.

24 Although on some occasions the party defended its neutrality in the conflict and different internal voices such as Luis Arana criticised this position harshly, the pro-Ally stance of *Euzkadi* and its party was obvious.

praised and defended more than any other Allied power in *Euzkadi*, which presented its actions as the heroic acts of a power committed to protecting small nationalities.

On the other hand, the two sides of the Great War knew how to exploit the so-called 'principle of nationalities', which became a crucial topic in international affairs during and after the war. In the words of Núñez Seixas, both sides of the war deployed the question of nationalities as a strategic weapon by exploiting the existing nationalist claims at the heart of the great multinational empires and thus weakening the enemy internally.[25] Like many other nationalist movements, the CNV thought that the Great War posited great hope for the oppressed nationalities of Europe. In particular, the Allies were regarded by Basque nationalists as the saviours of the small or 'weak' nationalities.[26] Ugalde has argued that for a large section of the Basque nationalists the Great War was a conflict between imperialism and nationalism.[27] Yet as demonstrated below, the CNV really saw it as a clash between savage imperialism – represented by the Central Powers – and benevolent or civilising colonialism, represented by the Allies, particular by Britain.

Finally, and perhaps most importantly, the Great War turned into a great opportunity to promote the pro-autonomy vision of the CNV. As Alejandro Pulido has argued, whoever was able to impose their judgement on the war could then determine the CNV's political path. If the party advocated for Britain, the pro-autonomy thesis would be reinforced, but if the dominant posture was either a pro-German stance or neutrality, the Aranist (and hence pro-independence) orthodoxy would be reinforced in the party.[28] In other words, the support of both a moderate and pro-autonomy strategy within the party and praise of Britain in the war went hand in hand.

Euzkadi's writers were probably aware that it was a bold statement to consider the Allies, and particularly Britain – one of the biggest imperialist powers of the time – the protectors of small nations. Even if the Great War is usually classified as a European conflict, the reality is that people from

25 Xosé Manoel Núñez Seixas, 'Espías, idealistas e intelectuales: La *Union des Nationalités* y la política de nacionalidades durante la I Guerra Mundial (1912–1919)', *Espacio, Tiempo y Forma, Serie V, Hº Contemporánea*, 10 (1997), pp. 117–50 (p. 118). See also Xosé Manoel Núñez Seixas, 'Introduction', in Núñez Seixas (ed.), *The First World War and the Nationality Question in Europe* (Leiden: Brill, 2020), pp. 1–14.

26 The example of Belgium, invaded by the Germans in 1914, was used repeatedly to highlight the cruelty of the Central Powers and to present the Allies as protectors of defenceless small nations. See Axe, '¡BelgienüberAlles!', *Euzkadi*, 1 November 1914, p. 1; G., 'Alemania al día. La represión en Bélgica', *Euzkadi*, 1 November 1915, p. 1.

27 Ugalde, *La acción exterior del nacionalismo vasco*, p. 232.

28 Pulido Azpíroz, *Neutralidad en pie de guerra*, pp. 104–05.

all over the world fought on it. Overall, unlike the Central Powers, the Allies were able to deploy about 650,000 colonial soldiers on European battlefields alone.[29] Britain's colonial power was undeniable and was made plain during the war: Britain had territories in five different continents and used its colonial population from across its vast Empire to fight in the European, African and Middle-Eastern fronts of the war. Figures vary, but Stephen Garton estimates that the British mobilised over one million men in India, 500,000 in Canada, 200,000 in Ireland, over 300,000 in Australia, 100,000 in New Zealand, over 120,000 in South Africa and 15,000 in the West Indies, amongst others.[30] Nevertheless, that did not seem to bother the writers of *Euzkadi*, who used the classic rhetoric of 'good colonialism' to justify the Allies' actions in general and Britain's in particular to differentiate them from the enemy.

The examples of the CNV's blatant Anglophilia are myriad. In an article published ten days after the outbreak of the war, *Euzkadi* stressed that the decline of the power of the House of Lords in England 'marked a new orientation in its colonial policy, which is much more humane and liberal'.[31] In fact, 'Home Rule, [and] India's autonomy ... prove that today English rapacity is nothing but a myth'.[32] Other articles such as 'Gloria a Inglaterra' ('Glory to England') went further and denied British imperialism whilst stressing that in the First World War 'all the major powers, with the exception of one, Great Britain, ground their policies in imperialism'.[33] This confirmed the CNV's vision of a war between benevolent and cruel old empires:

> the only country – ode to it! – which is not imperialist amongst all the belligerent powers is Great Britain. It [Britain] might have been imperialist, but it is not today. All its colonies are autonomous, because Britain has understood that there is a bigger force than imperialism: nationalism.[34]

---

29 Christian Koller, 'The Recruitment of Colonial Troops in Africa and Asia and their Deployment in Europe during the First World War', *Immigrants & Minorities*, 26.1-2 (2008), pp. 111-33 (p. 113). This number does not include white settlers from colonies or territories.
30 Stephen Garton, 'The Dominions, Ireland, and India', in Robert Gerwarth and Erez Manela, *Empires at War: 1911-1923* (Oxford: Oxford University Press, 2014), pp. 152-79 (p. 155).
31 Irrintzi, 'Hacia las nacionalidades', *Euzkadi*, 10 August 1914, p. 1.
32 Irrintzi, 'Hacia las nacionalidades', p. 1.
33 Euzkeldun-Bat, 'Gloria a Inglaterra. Nacionalismo e Imperialismo', *Euzkadi*, 26 September 1914, p. 1.
34 Euzkeldun-Bat, 'Gloria a Inglaterra', p. 1. David Martínez Fiol notes how in their propaganda the Allies themselves distinguished two different types of empire: aggressive (represented by the Central Empires) and civilising ones (represented by

When *Euzkadi* wrote about 'autonomous colonies' it was making a clear allusion to cases such as Ireland, which was granted Home Rule following the approval of the Third Home Rule Bill in 1912. Although this bill 'was really no more than an extended form of local government' with many limitations criticised even by Irish moderates, the CNV continued considering Britain as the protector of Irish autonomy.[35] Furthermore, Home Rule had been suspended indefinitely after the outbreak of the war, but *Euzkadi* believed that this was temporary and that it would resume after the end of the conflict. Thanks to the benevolence of the British, Basque nationalists believed, the Irish had finally achieved 'their holy desires of freedom' now that they had obtained Home Rule.[36] 'Whilst the great English nation', the article continued, 'sinned [in the past] like the rest of the powers [it] is now an honourable exception which has repaired the injustices committed and which deserves, once again, from today, the admiration of all men of good faith'.[37]

Similar arguments were made by Engracio de Aranzadi (Kizkitza), CNV's official ideologue and director of *Euzkadi*. In 1916 Aranzadi published a series of 21 articles in the Basque nationalist newspaper titled 'Inglaterra en la India' ('England in India'), which aimed to dismantle the arguments against Britain and its empire made during the Great War and sought to present Britain as the facilitator of progress and advancement. Aranzadi stated in the first article of the series that 'England is the only power that admits its [past] sin and makes amends to the countries that it oppressed in the past, granting them national freedom and protecting them from foreign intervention with the resounding power of its fleets'.[38] Aranzadi also expressed his aim to use the example of Britain in India to debate whether England was an oppressive power in India or if in contrast, India had entered the 'civilised world' thanks to the Empire and was advancing, thanks to English intervention, on its path towards national liberation.[39]

France and Britain). As we can see, the CNV clearly engaged with and elaborated on this propaganda. See David Martínez Fiol, '1916. Imperialismo, antiimperialismo, "Guerra de les Nacions" y principio de las nacionalidades desde Cataluña: a propósito de "Contra la idea d'Imperi" d'Eugeni Xammar', in Ucelay-Da Cal, Núñez Seixas, Arnau Gonzàlez i Vilalta (eds), *Patrias diversas ¿misma lucha?* pp. 343-44 (pp. 344-63).

35 Kieran Allen, *1916: Ireland's Revolution Tradition* (London: Pluto Press, 2016), p. 22.
36 Anon., '¡Viva Irlanda! ¡Viva Inglaterra!', *Euzkadi*, 22 September 1914, p. 1.
37 Anon., '¡Viva Irlanda! ¡Viva Inglaterra!', p. 1.
38 Kizkitza, 'Inglaterra en la India', *Euzkadi*, 2 April 1916, pp. 1-2 (p. 1). Although all these articles are attributed to him, sometimes they were not signed. However, for consistency, I include his signature in the footnotes each time.
39 Kizkitza, 'Inglaterra en la India', 2 April 1916, p. 2.

Although Aranzadi presented himself as the defender of the truth, his articles were replete with pro-Empire propaganda that presented the British as a superior and benevolent power and the Indian subjects as passive and complacent, stressing colonialism's role in civilising or 'improving' the local population. With this end, Aranazadi's series of articles examined issues related to Indian administration, society, economics and policy with the same repetitive and biased argument: India was a delayed and uncivilised country until the British, guided only by their good faith, facilitated what seemed impossible: order and progress. The British did not only allow the Indians to enter gradually into the 'demands of modern life' through their investment in railways, roads, education, healthcare or agriculture, but also managed to abolish the 'not few anti-human practices' that existed in India and other 'savage communities' as well as 'the spirit of anarchy' that prevailed before the British arrived.[40] But most importantly, in line with the CNV's pro-autonomy view, Aranzadi argued that the British promoted the adoption of projects that were increasingly in harmony with Indian aspirations: 'a pro-autonomy system, a veritable *self-government*' within the Empire, which contrasted with what happened in Euskadi.[41] It was thanks to this self-government model, Aranzadi argued in another article, that 'Indians are gradually getting into the habit of citizenship, as in the civilised countries of Europe'.[42]

According to Aranzadi, the improvement of India thanks to the British was undeniable, as it was proven by the help that Indians offered to the Empire during the Great War. Aranzadi made sure to stress this fact, which was the subject of five articles out of the 21 in the series.[43] Aranzadi's

---

40 Kizkitza, 'Inglaterra en la India. Hacia la civilización', *Euzkadi*, 5 April 1916, p. 1 and Kizkitza, 'Inglaterra en la India. Administración', *Euzkadi*, 8 April 1916, pp. 1–2.

41 Kizkitza, 'Inglaterra en la India. Legislación', *Euzkadi*, 11 April 1916, pp. 1–2 (p. 1). See also Kizkitza, 'Inglaterra en la India. Autonomía local', *Euzkadi*, 3 May 1916, p. 1.

42 Kizkitza, 'Inglaterra en la India. Libertad', *Euzkadi*, 31 May 1916, pp. 1–2 (p. 1).

43 The first article of the series stressed that the fact that 'former victims of British imperialism' such as Canada, Australia, the Transvaal, and Ireland spilled their blood in defense of Britain during the Great War was proof of Britain's greatness. See Kizkitza, 'Inglaterra en la India', *Euzkadi*, 2 April 1916. Many others stressed this too when discussing India's role in the Great War, but I only list here the articles devoted exclusively to India's contribution to the First World War and Indian public opinion on the conflict. See Kizkitza, 'Inglaterra en la India. Los indios en la milicia', *Euzkadi*, 5 July 1916, pp. 1–2; Kizkitza, 'Inglaterra en la India. El ejército anglo-indio', *Euzkadi*, 6 July 1916, p. 1; Kizkitza, 'Inglaterra en la India. La India en la presente guerra', *Euzkadi*, 10 July 1916, pp. 1–2; Kizkitza, 'Inglaterra en la India. La prensa india ante la guerra', *Euzkadi*, 14 July 1916, pp. 1–2; Kizkitza, 'Inglaterra en la India. El pensamiento indio ante la guerra', *Euzkadi*, 18 July 1916, p. 1.

arguments were supported by the statements of Imperial figures such as Queen Victoria and Lord Curzon, Viceroy of India, as well as those of Indian newspapers and intellectuals who praised the intervention of Britain in the Empire. In these seemingly well-informed and objective articles, Britain was portrayed as a tolerant and respectful nation which acted in line with the aspiration of its territories. As such, the average *Euzkadi* reader would find little to criticise about Britain and its actions in India. To conclude the series, Aranzadi wisely chose a quote by Abdur Rahim, a contemporary Indian intellectual and politician who agreed with his judgement of Britain: 'we believe that by remaining within the orbit of the British Empire, we can reach India's destination sooner than otherwise.'[44]

As mentioned above, the writings that stressed the image of Britain as the facilitator of a perfect system of autonomy served both to justify the CNV's pro-Ally stance as well as its pro-autonomy strategy. This pro-Ally and pro-autonomy vision were clearly dominant in the party by 1916. But not everyone in the movement agreed with this vision. Following his expulsion from the party in late 1915, Luis Arana and some of his followers criticised the official attitude of the party from *Bizkaitarra*, which symbolically recovered the name of his brother's first periodical.[45] Both the name of his newsletter and the reactivation of the Euskeldun Batzokija indicated that he was a firm defender of his brother's initial radical ideas and was unwilling to accept any deviation from this ideology.

As the next sections prove, *Bizkaitarra*'s radicalism implied the re-emergence of Sabino Arana's radical anticolonial language, which had barely been used since 1903. Nevertheless, the newsletter went further, as unlike Sabino Arana, it condemned all forms of colonialism – an important change that became a key characteristic of the Basque radical ideology from the 1920s onwards. *Bizkaitarra* deviated from Basque Anglophilia and challenged the arguments of 'good colonialism' to defend neutrality in the war.[46] This position was strengthened after the Easter Rising of 1916, when

---

[44] Quoted in Kizkitza, 'Inglaterra en la India. Con más prontitud', *Euzkadi*, 30 July 1916, p. 1.

[45] Luis Arana's expulsion from the party in late 1915 has been attributed to many different factors, including his self-marginalisation in the party, his authoritarianism, his poor economic management and electoral fraud. Without a doubt, the stance adopted by the different factions of the Basque nationalist movement in the First World War was also a key factor in the decision. See Pulido Azpíroz, *Neutralidad en pie de guerra*, pp. 103–10.

[46] As noted previously, the defence of neutrality in Spain often meant a defence of the Central Powers. This is perhaps why some have painted Luis Arana as a veiled Germanophile. Whether secretly an advocate of Germany and the Central Powers or

Bizkaitarra used the fierce repression of the Irish by the British to point out the malevolence of the latter. The next sections explore how international events such as the Easter Rising were essential to the radicalisation of sectors within Basque nationalism and to the polarisation of its branches.

The Easter Rising and the First Blow to the Theories of 'Good Colonialism'

On Easter Monday 1916, Ireland became a theatre of violence, insurrection and destruction when Irish insurgents rebelled against British rule. The rebels managed to seize key buildings in Dublin, including the General Post Office, from where Irish nationalist Patrick Pearse proclaimed an independent Irish Republic. The Easter Rising of 1916, which took Britain by surprise, involved no fewer than 1,300 insurgents who felt disappointed with the advances of constitutional nationalism and the indefinitely suspended Home Rule project. The British – threatened by a new war amid the existing devastating conflict – did not take long to suppress the Irish rebellion, which was met with fierce repression and which was suffocated in a matter of days. Still, the sacrifices of the Irish rebels were not in vain. What started as 'a blow against the greatest empire of the day' became the prelude to the establishment of the Irish Republic in 1919 and eventually the end of British rule in Ireland.[47] As Fearghal McGarry points out, in April 1916 the alternative future for Ireland that was set out with the state's approval of Home Rule in 1914 was destroyed.[48]

The Easter Rising did not only influence generations of Irish republicans who refused to be in the orbit of the British Empire. The failed attempt to overthrow British imperial rule in Ireland influenced anticolonial revolts across Europe and led to the creation of anti-imperial networks and alliances against the British with Indian and Egyptian nationalists. Some Irish republicans such as Gerry Adams have gone further and argued that the Irish nationalist movement played a 'crucial role in the international development of the struggle to overthrow colonialism'.[49] Although perhaps Adams's statement is exaggerated, the Irish rebellion certainly affected the development of Basque nationalism deeply.

---

not, he was also critical of Germany's actions and constantly defended the neutrality of the war. As demonstrated in this chapter, *Bizkaitarra* directly condemned the imperialism of the powers on both sides of the war.

47 Allen, *1916: Ireland's Revolutionary Tradition*, p. 53.
48 Fearghal McGarry, *The Rising: Ireland, Easter 1916* (Oxford: Oxford University Press, 2010), p. 9.
49 Quoted in Stephen Howe, *Ireland and Empire: Colonial Legacies in Irish History and Culture* (Oxford: Oxford University Press, 2000), p. 48.

As Núñez Seixas argues, the Irish question became a domestic dispute in Euskadi.[50] The events of Easter 1916 provoked important tensions in the local political arena and became a new topic of dispute between the pro-German newspaper *La Gaceta del Norte* and the pro-British *Euzkadi*. The stances both newspapers adopted during the Easter Rising were not exempt from contradictions and were determined by the position that each embraced during the Great War. Thus, the Germanophilia of *La Gaceta del Norte* led the Bilbao newspaper to sympathise with the Irish radical rebels who were challenging Germany's enemy in a period of crisis. Although *La Gaceta del Norte*'s interest in Ireland had been scarce before 1916, after the Rising the newspaper started to reproduce with enthusiasm the news arriving from Dublin and condemned the fierce repression by the British.[51] On the other hand, the Rising put *Euzkadi* – an allegedly nationalist newspaper – in a tricky situation: supporting the Irish would imply betraying their beloved English allies but condemning a group of rebels who wanted to assert their right to independence would mean a blow against their nationalist discourse. *Euzkadi* opted for the second option and openly defended the British and the moderate faction of Irish nationalism led by John Redmond. Naturally, *La Gaceta del Norte* did not take long to criticise *Euzkadi*'s position and its alleged nationalism.

In reality, *Euzkadi*'s stance was far from surprising. Apart from *Euzkadi*'s lack of neutrality during the Great War and its Anglophilia, the CNV shared and supported an approach and strategy based on the achievement of autonomy with the non-violent, moderate parliamentary strand of Irish nationalism. This was not the only aspect that united the CNV with Redmondism; they also shared its benign vision of the British Empire, which was challenged by the leaders of the Easter Rising. Like the CNV, and as demonstrated by Eleizalde's articles, which were partly published in parallel with the Irish revolutionary events, Redmond believed that the British Empire was 'an instrument of civilisation and progress whose existence was not incompatible with national freedom'.[52] Hence, according

---

50 Núñez Seixas, 'Ecos de Pascua', p. 458. See also Lorenzo Espinosa, 'Influencia del nacionalismo irlandés en el nacionalismo vasco, 1916–1936', p. 242. For a recent analysis of the Irish Rising and how it was interpreted by the different sections of the Basque movement, see Cullen, *Radical Basque Nationalist-Irish Republican Relations*, pp. 40–41.

51 For a detailed account between *La Gaceta del Norte*'s position in the Rising and the tensions it generated with *Euzkadi* see Pulido Azpíroz, *Neutralidad en pie de guerra*, pp. 95–103.

52 Allen, *1916: Ireland's Revolution Tradition*, pp. 16–17.

to this view, rebelling against the Empire by force would be detrimental to Ireland's future.

Euzkadi began to report on the events in Dublin on 26 April 1916, two days after the Rising had started. From that day until at least mid-May, many articles covered the conflict in detail. The majority of information used to report on the Irish events came from London, reflecting a pro-British bias. The articles tended to emphasise the atmosphere of 'terror' that the rebels had created on the island. However, *Euzkadi* reassured its readers by insisting that the Rising had been crushed thanks to the British authorities' actions. Although the Irish republican party Sinn Féin was not involved directly in the Rising, *Euzkadi* soon blamed them. Sinn Féin was described as a 'revolutionary nationalist party' whose aspiration was 'the independence of Ireland' and that used 'terrifying and revolutionary tactics'.[53] According to *Euzkadi*, this party, which inherited the 'violent tendencies of John Mitchell' – a leading Irish nationalist from the nineteenth century – represented only a 'revolutionary minority within Irish nationalism', in contrast with the moderate majority led by John Redmond.[54] Sinn Féin was for *Euzkadi* an organisation that was against everything the moderates had advocated for years, as they were 'proclaimed enemies of Home Rule, [and] of Parliamentarianism'.[55] Sinn Féin, and Fenianism in general, were a 'cult' formed by 'the terrorists of nationalism', which believed in the use of methods that, according to *Euzkadi*, had never worked at any point in the history of Ireland.[56]

Euzkadi's words of disapproval towards the leaders of the rebellion were even more extreme than those used to describe Sinn Féin. The plotters were presented as impatient revolutionaries who lacked any sort of preparation and contact with reality when planning the rebellion. *Euzkadi* did not show much mercy towards any of the Irish leaders who were condemned to death and executed after the rebellion. For instance, Irish nationalist Patrick Pearse was referred to as an 'insane dreamer'.[57] Irish socialist James Connolly, also executed by the British, was described frequently as an anarchist or syndicalist, and his violent and revolutionary ideas were usually emphasised.[58] The involvement of influential socialists such as Connolly in the Rising was another cause of disdain for Basque moderates.

53 Axe, 'Actualidad irlandesa. Sinn Fein', *Euzkadi*, 9 May 1916, p. 1 and Anon., 'Al pasar', *Euzkadi*, 8 May 1916, p. 2.
54 Axe, 'Actualidad irlandesa', p. 1.
55 Axe, 'Actualidad irlandesa', p. 1.
56 Anon., 'Los fenianos', *Euzkadi*, 1 May 1916, p. 2.
57 Axe, 'Actualidad irlandesa', p. 1.
58 See Anon., 'Los fenianos', p. 2; Anon., 'Al pasar', pp. 2–3.

Perhaps the Irish rebel who received the most coverage in *Euzkadi* was Roger Casement. Apart from being one of the most important leaders of the Rising, Casement is now known for being one of the first western political figures to denounce the horrors of colonialism.[59] Condemned to death for treason, he was hanged in London on 3 August 1916. His trial and death were followed internationally. Casement's trial divided the opinion of Basque nationalists: *Euzkadi* had published a note in early August demanding his pardon, but referred to him as an 'unfortunate patriot' who had been tricked by the 'enemies of Irish nationalism and England', something that did not go down well with the most radical sectors of the Basque Youth movement.[60] According to José María Lorenzo Espinosa, the young radical nationalist Eli Gallastegi – by then a member of the JVB and from 1919 its president – even petitioned for the removal of an article about Casement written by Aranzadi in *Euzkadi* and asked for the dismissal of its author.[61] Whilst Gallastegi's petition did not succeed, JVB celebrated a mass in honour of Casement following his execution by the British authorities.[62] Indeed, a very dynamic section of the Basque movement was starting to challenge the CNV's international vision.

Without a doubt, the leading force in defying *Euzkadi*'s (and the CNV's) official stance towards the Rising and the rebels was *Bizkaitarra*.[63] Instead of criticising the 'violent' character of the Irish rebellion, *Bizkaitarra* described the British presence in Ireland as oppressive, sanguinary and coercive.[64]

59 Casement was one of the first to denounce Belgium's abuses in Congo. As Vijay Prashad recounts, Casement – who worked in the Foreign Office – travelled to Congo in the early twentieth century and published a 'catalogue of outrages', only to then discover that British companies performed the same kinds of atrocities in other territories. See Prashad, *The Darker Nations*, p. 18.

60 Ruiz Descamps, *Historia de las organizaciones juveniles del nacionalismo vasco*, p. 85.

61 José María Lorenzo Espinosa, *Gudari. Una pasión útil. Eli Gallastegi (1892–1974)* (Tafalla: Txalaparta, 1992), p. 58. Cullen also argues that Gallastegi demanded the retraction of the article condemning Casement. As he argues, for Gallastegi 'the Rising had sparked a life-long engagement with Irish republicanism'. See Cullen, *Radical Basque Nationalist-Irish Republican Relations*, p. 41.

62 As Ruiz Descamps argues, other newsletters that were strongly associated with the Basque Youth movement such as *Euzko Deya* were more defiant with the party and not only defended Irish leaders such as Casement but also dared to condemn the CNV's pro-Ally stance. Ruiz Descamps, *Historia de las organizaciones juveniles del nacionalismo vasco*, pp. 87–88.

63 *Bizkaitarra* also tried to prevent the execution of Casement. For instance, at the start of August 1916, the newsletter sent a message, backed by around 30 women, to the British ambassador in Madrid asking the British monarch to pardon Casement. Ugalde, *La acción exterior del nacionalismo vasco*, p. 221.

64 Equis, 'Irlanda', *Bizkaitarra*, 6 May 1916, pp. 1–2.

The Irish rebels were, according to *Bizkaitarra*, martyrs and heroes of the Irish nation.[65] But aside from romanticising the Irish rebels, the novelty in *Bizkaitarra*'s arguments was that to defend their struggle and legitimise their actions, the newsletter condemned British imperialism directly and attacked the theories of 'good colonialism'. This meant a turning point for Basque nationalism, which had been characterised by its strong Anglophile leanings from its outset.

In a daring tone, *Bizkaitarra* condemned *Euzkadi*'s pro-British positioning on the Rising and claimed that '[we] condemn every nation that dominates other nations, especially when they are tough and their yoke is not gentle. And today, and not before, we need to include the powerful Britain ... among these.'[66] In this article, *Bizkaitarra* asked *Euzkadi* to rectify its pro-British position towards the Rising.[67] Another article in *Bizkaitarra* went further, comparing the German occupation of Belgium in 1914 with that of Ireland by Britain during the Rising: 'England has entered Dublin like the Germans entered Louvain, with bloodshed and fire.'[68] Thus, *Bizkaitarra* posited, England was not the defender and protector of small nationalities but instead, with the Rising 'England has been confirmed as a colonising nation'.[69] Different issues explicitly highlighted Britain's colonial nature. For instance, an article published in August 1916 against the execution of Casement described the British as 'supreme colonisers, owners of half of the world'.[70]

Stressing Britain's imperialist nature was also a way of equating it with the Central Powers and promoting a neutral position regarding the Great War. Indeed, *Bizkaitarra*'s writings completely challenged the Allied (and the CNV's) portrayal of powers such as Britain as 'civilising' empires, which contrasted with the aggressiveness of the Central Powers. According to *Bizkaitarra* both a 'fanatic *Germanophilia*' and a 'vain and unconscious support of the Allies' were equally reprehensible, as Basques 'cannot expect anything from any of those nations in the achievement of our claims, because neither England nor Germany, nor any other nation, does anything for the spirit of justice'.[71]

Although *Bizkaitarra*'s arguments have tended to be ignored by historiography, they would be repeated by subsequent generations of

65 Among others see K., 'Por Irlanda. Para el diario *Euzkadi*', *Bizkaitarra*, 13 May 1916, pp. 2–4.
66 K., 'Por Irlanda', p. 3.
67 K., 'Por Irlanda', pp. 2–3.
68 Anon., 'La revolución de Irlanda', *Bizkaitarra*, 13 May 1916, pp. 6–7.
69 Anon., 'La revolución de Irlanda', pp. 6–7.
70 Anon., 'Sinn Fein', *Bizkaitarra*, 5 August 1916, pp. 4–5 (p. 4).
71 A. Tar J., 'Labor estéril (conclusión)', *Bizkaitarra*, 23 December 1916, pp. 4–5.

Basque radicals from then on. These were based on the premise that all colonial powers (including not only Spain but also Britain) were equally evil and therefore, collaborating with the enemy and achieving autonomy was unfeasible. Independence, as the radical Arana and the third *Bizkaitarra* advanced, was the only option. Once the CNV pro-autonomy campaign failed and Ireland proclaimed its independence in 1919, the young Basque radicals who had shown signs of disagreement with the official party during the Rising began positing similar ideas to *Bizkaitarra*. The CNV's programme of gradualism and collaboration was in crisis.

Wilsonian Fever: Euphoria, Crisis and the Re-Emergence of Basque Anticolonialism

The Easter Rising of 1916 did not alter the CNV's vision of the First World War as a struggle in which the Allies were defending the right of small nations to achieve their national claims. If anything, the Irish moderate wing – which was willing to work within the orbit of the British Empire – had reinforced the belief that collaboration and autonomy was the best option for the Basques. Apart from the rebels of *Bizkaitarra* and some voices within the young sections of the movement, Basque nationalists largely seemed to agree with this vision. Yet the immediate years following the Great War were to have a profound impact on the ideas of the radical factions of the Basque movement. If the moderates, led by the CNV, were convinced that their campaign for autonomy would succeed in the context of Wilsonian euphoria, the most radical groups within the movement – represented by *Bizkaitarra* and *Aberri* – became increasingly convinced that the great powers would grant nothing to the weaker nations like Euskadi. Instead, inspired by the Irish War for Independence (1919–1921), the latter believed that if Basques were to achieve self-determination, they would have to do it by their own means.[72]

The radicalisation of some sections within the Basque movement was caused by a deep national and international disappointment. Nationally, in the last years of the Great War, the CNV led a parallel pro-autonomy campaign with the Catalan Lliga Regionalista and its leader Francesc Cambó, which represented the moderate and pro-autonomy branch of Catalanism. Cambó

---

72 Scholars have used different labels to refer to the war that led to the creation of two Irish states in 1921, the most common being the War of Independence. According to Irish nationalism expert Richard English this label, however, is not adequate given the 'far from fully independent outcome of 1921', and he refers to the conflict as the War for Independence. I agree with English and so use his term throughout this book. See Richard English, *Irish Freedom: The History of Nationalism in Ireland* (Pan Books: London, 2008), pp. 351–52.

had gained great popularity these years by becoming the champion of change and modernisation of a country that was on the verge of collapse.[73] Cambó and the Lliga – which encompassed Catalan nationalists and regionalists – posited that Spain was a moribund country and that Catalonia, a more modern and European nation or region, was qualified to undertake Spain's modernisation, which ultimately would allow the country to recover its imperial glory.[74] In order to bring the country to its former glory, Spain had to modernise itself and grant Catalonia political and economic autonomy. Although Cambó's imperial claims presented important contradictions within Sabino Arana's thought and therefore supposedly with that of the CNV, the party decided to ignore this and began collaborating closely with the moderate Catalans from January 1917, when Cambó visited Bilbao.[75] Later that year, *Euzkadi* – which fully backed the CNV's autonomy campaign – published an article that stressed the Basque nationalist desire (clearly shared by Cambó) to remain part of Europe through the achievement of autonomy: 'After 25 years of an autonomous regime, we the Basques could certainly commit to raising the moral and material level of our Country to the level of the most advanced and cultured countries of Europe.'[76]

As the campaigns for autonomy went on in the two regions, Basques and Catalans found an international ally in the Wilsonian principles of self-determination. In January 1918 US President Woodrow Wilson set out his influential 'Fourteen Points', which addressed the problem of the small nationalities and promised them self-determination. As Manela has stated, 'Wilson's promise of a new world order captured imaginations across the

---

73 See Angel Smith, 'Cataluña y la Gran Guerra: De la reforma democrática al conflicto social', *Hispania Nova*, 15 (2017), pp. 472–99.

74 Smith, 'Cataluña la Gran Guerra', p. 479.

75 Note 1: When Cambó visited Euskadi that year, he delivered a speech in which he encouraged Basques to join a movement that favoured not independence but territorial reform within Spain. Cambó also invited Basques, alongside the Catalans, to become 'the leaders of "imperial Spain ... empire of great peoples"'. Mees, *The Basque Contention*, p. 66. As Mees argues, not even Cambó's controversial statement about the future of the Spanish Empire received any critical comments in the Basque nationalist press, which cautiously dropped the world 'imperial' when reporting on Cambó's speech. Note 2: The driving force of the contact between Basques and Catalans was the proposal of an extra tax by the Minister of Finance, Santiago Alba. This tax, which aimed to levy the benefits generated during the Great War by the industries that benefited from the economic boom, generated strong opposition in Euskadi and Catalonia and united the bourgeoisie of the two regions.

76 Axe, 'Detrás ... el separatismo', *Euzkadi*, 23 September 1917, p. 1. To justify the collaboration with 'the enemy', *Euzkadi* and the CNV used Arana's 'pro-Spanish' texts.

world', achieving the attention of different audiences, including, naturally, nationalist groups.[77]

In Euskadi, Wilsonianism reinforced both the CNV's goal of autonomy and its pro-Allied position in the Great War: the benevolence of the Allies (including the US from 1917) would facilitate the achievement of Basque autonomy. *Aberri* expressed this idea very clearly when praising Cambó's ideas, declaring: 'tomorrow there will be a Lloyd George or a Wilson or another man who loves justice, who will be in charge of defending our rights'.[78] Following Wilson's principles and motivated by the electoral gains the CNV experienced in the general elections of February 1918, Basque nationalists felt more optimistic than ever. Thus, on 25 October 1918, the Euzkadi Buru Batzar (National Executive Committee of the PNV: henceforth EBB) published a long statement announcing the triumph of nationalism and argued that the Allies, led by Wilson, defended equally the interests of the weakest and the strongest.[79] On the same day, the elected Basque MPs and the members of the senate decided to approach Wilson directly through a telegram asking him to ensure that the rights of the small nationalities were respected once peace negotiations were reached.[80]

This Wilsonian 'euphoria' was no exception to Basque nationalism, as many other groups around the world also appealed to the perceived benevolence of Wilson with the hope their goals would be achieved. As Núñez Seixas points out, in the Basque case, the support for Wilson was certainly conditioned by the internal objectives of Basque nationalism, which had prompted the support of Cambó's regionalist campaign and now the adhesion to Wilson in the international sphere.[81] However, much to the CNV's dismay, the petitions for Basque autonomy were ignored both internationally and nationally and the first autonomy campaign led by peripheral nationalist movements in Spain failed in 1919.

This double failure certainly began to put into question the CNV's national and international programme: was Wilson really the leader of fair struggles if he, like the Spanish, had ignored the Basque petitions of self-determination? This de-mythologisation of Wilson and the other victorious powers would eventually drive to ideological change in the peripheries and the metropole.

---

77 Manela, *The Wilsonian Moment*, p. 7.

78 Reproduced in *Bizkaitarra*: Nekotxea, 'Cambó, Lloyd George y Wilson', *Bizkaitarra*, 11 May 1918, pp. 1-2. *Bizkaitarra* used this fragment to criticise the stance of the newsletter and question the benevolence of Lloyd George and Wilson.

79 Pulido Azpíroz, *Neutralidad en pie de guerra*, pp. 350-51.

80 Pulido Azpíroz, *Neutralidad en pie de guerra*, pp. 350-51.

81 Núñez Seixas, '¿Protodiplomacia exterior o ilusiones ópticas?', p. 258. See also Núñez Seixas, *Patriotas transnacionales*.

As Manela has pointed out, Wilson's principles affected not only the self-determination claims of the 'weaker nations' of Europe towards which he had intentionally directed his thought, but it also reached 'unintended audiences' of the colonial world.[82] Once it was clear that the Wilsonian principles were not designed for non-Europeans, a wave of Third-World anticolonial nationalism arose.[83] As we will see in the following chapters, this wave of thought clearly reached Euskadi and affected Basque radicals, who imagined themselves as part of the unintended colonial audiences that Wilson had ignored and, significantly, as one of the colonised.

Even before the failure of the autonomy campaign, the radicals of *Bizkaitarra* had voiced their scepticism about the benevolence of the Allies and, of course, about the CNV's autonomy campaign. *Bizkaitarra* disagreed with the autonomy campaign, accusing the CNV of killing off and replacing the party that Sabino Arana had established in his lifetime, whilst condemning Catalan influence on Basque nationalism.[84] In an attempt to recover Sabino Arana's radical doctrine and stress the necessity of independence, anticolonialism became a key feature in *Bizkaitarra*. According to the radical newsletter, it was impossible to trust Spain to achieve Basque nationalist claims and to collaborate with what *Bizkaitarra* described as a government that in 1839 destroyed the life of a nation (Euskadi) through 'brute force, conquest, ambition, imperialism, assimilation through domination'.[85] The same could be said about the two sides of the Great War, which were equally imperialist and therefore would not assist Basques in advancing their claims:

> When it comes to the subjugation of small nationalities, we do not see the differences that others do [referring to the newspaper *Euzkadi*] between the Allies and the Central-European Empires, as the history of all of these actors contain pages of abuse and domination of small nations.[86]

---

82 Manela, *The Wilsonian Moment*, p. 17.

83 See Manela, *The Wilsonian Moment*.

84 See, among many anti-autonomy writings, Zuri, 'Corrupción comunionista', *Bizkaitarra*, 2 February 1918, pp. 1–2; and AGK, 'Votos son triunfos. El 27 de enero de 1918', *Bizkaitarra*, 2 February 1918, pp. 2–6. For anti-Catalanism see, for instance, A.G.K. 'Después de las elecciones', *Bizkaitarra*, 2 March 1918, pp. 1–3; Trampolín, 'Comunionadas', *Bizkaitarra*, 29 March 1918, pp. 5–6; Agaka, 'Anotaciones', *Bizkaitarra*, 22 June 1918, pp. 3–4.

85 Baserritarra, 'La derecha o el buen camino y las derechas', *Bizkaitarra*, 7 December 1918, pp. 4–5 (p. 5).

86 Urregorri, 'Movimiento irlandés antimilitarista. El ayuntamiento de Limerick', *Bizkaitarra*, 13 July 1918, pp. 5–6 (p. 6).

Bizkaitarra did not change its position after the end of the Great War and continued exposing the imperial aspirations of the winners of the war and questioning their benevolence towards oppressed nations. For instance, in an article published on 14 December 1918, *Bizkaitarra* criticised the decision (backed by members of the CNV) to name some streets of Bilbao in commemoration of the Allies.[87] According to *Bizkaitarra*,

> the [CNV] blindness does not allow them to see that the struggle of oppressed nationalities remains the same or is even worse than before, following the end of the war with the Allied victory. This crucial question [the struggle of the oppressed nationalities] would have been no different if the Central Powers had won.[88]

As we can see, the alleged benevolence of certain Empires was a crucial point of contention within certain sectors of the Basque nationalist movement.

But this time *Bizkaitarra* was not alone. If prior to 1919, the young Basques and their newsletter *Aberri* had endorsed the national and international vision of the CNV, the failure of the autonomy campaign and the international silence around the Basque question was translated into a period of radicalisation which made them reconsider the official ideas of the party.[89] Like *Bizkaitarra*, as *Aberri* began to question the pro-autonomy approach of the CNV and endorse independence, the rhetoric of the newsletter increasingly featured anticolonial language. Spain was portrayed as an imperialist country or 'metropole' and Euskadi as one of its victims, 'the indigenous of the [Spanish] colonies'.[90] Euskadi's ills were all attributed to 'obstinate Spanish imperialism'.[91] Furthermore, *Aberri* condemned Spanish colonialism in north Africa, mocked Africanist and pro-colonial discourses and explicitly defended Spain's colonial insurgents.[92] In other words, like Sabino Arana, *Aberri* began to read the Basque

---

87 See Trampolín, 'Murmuraciones', *Bizkaitarra*, 14 December 1918, pp. 5-6.
88 Trampolín, 'Murmuraciones', p. 5.
89 For examples of articles about the Allies and Wilson being presented as the defenders of the small nationalities see, for instance, Anon., 'Afirmación de la Nacionalidad. Mañana en Sukarrieta', *Aberri*, 20 January 1917, pp. 1-2 or Jour, 'Temas actuales. Antes y más claro que Wilson, otros', *Aberri*, 12 October 1918, p. 2.
90 Betikua, 'Civilización española y separatismo vasco', *Aberri*, 6 December 1919, p. 2. See also Raisulitzale, 'Bellotas paradisíacas', *Aberri*, 10 January 1920, p. 3 and Maceotzale, 'Pífias de un plumífero yabana', *Aberri*, 24 January 1920, p. 2.
91 Rainsulitzale, 'Bellotas paradisíacas', p. 3.
92 See for instance Z, 'El fusilamiento de los leales de Malalien', *Aberri*, 6 December 1919, p. 2; Betikua, 'Civilización española y separatismo vasco', p. 3. It is worth noting that the moderates also began condemning Spanish imperialism. In fact, both *Euzkadi* and *Aberri* rejected the Spanish campaign for the formal occupation

situation in colonial terms and to develop and adapt its anticolonialism to the period. Indeed, for *Bizkaitarra* and *Aberri*, independence and anticolonialism clearly went hand in hand.

Furthermore, as Cullen and Kyle McCreanor argue, this double national and international disappointment prompted young Basque radicals to begin identifying 'revolutionary alternatives'.[93] Once again, Ireland became a source of inspiration for Basque nationalists. The start of the Irish War for Independence coincided with the failure of the Basque autonomy campaign. Thus, the new Irish conflict became an example for young Basque nationalists who were starting to consider the advantages of violence in the nationalist struggle. The Irish War for Independence started in 1919 following the sweeping victory of Sinn Féin in the general elections of December 1918. After refusing to take their seats at Westminster, the Dáil Éireann (assembly of Ireland) was constituted. On 21 January 1919, the Dáil met for the first time and issued a message to the 'free nations of the world', calling for independence and international recognition.[94] This document, aimed at the delegates of the Paris Peace Conference of 1919, was read aloud in French, Irish and finally in English. Despite these efforts, the Irish petition was ignored. The same day on which the Dáil issued this message, the Irish Republic was proclaimed and the Irish War for Independence began, confronting the Irish Republican Army (henceforth IRA) and the British. This was an important blow for the CNV's theories of 'good colonialism', which trusted the benevolence of the Allies to see their autonomy desires fulfilled. In fact, after 1919, Basque moderates even recognised that the Basques had much to learn from the Irish.[95] Nevertheless, the moderates had many differences with the Irish rebels, as they could not embrace an anti-British movement that rebelled using violence. As we will see in the next chapter, their support for the Irish did not last.

The Irish War for Independence had important effects on the imagination of young Basque radicals. First, it became a symbol of resistance against

---

of northern Morocco which had started in 1919 following the establishment of the Spanish Protectorate.

93 Niall Cullen and Kyle McCreanor, '"Dangerous Friends": Irish Republican Relations with Basque and Catalan Nationalists, 1916–26', *International History Review*, 44.6 (2022), pp. 1193–210 (p. 1196).

94 First Dáil of the Republic of Ireland, 'Message to the Free Nations of the World', 21 January 1919, https://www.difp.ie/docs/1919/Message-to-the-Free-Nations-of-the-World/2.htm. This text highlighted the differences between the Irish and the English: 'nationally, the race, the language, the customs and traditions of Ireland are radically distinct from the English.' It also pointed out the ancientness of the Irish nation, using similar language to that used by Basque nationalists.

95 Núñez Seixas, 'Ecos de Pascua', p. 460.

tyranny and colonialism, and the 'fallen Irish' were mourned and praised by subsequent generations of Basques. Ireland had shown once more that violence could be used when parliamentary methods failed. Inspired by the Irish example, *Aberri* was to write texts that alluded to the use of violence from the 1920s onwards.[96] Second, the Irish War demonstrated, once again, that 'good colonialism' was nothing but a myth. Wilson and the Allies had ignored the petitions of one of the European nations that had been fighting for centuries to achieve its aims, causing a new armed conflict. This also demonstrated that Wilson's new peace order did not work. Although from 1919 to 1921 *Aberri* barely talked about the Allies, from the moment in which the PNV split in two, Basque radicals constantly attacked Wilson and the imperialist character of the League of Nations (henceforth LN). This reflected the new form of anticolonialism that the Basque radicals embraced from 1921: one that was directed not only at Spain but against all imperial powers.

The Irish example also reinforced *Aberri*'s pro-independence ideas and brought them closer to *Bizkaitarra*, which had already challenged the CNV's ideas. Unsurprisingly, *Bizkaitarra*, which had already seen in the Irish Rising of 1916 an example to follow and an opportunity to legitimise its ideas about independence, applauded the victory of the Sinn Feiners. In the last issues it published, Ireland was the only international reference for *Bizkaitarra*, which praised the actions of 'Casement's peers', who 'prompted Basques to imitate their great example' and condemned the Anglophile bias of *Euzkadi* when talking about the Irish struggle.[97] Both *Aberri* and Luis Arana's group would ultimately join after the split of the party in 1921 and, as we will see, the Irish struggle would continue being a constant point of tension between Basque radicals and moderates.

The split in the Basque nationalist movement eventually came in summer 1921, after an intense period of heated debates in the pages of *Aberri* condemning the CNV strategy and *Euzkadi* rejecting the separatist and revolutionary thesis of the radicals. Following an article by Eleizalde (approved by the EBB) in May 1921 arguing that independence was not inherent to nationalism, *Aberri* launched a campaign in defence of Basque pro-independence principles, which the newsletter claimed was backed by 50 nationalist organisations.[98] As a result, in July 1921, *Aberri* and the main

---

96 The authors of *El péndulo patriótico* argue that one of the first texts in which Basque nationalists openly admitted the possibility of violent methods in the nationalist struggle can be found in a text published by *Aberri* in December 1918. De Pablo and Mees, *El péndulo patriótico*, p. 127.

97 See A. Tar. J., '¡Gora a Irlanda! El triunfo de los Sin-Feiners', *Bizkaitarra*, 4 January 1919, p. 2 and Atarbe, 'Siempre avechuchos!', *Bizkaitarra*, 18 January 1919, p. 4.

98 Camino and Guezala, *Juventud y nacionalismo vasco*, p. 89.

representatives of the JVB were expelled from the party and a month later, the CNV also expelled all the organisations that had backed *Aberri*'s radical campaign. The process that had divided nationalists for nearly 20 years culminated on 4 September 1921 when those who were expelled alongside other radical sympathisers created the new Basque Nationalist Party or the PNV-*Aberri* (whose members were commonly known as Aberrianos). These were later joined by Luis Arana and his Euskeldun Batzokija which, as demonstrated in this chapter, posited very similar ideas to *Aberri* towards the end of this period. The local and international events explored in this chapter contributed to the rapprochement of these two radical groups. From then onwards, the radicals became an influential faction that considered the fight against global colonialism an essential part of its political agenda.

Conclusion

Although scholars have generally overlooked how different strands of Basque nationalism regarded colonialism, this chapter has proved that this issue became an important point of division within the movement prior to 1921. This differing view of colonialism – which divided those who praised the existence of benevolent forms of colonialism that could help small nations achieve their national claims and those who condemned every type of empire – had much to do with the recurrent dividing topic of autonomy and independence. Whilst those who favoured autonomy considered the relationship that the British Empire had with its colonies a perfect model of self-government, those who advocated for separatism and independence rejected every form of imperialism. In other words, Basque pro-colonial or anticolonial claims were determined by the national goals each section pursued.

As this chapter has demonstrated, the third *Bizkaitarra* was the first Basque newsletter to condemn colonialism generally, and to challenge the theories of 'good colonialism' that did not fit with its pro-independence stance. Thanks to the radicalisation that *Aberri* experienced in the late 1910s, the newsletter would adopt a very similar position to that of Luis Arana and his followers during the 1920s. As demonstrated in the next chapters, which focus on Basque radicalism alone, Basque radicals – grouped under the PNV-*Aberri* from 1921 – stepped away from western forms of nationalism and gravitated towards a model of anticolonial nationalism that even considered violence as a plausible method to achieve independence.

CHAPTER FOUR

Towards a Global Insurrection System? International Networks, Brotherhood and Anticolonial Solidarity in the PNV-*Aberri* (1921–1923)

The period that ran from the split of the PNV from the CNV in 1921 until Miguel Primo de Rivera's coup in 1923 was short but intense. Internationally, these two years saw the first tangible consequences of the Paris Peace Conference of 1919–20, with the disintegration of old empires, the strengthening of others and the expansion of totalitarian regimes in countries like Italy following the ascension to power of Benito Mussolini in 1922. The Allies also suffered the consequences of the post-war order with the emergence of widespread anticolonial resistance across the British and French Empires. Despite its neutrality in the Great War, Spain was not immune to the international situation either and had to face strong anticolonial revolts in northern Morocco.

These anticolonial revolts are an example of the process of internationalisation that anticolonial nationalism underwent after the Great War. Manela suggests that this process occurred at both a theoretical and practical level. Wilson's right of self-determination was appropriated and reinterpreted by nationalists in colonised territories as a challenge to the logic of imperialism. In addition, the Paris Peace Conference presented a great opportunity for international action within anticolonial nationalist circles.[1] The twin spheres of theoretical and practical internationalisation also affected the Basque radicals or the Aberrianos. As Ugalde has suggested, during this period Basque radicals combined claims for national independence with international anti-imperial demands.[2] The Aberrianos, who proclaimed themselves as anticolonial champions, added Euskadi to the list of colonised, oppressed and stateless nationalities and questioned the principles of imperialism, establishing both tangible and symbolic links with other movements including the Irish, Catalan, Galician and Riffian movements.

---

1 Manela, *The Wilsonian Moment*, pp. 61–62.
2 Ugalde, *La acción exterior del nacionalismo vasco*, p. 317.

This chapter places the PNV-*Aberri*'s activity within the global framework of anticolonial nationalism and analyses the nature of Basque anticolonial ideas during the early 1920s. I do this by examining the direct influence of, contacts with and reactions to the Irish and the Riffian struggles, as well as the formation of an alliance (called the Triple Alliance) that united Spain's three sub-state nationalities: Euskadi, Catalonia and Galicia. By examining these case studies, I explore the development of Basque anticolonialism, as well as its theoretical and practical uses. I argue that although Basque radicals condemned colonialism globally and compared Euskadi with extra-European nations, the racist, paternalistic and Orientalist ideas that had characterised Basque nationalism from the outset did not disappear from the Basque anticolonial corpus. The coexistence of anticolonial and colonial ideas, I argue, can be explained by the strategic nature of Basque anticolonialism. From the early 1920s, Basque anticolonialism served two main purposes, namely the justification of independence claims and the internationalisation of the Basque cause.

The PNV-*Aberri*: Organisation, Composition and Rhetoric

In September 1921, the new PNV (commonly known as PNV-*Aberri*), which recovered the original name of the party founded by Sabino Arana in the 1890s, was established after an assembly in the JVB's headquarters. From that moment, the activities of the PNV-*Aberri* were strongly linked to those of the JVB and, as Ruiz Descamps has argued, sometimes it was difficult to distinguish them.[3] Yet as the same author has pointed out, there was more to the PNV-*Aberri* than the JVB.[4] In fact, the new party counted on the support of veteran nationalist and radical leader Luis Arana and his Euskeldun Batzokija, whose fusion with the PNV-*Aberri* was officially approved in early 1923. The JVB and some of its leaders such as Eli Gallastegi – who became one of the leading voices of Basque radicalism – had supported Luis Arana's dismissal from the party in late 1915 but had no problem welcoming him back after the split with the CNV. In fact, Luis was elected president of the new radical party in 1922 and was also responsible for drafting its manifesto, which advocated for the full independence of Euskadi.[5] Indeed, the ideological similarities between Luis Arana's group

---

3 Ruiz Descamps, *Historia de las organizaciones juveniles del nacionalismo vasco*, p. 319.
4 Ruiz Descamps, *Historia de las organizaciones juveniles del nacionalismo vasco*, p. 319.
5 As authors such as de la Granja and Mees have pointed out, apart from the explicit defence of independence, the manifesto of 1922 was not substantially different from that of the CNV. For instance, both parties put Catholicism at the centre of their programme and used the same slogan (JEL: God and Old Laws). See

and the young radical nationalists who re-founded the PNV brought these groups closer: they shared their admiration for the Irish separatists who had risen against the British Empire in 1916 and were equally concerned by the CNV's pro-autonomy and possibilist praxis.

Unlike the CNV, the PNV-*Aberri* would not contemplate collaboration with the central state by accepting autonomy over independence, and declared itself the rightful heir to the classic principles of Basque nationalism put forward by Sabino Arana in his radical period. As such, the PNV-*Aberri*'s publications constantly stressed their differences with the CNV, which was labelled as 'anti-nationalist' or 'regionalist' due to its collaborationist approach.[6] Another aspect that distinguished the two parties was their geographical area of influence and their social composition. Support for the PNV-*Aberri* was limited to Biscay, and more specifically to Bilbao, where it was able to defeat the CNV in the municipal elections of 1922. In contrast, its influence in rural Biscay and Gipuzkoa was limited, and it was non-existent in Alava and Navarra.[7] It is thus hardly surprising that the new party was formed mainly by urban middle and lower-middle classes with its centre in Bilbao in contrast to the more upper-class composition of the CNV. Needless to say, the new 'popular' identity of the PNV-*Aberri* did not translate into the adoption of socialist ideas. Although some of its leaders like Gallastegi tried to develop Arana's concern for the (Basque) working classes, the PNV-*Aberri*'s programme, like that of the CNV, did not include any allusions to how to tackle social or economic problems.

As de Pablo and Mees argue, the PNV-*Aberri* was also a more popular party than the CNV in the sense that it understood the importance of popular culture.[8] As a result, during these years the PNV-*Aberri* organised multiple activities and events that ranged from theatre plays and musical *soirées*, to local festivities and sportive events. Apart from theatre – which became an essential method of spreading both nationalism and the use of Euskera – the propagandistic activity of the *mendigoxales* stood out. Additionally, as I will detail further, the party made efforts to integrate sectors of society that had been previously neglected within the movement. This was confirmed with the creation of the first organisation of Basque nationalist women,

de la Granja, 'El nacionalismo vasco en el tiempo de las Irmandades da Fala', p. 285 and Mees, 'El nacionalismo vasco entre 1903 y 1923', p. 136.

6 See amongst many others: Dorkaitz, 'Preciosidades comunionistas', *Aberri* (newsletter), 25 November 1921, p. 3; Anon., 'Nacionalismo vasco. Dos interpretaciones distintas', *Aberri* (newsletter), 6 May 1922, p. 2; Anon., 'Dos interpretaciones distintas', *Aberri* (newsletter), 27 May 1922, p. 3.

7 Mees, 'El nacionalismo vasco entre 1903 y 1923', p. 135.

8 De Pablo and Mees, *El péndulo patriótico*, p. 80.

Emakume Abertzale Batza (Association of Nationalist Women: henceforth EAB) in 1922, which would become one of the most popular and accepted Basque nationalist organisations within the Basque Youth.[9]

The PNV-*Aberri* was in part able to carry out this intensive cultural, political and social activity thanks to the invaluable help of the JVB, which in previous years had been responsible for organising propagandistic and cultural activities for the benefit of the movement. Although following the split of 1921 the CNV also had its own youth organisation – the so-called Juventud Nacionalista de Bilbao (Bilbao's Nationalist Youth: henceforth JNB), which was born to counteract the influence of the JVB – the JNB was never a significant rival for the JVB's solid organisation.

Furthermore, the new party also had an influential publication at its service that could be used both to promote cultural activities and spread its pro-separatist message. This was the case of the previously mentioned weekly newsletter *Aberri*, which turned into a daily newspaper for about three months in 1923.[10] Like *Euzkadi*, both versions of *Aberri* (newsletter and newspaper) were greatly concerned with international affairs, although the radical publications paid more attention to extra-European issues. Shortly before launching the *Aberri* newspaper, its predecessor stated with pride that the new paper 'will follow with special attention the life of the nations that have not yet resolved the nationalist problem'.[11] To do this, the *Aberri* newspaper had correspondents and collaborators in different parts of Spain, as well as in Paris, London, Berlin, New York, Buenos Aires, Mexico, Moscow and the Spanish Protectorate of Morocco. The fact that the paper devoted at least one of its six to eight daily pages to international affairs with information from different places around the world reflected not only *Aberri*'s interest in other nations but its desire to be part of a wider international movement. This suited the internationalist stance of the PNV-*Aberri*. As Ugalde has argued, the international recognition of Euskadi was one of the main goals of the party, as proven by its manifesto of 1922.[12]

From *Aberri*, the PNV-*Aberri* developed and articulated a strong verbal radicalism that differed from the more cautious *Euzkadi*. The defence of independence as the main goal of Basque nationalism entailed the articulation of a more aggressive language against Spain inspired by

---

9 Lorenzo Espinosa, 'Influencia del nacionalismo irlandés en el nacionalismo vasco', p. 244.
10 To avoid confusion, throughout the next chapters I refer to *Aberri* (1916–1923) as *Aberri* newsletter and to *Aberri* (1923) as *Aberri* newspaper.
11 Aberri, 'Próxima aparición del gran diario nacionalista *Aberri*: órgano del Partido Nacionalista Vasco', *Aberri* (newsletter), 21 April 1923, p. 4.
12 Ugalde, *La acción exterior del nacionalismo vasco*, p. 291.

Sabino Arana's radical rhetoric. In particular, the Aberrianos recovered and developed Sabino Arana's anti-Spanish 'racism' and anticolonial rhetoric, which had been toned down in the previous period. These were used to defend the necessary independence of Euskadi from Spain.

First, as Fernández Soldevilla has argued, the PNV-*Aberri* recovered and exalted the purest version of the Aranist discourse, which included amongst other things Sabino Arana's hatred towards the *maketos*, considered an inferior race.[13] Thus, race was a recurrent point of reference and identity in both the *Aberri* newsletter and the *Aberri* newspaper.[14] Like Arana, *Aberri* presented the Basques as the oldest race in Europe, a race whose purity was threatened by the vice and degradation that Spaniards – mixed-blood and inferior – brought to Euskadi. As the *Aberri* newsletter claimed, for example, the Basque race 'was disappearing physically and morally'.[15] For this reason, the two periodicals frequently called for the eviction of the 'foreign' race and for the rejection of customs that could harm Basque purity including alcoholism, atheism, vice and sex; characteristics that were believed to be intrinsic and inherent to the foreign Spanish 'race'. Racist discourses legitimised the PNV-*Aberri*'s separatist programme: without 'national independence', the *Aberri* newsletter argued, measures to protect the Basque race were pointless as 'the invader [Spain] can flood the homeland with foreign blood; can impose an alien language; can destroy secular legislation; can accept exotic games; can introduce neighbouring customs and destroy racial characteristics'.[16] The article continued arguing that rather than knowledge, action was necessary, so 'the germs that produce ethnic characteristics are nourished'.[17]

---

13 Gaizka Fernández Soldevilla, 'De *Aberri* a ETA, pasando por Venezuela. Rupturas y continuidades en el nacionalismo vasco radical (1921-1977)', *Bulletin d'histoire contemporaine de l'Espagne*, 51 (2015), pp. 219-264 (p. 222).

14 It is worth pointing out, however, that we observe a slight decrease in its use in *Aberri* newspaper: whilst from 1916-1923 race appears as an obsessive point of reference and is present in virtually every issue of the *Aberri* newsletter, in the *Aberri* newspaper references to race are not as frequent. This is possibly explained by the fact that from 1923 onwards, *Aberri* sought direct collaboration with non-white movements with which Basque nationalists were attempting to establish fraternal links. Despite its decrease, ideas of racial purity and whiteness were still present in both publications.

15 U.T.S., 'Colaboración femenina. Comentando', *Aberri* (newsletter), 20 January 1923, p. 2. This article assured readers that with the Spanish invasion, the Spanish infiltrated every aspect of the Basque life, in this case religion.

16 Azkonara, 'Engañifa', *Aberri* (newsletter), 1 September 1922, p. 3. Note: 'Juegos' in Spanish could mean both sport games and board games. I have translated it as 'games'.

17 Azkonara, 'Engañifa', p. 3.

An excellent example of the obsession with racial purity can be found in an article written in 1923 by Arana's follower Adolfo de Larrañaga, published in the *Aberri* newspaper. This article advocated the conservation of the Basque race and hence its purity which had to be achieved by ending racial mixing and mixed marriages.[18] Racial mixing, according to de Larrañaga, was easily identified by one's last name.[19] These ideas about last names as an indicator of purity and Basqueness recall Sabino Arana's belief that a person's race could be affirmed by asking their second name: as MacClancy states, for Arana 'a person called Rodríguez could not be Basque under any circumstances; one called Garaicoetxea Aguirreazkuenaga Zigorraga could not be anything but'.[20] De Larrañaga concluded his article with a word of warning for the Basques:

> Do you know that the Aryans, that chosen race, refined over centuries, stylised with purity and selected by aristocratic pride, disappeared forever due to not having forbidden marriage with other races? When the death penalty was imposed on anyone who married a foreigner, it was too late, they already had cancer in their souls.[21]

Writings like this suggest that de Larrañaga was engaging with similar ideas about mixed marriage and the end of racial purity to those developing in Germany at the time, where antisemitic publications claimed that 'when an Aryan man married a full-blooded Jewess, their children approached the Jewish type'.[22] Furthermore, references to inter-racial marriage suggest an awareness of the eugenics movement and its views on 'selective breeding', which was gaining growing popularity in many parts of the world, including Spain.

Second, if Sabino Arana's fervent racism and anti-*maketismo* had proved helpful in articulating a more radical doctrine, the same can be said about his ideas against empire. Like Arana, the Aberrianos appropriated anticolonial language to legitimise their aspirations and argued that their situation was no different to that encountered by other colonial subjects

---

18 Adolfo de Larrañaga, 'Matrimonios de raza', *Aberri* (newspaper), 15 June 1923, p. 6. These ideas had already been posited in *Aberri* newsletter. See for instance, the article in Euskera titled 'Abertzaletasuna zer da?' ('What is patriotism?'), which posited that finding a spouse outside Euskadi was detrimental for the Basque cause. U. Tar K., 'Abertzaletasuna zer da?', *Aberri* (newsletter), 31 March 1922, p. 1.
19 De Larrañaga, 'Matrimonios de raza', p. 6.
20 MacClancy, *Expressing Identities in the Basque Arena*, pp. 106–07.
21 De Larrañaga, 'Matrimonios de raza', p. 6.
22 Amir Teicher, *Social Mendelism: Genetics and the Politics of Race in Germany, 1900–1948* (Cambridge: Cambridge University Press, 2020), p. 114.

of the period. As I demonstrate later, the colonial war that Spain was battling in Morocco turned into the perfect opportunity to develop *Aberri*'s anticolonial repertoire. De Pablo and Mees argue that ultimately the CNV shared *Aberri*'s anticolonialism, but that the latter was more verbal about it than the former.[23] However, the differences between the PNV-*Aberri* and the CNV's anticolonialism went beyond their frequency and boldness. As the first section of this chapter proves, unlike Sabino Arana and the CNV, *Aberri*'s anticolonialism was not focused on Spain alone but condemned every form of colonialism.[24] In other words, during this decade the Aberrianos completed the transition from a selective form of anticolonialism to one that advocated the global end of colonialism. Inspired by international anticolonial movements, the Aberrianos increasingly regarded violence as a plausible method to end colonial rule.

As I have advanced before, this shift towards a new form of global colonial opposition and the willingness to be part of a global struggle against colonialism with extra-European nations did not imply a lack of racist and imperialist attitudes within the movement. Although Basque radicals denounced the imperialist actions of Spain in Morocco during the 1920s and attempted to forge direct contacts with rebel Riffians, they still held problematic ideas about them. At the end of the day, Riffians were not white and, despite being an ideal ally due to the circumstances, were seen as different, exotic and barbaric by a movement for which race was an object of obsession.[25]

The reason these contradictory ideas coexisted, I argue, is that Basque anticolonialism must be understood as a strategy serving important political purposes. First, by framing the Basques in a struggle against colonialism, the Aberrianos led important internationalisation attempts, which had been one of the PNV-*Aberri*'s central priorities since its formation. By equating their struggle to that of other colonised nations, Basque nationalists aimed to be recognised and acknowledged by other movements. Second,

---

23 De Pablo and Mees, *El péndulo patriótico*, p. 80.

24 It is worth noting that although Basque radicals stopped praising the British in their newsletters so often, they still demonstrated residual Anglophilia.

25 The whiteness of the Basques was cited as an element of difference between them and other subjugated or colonised 'races'. For instance, in an article that aimed to equate Spain's African dominions to Euskadi, the *Aberri* newsletter stressed the whiteness of Euskadi's citizens when arguing that in Euskadi Spain also had white subjects. See Arkaitz, 'El Clero diocesano en Gazteiz', *Aberri* (newsletter), 28 October 1922, p. 2. In this article, the author complained about the fact that in other parts of the world missionaries spread and taught religion in the same language that was spoken by the indigenous population of the area, whereas in Euskadi religion was taught in Spanish.

these anticolonial claims were used by the PNV-*Aberri* to present Basque self-determination, independence and non-collaborationist theories as a logical and necessary step for the Basque population. Drawing from Sabino Arana, *Aberri* argued that Euskadi had been colonised by Spain in the nineteenth century and that therefore, independence was the only solution. In sum, although anticolonialism became a recurrent rhetorical device in this period, its sincerity must be questioned.

Gora Irlanda Azkatuta: Ireland's Anticolonial Example in Basque Radical Nationalism

The years that followed the First World War saw a new wave of worldwide anticolonial nationalism, and with it the forging of international networks that sought to defeat colonial rule collectively. These included nationalist individuals and organisations from the British territories of Egypt, India and Ireland. Although, as Kate O'Malley has argued, the latter has traditionally been left out by scholars when recounting the history of British decolonisation, Ireland played a key role in the decomposition of the British Empire.[26] The mutual influence that Irish, Egyptian and Indian nationalists had on each other, as well as the alliances they established against Britain, should not be overlooked.[27] Although India had to wait, Ireland and Egypt had more success with their respective independence claims during the 1920s. The Aberrianos were not immune to this global anticolonial insurrection, which they regarded as the perfect model to emulate. Among the insurgents that rebelled against the British Empire during this period, Basque nationalists paid particular attention to Irish republicans. Once again, the different strands of Irish nationalism became a point of reference for both Basque moderates and radicals, who used the Irish example to consolidate their different nationalist programmes.

---

26 Kate O'Malley, '1919, un punto de inflexión antiimperialista: Irlanda, Egipto y la India', in Ucelay-Da Cal, Núñez Seixas, Gonzàlez i Vilalta (eds), *Patrias diversas ¿misma lucha?*, pp. 131–50 (p. 132).

27 For a detailed account of these mutual influences see M. C. Rast, '"Ireland's Sister Nations": Internationalism and Sectarianism in the Irish Struggle for Independence, 1916–22', *Journal of Global History*, 10.3 (2015), pp. 479–501 and O'Malley, '1919, un punto de inflexion antiimperialista'. See also Durba Ghosh and Dane Kennedy (eds), *Decentring Empire: Britain, India and the Transcolonial World* (New Delhi: Orient Longman, 2006). In particular, Kevin Grant's chapter compares the hunger strikes of Irish and Indian nationalists in the first half of the twentieth century. See Kevin Grant, 'The Transcolonial World of Hunger Strikes and Political Fasts, c. 1909–1935', in Ghosh and Kennedy (eds), *Decentring Empire*, pp. 243–69.

Unsurprisingly, unlike the CNV, the Aberrianos paid particular attention to the developments of the radical branch of Irish nationalism, represented by Sinn Féin and the newly formed IRA. This branch of Irish nationalism reinforced Basque radicals' commitment to independence, sacrifice and anticolonialism.

Irish republicans such as the Irish Argentinian Sinn Féin member Ambrose Victor Martin were able to spread these values in Euskadi themselves.[28] Martin visited Bilbao on his way to Ireland from Argentina, where he had been deported by the British authorities in 1919. During his stay in Bilbao in the spring of 1922, Martin gave lectures on Irish nationalism at different Basque Youth headquarters and inspired those Basque nationalists who believed that the only way to achieve independence was by imitating the Irish example. In one of his speeches, Martin gave a talk about the role of women in the movement through the example of the Irish Cumann na mBan, a women's paramilitary and nationalist organisation formed in Dublin in 1914. Days later, Gallastegi encouraged Basque women to create a similar organisation, and on 10 April 1922 the EAB was established as the first women's association of the PNV.[29] Indeed, the Irish movement was viewed as a valuable test case: the events that took place on the island were closely watched and copied according to their effectiveness by Basque nationalists.

With the hope that Basque readers would support and lead a similar insurrection soon, the pages of the *Aberri* newsletter and newspaper followed with enthusiasm the so-called Irish Revolution of 1916–1923. An article published in December 1921 stated, 'let's learn, Basques. The History of the nations has never seen a struggle as exemplary as this seven-century-long

---

28 Martin's first stay in Euskadi and its influence on Basque nationalism and contacts with Basque nationalists has been the object of numerous studies. In his book, Ugalde studied these contacts closely: Ugalde, *La acción exterior del nacionalismo vasco*, pp. 295–99. Ever since, different studies have also emerged: see, for instance, Núñez Seixas, 'Ecos de Pascua', pp. 465–67; Pere Soler Paricio, 'Ambrose Martin: Nacionalista irlandès. Del quarter d'Estat Català a la defensa del govern d'Euzkadi', *Butlletí de la Societat Catalana d'Estudis Històrics*, XXXII (2021), pp. 91–122; Cullen and McCreanor, 'Dangerous Friends' and Cullen, *Radical Basque Nationalist-Irish Republican Relations*, pp. 50–53.

29 As Núñez Seixas argues, the EAB was not, however, an exact replica of the Irish women's organisation. In the Basque case, the role of women was considerably more secondary than in the Irish case. See Núñez Seixas, 'Ecos de Pascua', p. 467. For a detailed study on the EAB, see Mercedes Ugalde Solano, *Mujeres y nacionalismo vasco: génesis y desarrollo de Emakume Abertzale Batza (1906–1936)* (Bilbao: Universidad del País Vasco, 1993).

titanic fight for independence.'[30] The proclamation of the Irish Republic in 1919 was, according to this article, the greatest episode within the 'most impressive epic that humanity has witnessed'.[31] The article concluded with a warm solidarity message to the Irish nationalists: '[Basque nationalists] warmly congratulate the Irish nation, a model of heroism and love of nationalism, and vow that Ireland can achieve eternal prosperity and absolute independence. LONG LIVE FREE IRELAND!' (capitals in the original).[32]

The values of sacrifice, martyrdom and violence featured heavily in the speeches and writings of *Aberri* when talking about Ireland and its struggle for independence. Articles published in *Aberri* commemorated key episodes of Irish history. For instance, an issue of *Aberri* newsletter published in April 1922 recalled the Easter Rising of 1916 and documented the advances of Irish republicanism since. The issue – written in profoundly patriotic and romantic language – recalled some key events of the Irish Revolution, including the Irish War for Independence, and stressed the cruelty of the British Empire and the heroism of the Irish leaders. The latter were labelled as 'martyrs', and *Aberri* ensured that its readership remembered the names of some of the most exemplary ones, including Patrick Pearse, Thomas Clarke and James Connolly.[33] The second page of the issue included images of some of the charismatic martyrs, including a 'martyr kid' (Kevin Barry) who died after being brutally tortured by the British Black and Tans, Roger Casement, Éamon de Valera, Terence MacSwiney and Thomas Ashe, the latter two having died on hunger strike.[34]

Supporting the most radical branch of Irish nationalism and romanticising the Irish republican struggle had important advantages for the Basque radical cause. The articles published in nationalist papers inspired young Basque radicals, who dreamed about imitating the Irish and defeating what they still considered a second-class power, whose civilising abilities were questioned by *Aberri*.[35] Basque radical nationalists expressed this thought themselves. An article published in 1923 started and finished with the

---

30 Anon., 'El estado libre de Irlanda', *Aberri* (newsletter), 17 December 1921, p. 1.
31 Anon., 'El estado libre de Irlanda', p. 1.
32 Anon., 'El estado libre de Irlanda', p. 1. Note: ETA used a similar motto to defend their cause 50 years later with the slogan *Gora Euskadi Askatuta* (Long Live Free Euskadi).
33 See Anon., 'Algunos héroes de la rebelión irlandesa de 1916', *Aberri* (newsletter), 15 April 1922, p. 1.
34 Anon., 'Del movimiento nacionalista irlandés', *Aberri* (newsletter), 15 April 1922, p. 2.
35 See, for instance, Anon., 'Toros y barracas', *Aberri* (newspaper), 13 September 1923, p. 5, which ironically refers to the Spaniards as 'the "civilised" colonisers'.

same sentence: 'when powerful England was at the peak of its maritime and terrestrial power, during the European war, a mere handful of Irish patriots rose up against her in the week of Easter 1916.'[36] The power of national unity and sacrifice could break empires. In contrast to powerful Britain, Spain was 'one of the most backwards nations in the world' and was in a state of total decomposition.[37] Whilst that same article recognised that Basque nationalists had had many opportunities to rebel against Spain in the past, the author encouraged readers to take advantage of the situation of total crisis that Spain was experiencing to revolt.[38] If Irish nationalists had successfully challenged one of the biggest empires in the world, the Basques could surely do the same against the sickly and virtually empire-less Spain. As I show in the next sections, this confidence led to action.

Furthermore, the Irish Revolution served to consolidate some beliefs that have been at the core of Basque radicalism ever since, and that some Basque radicals had already advanced in the previous decade: contrary to what the moderates thought, independence would not be granted by the generosity of the oppressors. Irish independence had not been achieved thanks to the benevolence of Britain or thanks to Wilson's self-determination policies but through revolution, national sacrifice and violence. The Irish example had taught the Basques a lesson: 'only sacrifice can make peoples bigger, only sacrifice can ... free peoples from the power of the oppressor!'[39] 'Nationalism without sacrifice', the same article argued, 'is not nationalism'.[40]

The Irish struggle also put into question a second belief that had been the cause of previous tension between Basque radicals and moderates: the alleged generosity of Britain to its colonies.[41] *Aberri* constantly highlighted the oppressive and imperialist character of the British and frequently condemned Britain's viciousness towards its oppressed colonies.[42] This belief

36 Iker, '¡Alertas, mendigoxales!', *Aberri* (newspaper), 20 July 1923, p. 3.
37 Iker, '¡Alertas, mendigoxales!', p. 3.
38 Iker, '¡Alertas, mendigoxales!', p. 3.
39 Anon., 'Del movimiento nacionalista irlandés', p. 2.
40 Anon., 'Del movimiento nacionalista irlandés', p. 2.
41 Although following the declaration of Irish independence in 1919, the moderates wrote some texts in support of the Irish rebels apparently indicating that moderate Anglophilia was declining, this did not last long and Basque moderates soon continued defending Britain and condemned the radical sections of Irish nationalism who opposed the the Anglo-Irish Treaty of 1921.
42 Irish radicals used similar anticolonial arguments to advocate for the complete independence of Ireland. For instance, influential Anti-Treaty leader Liam Mellows, who had established direct contacts with Indian nationalists in the US, used the 'colonial question' as a main argument for rejecting an agreement with Britain. See Howe, *Ireland and Empire*, p. 58. Basque nationalists were clearly aware of Mellows

was reinforced further by the events that took place after the Irish War for Independence. Following the war, Ireland was partitioned into two different states: the Catholic Irish Free State and the Protestant-leaning six counties of the north-east, which were excluded from the new state. According to Basque radicals, the partition of Ireland and the limited independence of Egypt granted in 1922 confirmed that the generosity of the war victors and more specifically, Britain, was nothing but a myth. As an article published in the *Aberri* newspaper stated,

> England has seen itself obliged ... to solemnly proclaim the independence of Egypt. But what [England] gave with one hand, it took away with the other; because this independence is surrounded by such limitations that it makes independence a mere myth.[43]

Furthermore, the proclamation of the Irish Free State led to the start of a civil conflict among Irish nationalists. The Irish Civil War of 1922–1923 pitted a majority faction that defended the Anglo-Irish Treaty, signed following the Irish War for Independence in 1921, against those who saw the treaty as a betrayal of the new state and advocated the complete independence of Ireland (anti-Treatyites).[44]

Aberri supported the anti-Treaty forces during the Irish Civil War and used the conflict to stress the evilness of British imperialism.[45] According to the periodical, pro-Treaty nationalists 'had forgotten their common enemy and the blood that runs through their veins' and they 'had been unconsciously turned into playthings of the British Empire'.[46] As the same article stated, 'the Anglo-Irish treaty will be known in history as the greatest product of

and his ideas. See for instance, U., 'La tragedia de Irlanda', *Aberri* (newsletter), 9 September 1922, p. 2.

43 U.E., 'Información nacionalista mundial', *Aberri* (newspaper), 17 June 1923, p. 1. This article argued that the Egyptian nationalist problem would only be resolved once British troops abandoned Egypt and the Egyptian government was elected independently with no restrictions. It also indirectly condemned the passivity of the war victors and the lack of representation of weak nations in the Lausanne Conference of 1922.

44 The treaty integrated the Irish Free State into the orbit of the British Empire. As such, the MPs of the newly created state were required to swear an oath of faith to the British Monarchy.

45 Cullen argues that most Basque nationalism welcomed the Anglo-Irish Treaty until the start of the Irish Civil War, when the Aberrianos began to support the anti-Treaty Republicans. Cullen, *Radical Basque Nationalist-Irish Republican Relations*, p. 52.

46 U., 'La tragedia de Irlanda', p. 2.

the cunning and intrigue of British imperialism'.[47] *Aberri* constantly claimed that the British were to blame for the Irish Civil War. The new Irish Free State, *Aberri* claimed, was not a state, nor was it free or Irish, because it went against Irish desires and had been propagated by the British, 'whose only objective was to defeat and break the Irish nation'.[48] *Aberri* used examples of British cruelty to dismantle some of the pro-British arguments CNV ideologues had posited: as *Aberri* argued – directly referring to the 'England in India' articles that Eleizalde wrote in 1916 – the situation in Ireland post-1921 proved that 'England is the nation that has the most slaves'.[49] Alluding to the situation in Ireland, the article questioned the benevolence of the British and ironically challenged Eleizalde to write a new series of articles titled 'England in Ireland'.[50]

Indeed, the Irish conflict provided a new opportunity for Basque radicals to defend their new separatist, anti-collaborationist and anticolonial programme, which resembled that of the Irish anti-Treaty nationalists. Significantly, *Aberri* used the Irish Civil War to stress its differences with the moderate and pro-Treaty CNV. Although unlike the Irish, Basque nationalists did not fight physically among themselves, the similarities between the two strands of Irish and Basque nationalism were strong enough to compare the ongoing clashes between nationalists in Ireland and Euskadi. On the one hand, both the PNV-*Aberri* and the Anti-Treatyites rejected any plans for gradual change or collaboration with the state, believing that nothing less than the complete independence of the nation could satisfy their national claims. On the other hand, both the CNV and the Pro-Treaty faction were much more pragmatic. Although they did not reject independence as the ultimate goal, they sought immediate solutions that implied collaboration with the dominant nation.

The strong similarities that the Aberrianos observed between the nationalist struggles in Ireland and Euskadi made them fear that a conflict like the Irish Civil War could happen in the Basque Country. In an article summarising the Irish revolutionary period, Gallastegi sympathised with 'the tireless republicans who ... reject every relationship, every deal, every submission to the crown of the oppressive King', and stated that in Euskadi 'there is already an organisation, the CNV, which from now on fights separatism, which seeks union with Spain, which supports the regionalist

---

47 U., 'La tragedia de Irlanda', p. 2.
48 Editor's Note, 'Las próximas elecciones generales', *Aberri* (newspaper), 4 July 1923, p. 1.
49 Anon., 'Naskaldija. Kizkitzianas', *Aberri* (newsletter), 27 January 1923, p. 4.
50 Anon., 'Naskaldija. Kizkitzianas', p. 4.

and autonomist movements against independentism'.[51] Gallastegi suggested that once Spain granted Euskadi extensive autonomy, events similar to those in Ireland would follow: 'the Communion [CNV] will then form a Basque regular army equipped by Spain and will fight with it, with bloodshed and fire, without mercy, against the "Basque separatist rebels" [the PNV-*Aberri*] ... and then they will shoot us.'[52]

Such comparisons not only illustrate the growing tension between the CNV and the PNV but also indicate that Basque radicals believed that the situation of Ireland as an oppressed territory mirrored that of Euskadi. As Sabino Arana and the third *Bizkaitarra* had done in the previous decades, during the 1920s the Aberrianos globalised the effects of colonialism by portraying both European and non-European nationalities as imperial victims. The oppression of the Irish was compared in equal terms to that of the Egyptians, the Indians and, of course, the Basques.[53] To stress the similarities between Euskadi and Ireland's situation, different articles even labelled Biscay's region 'Las Encartaciones' (which was considered less Basque than the rest of Euskadi) the Biscayan Ulster.[54]

Irish republicans had not achieved full independence in the 1920s. Yet the advances that Irish republicanism had experienced since 1916 were enough to convince Basque radicals of the power of national sacrifice and violence. Basque radical newsletters stressed the similarities they shared with Ireland so their readers could imagine a similar insurrection in Euskadi. In a way, a successful revolution was more feasible in Euskadi than in the new Irish

---

51 Gudari (Gallastegi), 'Pascua revolucionaria. ¡Y un día nos fusilarán!', *Aberri* (newsletter), 31 March 1923, p. 1. Gallastegi signed most of its articles as Gudari (warrior).

52 Gudari, 'Pascua revolucionaria', p. 1.

53 See for instance Garatza, 'En el XIX aniversario. Solidaridad de Patronos Vascos', *Aberri* (newsletter), 24 November 1922, p. 5, which shows how Basque radicals believed their situation was analogous to that of Morocco, India, Egypt and other colonies. Both *Aberri* newsletter and newspaper wrote texts in support of the national causes of the British colonies and compared them to the Basque case. For Egypt see for instance U.E., 'Información nacionalista mundial'. For India see Bingen, 'Ejemplos a seguir. India y nosotros', *Aberri* (newspaper), 11 September 1923, p. 6, which compared the figures of Sabino Arana and Gandhi, implying that the situation of both nations was analogous.

54 *Aberri* argued that Las Encartaciones was more Spanish due to the higher effects of the Spanish invasion. See for instance Dorkaitz, 'La encartación es euzkadiana', *Aberri* (newsletter), 18 June 1921, p. 2, which refers to the Encartaciones as the 'Biscayan Ulster' and Anon., 'Banquete a Elías de Galastegi', *Aberri* (newspaper), 19 June 1923, p. 1, which reproduces a telegram in which a part of Biscay is referred as the 'Basque Ulster'.

Free State: the former was far more industrial and economically independent from the dominant state than the latter. Furthermore, as explored below, in the early 1920s Spain was in a situation of total crisis that could be compared to the Disaster of '98. If a revolution were to happen, Basque radicals needed to imitate the Irish example and forge alliances with non-Basque forces. Most likely inspired by the networks that Irish nationalists had forged with other anticolonial insurgents within the British Empire, Basques began to do the same. The following sections explain how fortunate timing led the new Rif Republic, Catalonia and Galicia to become Euskadi's strategic allies against Spanish colonial rule.

Same Oppression, Same Enemy: Basque Radical Nationalism and the Rif War

In the 1920s, Spain was still haunted by the date of its Empire's collapse in 1898. As already mentioned, the small territory that Spain held in northern Morocco was Spain's last opportunity to demonstrate its imperial authority and to reverse the international and national crisis in which it was mired. Yet much to the Spanish government's dismay, its presence in Morocco was strongly opposed by the Berber indigenous communities, which were only loosely controlled by the Moroccan Sultanate when the Spanish arrived in the region. Spaniards encountered the most resistance in the Rif area, with its influential leader Muhamed Abd el-Krim Khattabi. Abd el-Krim was a teacher and journalist who in his early years worked in the Spanish administration and hoped that Europe would contribute to the 'modernisation' of the Rif region. Eventually, he became Spain's number one enemy during the last phase of the so-called Rif War, which was fought from 1909 to 1927.

The most humiliating defeat for Spain in this long conflict came in summer 1921, when Abd el-Krim led an unexpected victory over Spanish troops with barely 4,000 men defeating a modern army of 10,000 to 15,000 soldiers.[55] Despite the evident numerical advantage of Spain's forces, its army was forced to withdraw in the hot Riffian summer, leaving everything behind, from weapons to wounded men. Between 8,000 to 12,000 Spanish men perished in what became one of the biggest blows in Spain's modern history.[56] In events which strongly echoed the '98 crisis, the so-called Annual

---

55 Julián Casanova and Carlos Gil Andrés, *Twentieth-Century Spain: A History* (Cambridge: Cambridge University Press, 2014), p. 72.
56 As Balfour has noted, calculations of the scale of the Disaster have varied. See Sebastian Balfour, *Deadly Embrace: Morocco and the Road to the Spanish Civil War* (Oxford:

Disaster saw Spain lose a considerable amount of its protectorate as Abd el-Krim proclaimed the new Rif Republic (1921–1926). As María Rosa de Madariaga has noted, following the Annual Disaster, the territory that had taken 12 years to be conquered was lost in 21 days.[57] Furthermore, the new Disaster evidenced that Spain was not ready for another colonial conflict: its army was badly trained, equipped and fed, and its infrastructure was inadequate. What is more, the colonial crisis had exposed the limitations of an archaic political system that was unable to recruit soldiers to fight in what was an extremely unpopular war and was succeeded by a period of general unrest in Spain. As Balfour highlights, whilst the history of colonial campaigns is plagued by disasters, 'none of these disasters, however, was as severe as that suffered by the Spanish colonial army in Morocco in July 1921, nor did they have the same depth of domestic repercussion'.[58]

After Spain's latest humiliating national trauma, a new opportunity arose for Basque nationalists. During the early 1920s, as Abd el-Krim made the moribund Restoration system tremble with his ill-equipped but skilled troops, *Aberri* led a powerful campaign in support of the Riffian insurgents. This campaign went in line with the anticolonial stance of *Aberri*. The newsletter presented the Aberrianos as 'lovers of the triumph of justice and freedom of all the nations, fundamentally anti-imperialists and enemies of all wars of conquest'.[59] The newspaper agreed arguing that the PNV-*Aberri* was 'the enemy of every war of conquest and an anti-militarist party'.[60]

Basque radicals were one of the first movements to romanticise the figure of Abd el-Krim, who eventually 'became a mythical point for the leaders of anticolonial movements all over the world'.[61] The struggle that Abd el-Krim was engaged in broadened to challenge the French colonial presence in Morocco in the mid-1920s, and voices from all over the globe joined in solidarity with the Riffians and condemned the brutality of the Rif War. In 1925, Abd el-Krim was featured on the front page of *Time* magazine. His popularity transcended continents, with his war against France and Spain

---

Oxford University Press, 2002), p. 70. De Madariaga estimates that between 8,000 and 10,000 men died in the withdrawal. She also notes that in 1921, it was stated in Congress that 8,668 men had perished. De Madariaga, *Marruecos, ese gran desconocido*, p. 128.

57 De Madariaga, *Marruecos, ese gran desconocido*, p. 125.
58 Balfour, *Deadly Embrace*, p. 52.
59 Anon., 'El árbol malato', *Aberri* (newsletter), 10 March 1923, p. 3.
60 Anon., 'Los soldados de cuota y de haba. ¡Guerra a la guerra!', *Aberri* (newspaper), 21 July 1923, p. 3.
61 Casanova and Gil Andrés, *Twentieth-Century Spain*, p. 72.

sparking claims of anticolonial solidarity in South Asia, Europe and all over Latin America from 1925.[62]

The PNV-*Aberri*'s support of the Riffians was not, in any way, an exception among Spanish peripheral nationalist movements either. Although the Aberrianos went much further in their radicalism and dedication to the Moroccan cause, Spanish colonialism in Africa was criticised by others within the Basque movement, such as the CNV, and by some groups of Catalan and, though less widely, Galician nationalists.[63] Yet the extent to which these movements are understood to have sympathised with the Riffians needs to be nuanced. As Iglesias Amorín suggests, 'the defence of Morocco [by sub-state nationalist movements in Spain] often seems more practical than sincere'.[64] Dalmau agrees and argues that although a radical strand of Catalan nationalism shared important goals with the Riffians, 'Catalan separatists never came to see their fight as aligned with that of the Rifi', distinguishing their situations by citing 'civilisation' as a prior requirement for any who sought recognition as a nation.[65]

Basque and Catalan nationalists perceived the Riffians similarly. At least superficially, Basque radicals constantly aligned their cause with the Riffian struggle and even aimed to establish direct links with the Riffians. Yet their support for the anticolonial insurgents had limits, and indeed a close look at *Aberri*'s texts reveals what the Aberrianos really thought about the Riffians. Unlike the Irish, the Riffians were not the perfect allies because, among other things, they were not white, western or Catholic. This confirms that despite the re-emergence of Basque anticolonialism, the nature of Basque nationalism had not changed as much as it might appear. A further

---

62 See Dalmau, 'Catalans and Rifis during the Wilsonian Moment', pp. 141–42; and Lindner, *A City Against Empire*, pp. 135–39. See also Tony Wood, 'Indoamerica against Empire: Radical Transnational Politics in Mexico City, 1925–1929', in Manela and Streets-Salter (eds), *The Anticolonial Transnational*, pp. 64–89 (p. 75).

63 See de Pablo, '¡Grita Libertad!'; Martín Corrales, 'Catalunya i el Marroc'; Ucelay, 'Els enemics dels meus enemics', pp. 36–37; Watson, *Basque Nationalism and Political Violence*, pp. 120–23; Ugalde and Ucelay-Da Cal, 'Una alianza en potencia en un contexto más amplio', p. 395.

64 Alfonso Iglesias Amorín, 'Sub-state nationalisms in Spain during the Moroccan War and the Rif War (1909–1927)', *Studies on National Movements*, 8 (2021), pp. 2–25 (p. 12).

65 Dalmau, 'Catalans and Rifis during the Wilsonian Moment', p. 142. Interestingly, in this same article Dalmau shows how Abd el-Krim himself appropriated the classic binaries of civilisation and barbarity when demanding international recognition, as he demanded that the self-proclaimed civilised nations had an obligation to protect the 'weak' ones. See Dalmau, 'Catalans and Rifis during the Wilsonian Moment', p. 138.

analysis of *Aberri*'s writings during the Rif War demonstrates that Basque nationalism still had strong imperialist leanings. I now explore this through a close reading of *Aberri*'s issues produced during the war in Morocco.

During the Rif War, *Aberri*'s criticism of Spain and its involvement in the Rif was varied. The *Aberri* newsletter mostly criticised the conscription system, participating in the wider opposition to the recruitment of troops seen across the country. This opposition was widely popular amongst the working classes, who were most affected by a system that benefited those who could pay a fee to avoid going to war and saw many riots and mutinies from 1921 onwards. The *Aberri* newsletter consistently stressed the consequences of the Rif War for the Basque nation and its youth, as younger men were forcibly sent to Morocco regularly in order to 'fight against a nation that like us wants to be free'.[66] The *Aberri* newsletter complained that the Basques had to fight in a war that was not theirs, 'an unfair war, a war of conquest' that was fought in order to satisfy Spain's 'unstoppable imperial desires'.[67]

Both the *Aberri* newsletter and newspaper also denounced the inhumane conditions that Basque soldiers suffered in the military camps in Morocco. From 1921 the newsletter began to include extracts from diaries written by Basque soldiers sent to fight in north Africa, who condemned the situation in the military camps firsthand. The periodical also sought aid and funds for the Basque soldiers. The newsletter regularly advertised the charity events organised by the Basque youth to aid the soldiers, which also saw the creation of a board of aid, made up mainly of women.[68] On a weekly basis, the *Aberri* newsletter wrote with enthusiasm about these fundraising events and informed readers about the money that was being raised in order to help Basque soldiers and their families, 'victims of the war that Spanish imperialism was fighting in Morocco'.[69]

Anticolonial claims and opposition to the war intensified in the radical newspaper's daily coverage, which argued that Basques were not willing to 'help our own oppressor in their worthless attempts to broaden their slave territories'.[70] Like the newsletter, the newspaper *Aberri* centred all its efforts

---

66 Ibargaraondo tar Kepa, 'El viaje de la muerte', *Aberri* (newsletter), 30 September 1921, p. 3.
67 Sorgiña, 'Razones que no convencen', *Aberri* (newsletter), 5 November 1921, p. 1, and Anon., '¡Cobardes! ¡Cobardes! ¡Cobardes!', *Aberri* (newsletter), 29 October 1921, p. 2.
68 *Aberri* also criticised *Euzkadi* for not contributing to the charity campaign organised by *Aberri*. See for instance, Sorgiña, 'Razones que no convencen', p. 1.
69 Anon., 'Por nuestros soldados en África. La Velada del domingo', *Aberri* (newsletter), 25 November 1921, p. 3.
70 Anon., '¡Guerra a la guerra! Aspecto nacionalista vasco', *Aberri* (newspaper), 7 August 1923, p. 1.

on launching an anticolonial campaign that supported Abd el-Krim's troops, celebrated Spain's defeats, encouraged the rebellion of Spanish soldiers and mocked Spain's 'pro-civilisation' arguments to justify the war. This campaign, called 'guerra a la guerra' ('war against war') lasted from mid-July 1923 until the newspaper's closure in September that year. Despite the apparent pacificist tone suggested by the name of the campaign, the violent actions of the Riffians were justified and praised as these were considered self-defence against an unjust occupation. The *Aberri* newspaper proclaimed its solidarity with the Riffians when stating that 'Abd-el-Krim, the glorious defender of his homeland, has all the sympathies of Basque nationalists'.[71] Basque radicals' explicit support for the Riffian cause is hardly surprising, considering the strategic and opportunistic nature of Basque anticolonialism. As an article in *Aberri* newspaper argued: 'it is obvious that when considering Euskadi's liberation, Spain's disasters [in Morocco] are favourable to us and they facilitate our path in leaps and bounds'.[72]

It is no coincidence that *Aberri* newspaper stepped up its support for the Riffian rebels in the summer of 1923. By then, the aftermath of the Annual Disaster was still very much present, and the cracks of the Restoration system seemed more open than ever. Following Sabino Arana's tradition, *Aberri* took advantage of the crisis Spain was experiencing to reverse the traditional binaries of civilisation and barbarism and to question the validity of Spanish colonisation in Africa.[73] According to the *Aberri* newspaper, it was not the Riffians who needed to be civilised but the Spanish themselves: 'Abd-el-Krim, Abd-el-Krim, how necessary it is that you go to civilise Spain', said an editor's note next to information about Morocco.[74] In an article

---

71 Editor's Note, 'La aventura de Marruecos. Patrióticas frases del caudillo Abd-el-Krim', *Aberri* (newspaper), 9 August 1923, p. 2.

72 Anon., '¡Guerra a la guerra! Aspecto nacionalista vasco', p. 1.

73 In the late 1910s, the *Aberri* newsletter had used a similar strategy to condemn Spanish imperialism. For example, in 1919 *Aberri* commented Spain's pro-civilisation prose in a mocking tone: 'Spain goes to Morocco to fulfil a noble civilising mandate, it goes in the name of the sacred European civilisation, to spill their beneficial gifts over those that are savage, making their life beautiful and cheery.' Z, 'El fusilamiento de los leales de Malalien', p. 2.

74 Editor's Note, 'Información mundial. España', *Aberri* (newspaper), 1 September 1923, p. 2. These arguments were not made by Basque radicals alone. During the Rif War Spanish socialists such as Pablo Iglesias and newspapers such as *El Socialista* ('The Socialist') also condemned the Rif War. As Elisabeth Bolorinos Allard has pointed out, one of Iglesias's arguments against the war was that Spain could not colonise another region when the country itself was uncivilised. See Elisabeth Bolorinos Allard, *Spanish National Identity, Colonial Power, and the Portrayal of Muslims and Jews during the Rif War (1909–27)* (Woodbridge: Tamesis, 2021), p. 86.

condemning the brutal violence that convicts suffered in Spanish prisons, Gallastegi argued that with this information Abd el-Krim would be able to demonstrate to other nations how 'the Spanish state cannot justify a war that they label as a war of civilisation against African barbarism' when the Spanish themselves proved their savagery.[75]

A cartoon published in *Aberri* newsletter in July 1923 illustrates perfectly how Basques radicals perceived the Spanish. The drawing showed three men facing each other in what appears to be a very sunny, nearly desert-like landscape: to the left, a strong, tall white man dressed in a Basque traditional dress is standing, and to the right are two men who are visually physically weak, extremely thin and have black faces. Whilst this appears to be a highly racist, Orientalist depiction of the Riffians, it seems that the men with black faces might be intended as a depiction of the Spaniards fighting in the Rif. This is evidenced by the fact that one of them is wearing a pith helmet, as well as the caption, in which the Basque man tells the two men, in a warning tone: 'Do you know what I'm going to tell you, innocents? If you continue to sunbathe, soon you won't have a shadow.'[76] This illustrates the ambivalent way in which the Basques viewed the Spaniards: a despicable coloniser with traits characteristic of the colonised. Furthermore, it confirms the contradictory ideas that had been present in the Basque movement since its onset: a movement that professed to be anticolonial but continued using the racism that stemmed from European colonialism to mock and criticise the Spanish.

Certainly, the Rif War was the perfect opportunity for the Aberrianos to elaborate its anti-Spanish arguments, whilst also expanding its anticolonial agenda. It was also a good moment to emphasise to readers that the situation that Riffians and Basques experienced was similar and that therefore independence was the only option. Thus, the declarations of solidarity with the Riffians were usually accompanied by analogies between the Basque and the Riffian situation, which likely resonated strongly with a readership traumatised by the colonial war. Both *Aberri* newsletter and newspaper recognised the similarity of both struggles in many texts:

> The question of Spanish Morocco is simply a question of nationalism and imperialism. It is the struggle of a stronger 'imperialism' that smashes a weaker 'nationalism' with its weight. It is a coincidence that

---

75 Gudari, 'Humanidad. De hombre a hombre', *Aberri* (newspaper), 8 September 1923, p. 1.
76 'Eguzkitan', *Aberri* (newspaper), 4 July 1923, p. 4. In Euskera in the original. Translated for the author by Echanojauregui Ripa.

our [Basque] nationalism, which is also weak, finds itself smashed by precisely the same imperialism.[77]

The situation of the Riffians and the Basques was just another 'crime committed in the name of hateful imperialism ... Africa for the Africans! Spain for the Spanish! AND EUSKADI FOR THE BASQUES' (capitals in the original).[78] Riffians and Basques were united not only in a fight of a similar nature but also in a struggle against the same enemy. As Gallastegi wrote, the same people that enslaved Euskadi on 21 July 1876 were responsible for the 'Rif's Hispanic tragedy'.[79]

Echoing Sabino Arana's comments, *Aberri* claimed that the Basques were experiencing a conquest firsthand. In Euskadi, however, 'the invader was not coming, but was already home'.[80] As Basque radicals claimed, like the Riffians, they had also suffered a 'war of conquest' during the Carlist Wars, which marked the beginning of the 'foreign' invasion. To compare explicitly the situation of both Riffians and Basques explicitly, the *Aberri* newspaper occasionally labelled Euskadi as a protectorate: 'we [the Basques], know the Spanish very well thanks to the time that they have been in our country as a protectorate'.[81]

These symbolic comparisons with the Rif alongside *Aberri*'s large solidarity campaign towards the Riffians served two important purposes which aligned with the principles of Basque radicalism. First, by condemning the war and the Spanish presence in Morocco, *Aberri* established symbolic solidarity links with the Riffians and placed the Basque struggle as one against colonialism in a period in which anticolonial movements emerged in every part of the world. Second, by justifying and presenting the response of the Riffians against the Spaniards as a necessary one, the Basque struggle – which fought against the same enemy – and its separatist claims were equally justified. In other words, *Aberri*'s anticolonial campaign in Morocco

---

77 Dorkaitz, 'Preciosidades comunionistas', p. 3.

78 Editor's Note, 'Información del extranjero. Marruecos', *Aberri* (newspaper), 24 July 1923, p. 1.

79 Gudari, 'El proceso de Berenguer. El País Vasco debe exigir responsabilidades', *Aberri* (newspaper), 27 June 1923, p. 1. In this example Gallastegi uses the date when the *Fueros* were finally abolished to mark the beginning of Basque slavery.

80 Anon., 'Al paseo de una burda maniobra. ¿Quiénes son los verdaderos enemigos de la integridad nacional vasca?', *Aberri* (newsletter), 24 February 1923, p. 2.

81 Editor's Note, 'Información del extranjero. Marruecos', *Aberri* (newspaper), 28 July 1923, p. 1. Oddly enough, in the next issue *Aberri* stated that the Basque Country and Catalonia had not directly experienced the Spanish protectorate.

served to place Basque independence claims in an international context and to present them as necessary.

The strategic and opportunistic nature of Basque anticolonialism explains the contradictions in these publications.[82] As seen above, Basque nationalists relied on and reproduced colonial stereotypes to distinguish themselves from the 'other' (this being Spain or its colonial subjects). Ultimately, Basque nationalists considered themselves distinctly European, 'the representatives of the oldest race of Europe', and hence, were 'the only civilised race that remains subjugated'.[83] Their ancient and civilised status distinguished them from other cultures and religions. As an article published in February 1921 argued, the laws that had been imposed in the Basque territory – which were 'considerably less human and social' than the Basque ones – 'could be accepted perhaps by a Muslim, Jewish or African temperament but they were completely opposed and repulsive to the character of our [Basque] peoples'.[84]

A series of articles, allegedly written by *Aberri*'s collaborator Adul Rabi Arab in 1923, are particularly revealing of the Aberrianos' views.[85] These articles – which aimed to explain Islam to Basque and western readers – focused mostly on Morocco and on the effects that western imperialism had on the country. Although at first glance the articles appear to offer an anticolonial perspective in line with the rest of the newspaper, the language used to describe Moroccans is remarkable. In one of his articles devoted to the height and the decline of the historic Moroccan Empire, Adul Rabi Arab attributed the fall of Morocco into European hands to the inability of the country's rulers, which he stated lacked the capacity to 'revive the poor

---

82 Iglesias Amorín has argued that 'prejudices and pejorative stereotypes' used against Moroccans were common in the anticolonial claims of Basque and Catalan nationalists, although his article mostly provides examples from the latter. Iglesias Amorín, 'Sub-state nationalisms in Spain during the Moroccan War and the Rif War (1909–1927)', p. 20.

83 Anon., 'El estado libre de Irlanda', p. 1. This clearly agreed with the nineteenth-century debates about the Basque race led by European anthropologists (see Chapter 1 for reference).

84 Uritare, 'Comentario social', *Aberri* (newsletter), 26 February 1921, p. 5.

85 It is very likely that no such person existed and that this was a pseudonym. Although the pseudonym takes the form of an Arabic name, we can conclude from the series of articles that they were certainly written by someone who (although perhaps familiar with the Islamic world) was writing from a distant and European perspective, and who saw the culture of the Riffians as very 'different from ours'. See Adul Rabi Arab, 'En torno al resurgir del Islam. Los errores de la política española en Marruecos', *Aberri* (newspaper), 24 August 1923, p. 8.

and sick Moroccan [people]'.[86] In another article he went further. Assessing the present day and the work that the 'protector states' (Spain and France) had done in Morocco, the author began describing the splitting of Morocco between France and Spain and cited the Spanish nationalist Ramiro de Maeztu, most likely with irony, when arguing that France was willing to 'open the routes of civilisation' to the 'untamed and dying ex-empire'.[87] After questioning the success of some French colonial enterprises, he then talked about the vices that had invaded an indigenous 'city', placed next to Casablanca – European and modern – which he did not name but referred to as a non-white city that was dominated by alcoholism, prostitution and sexual violence. The article claimed that this city 'devoted to the lowest prostitutions' was reserved exclusively for the indigenous; where the *toniqués* and the black, the Moroccan and Algerian, the Indochinese and Senegalese, mix their bloods in filthy orgies, brutalised by alcohol'.[88] Although he attributed these vices to the European and western invasion, this article portrayed the indigenous people as childlike people guaranteed to fall into any vices unless they were protected or 'supervised' by the coloniser, thereby reproducing a highly Orientalist discourse.

This attitude was confirmed in another article published on 24 August 1923. In this article, the author discussed Spain's colonisation methods in Morocco, condemning its lack of justice and integrity and stating it had brought no advantage to anyone on either side of the Strait of Gibraltar. However, the author suggested that the Spaniards had not fully exploited the opportunity presented by Morocco and argued that this should have been relatively easy because:

> Everyone that has been in contact with the indigenous Moroccan knows immediately that the way in which you can gain their confidence and gain authority is fundamentally distinct to the way of achieving the same with a nation in western Europe. The state of civilisation of such territories, and the particular idiosyncrasies of its inhabitants is evidently the result of a system of resentment and a way of seeing facts which reflects a childish mindframe; easily impressionable but delicate.[89]

---

86 Adul Rabi Arab, 'En torno al resurgir del Islam. Aspecto de la civilización que se impone en Marruecos', *Aberri* (newspaper), 12 July 1923, p. 3.

87 Adul Rabi Arab, 'En torno al resurgir del Islam', *Aberri* (newspaper), 2 August 1923, p. 8.

88 Adul Rabi Arab, 'En torno al resurgir del Islam', p. 8.

89 Adul Rabi Arab, 'En torno al resurgir del Islam. Los errores de la política española en Marruecos', *Aberri* (newspaper), 24 August 1923, p. 8.

This article blatantly presented the Riffians as inferior, childlike and clearly different from their superior western antagonist. This illustrates how Basques (who perceived themselves as being colonised) regarded the non-western subject and adopted the lenses of the coloniser when doing so. Of course, this should not be overlooked as it indicates that Basque nationalists considered whiteness to be a sign of superiority: whilst Ireland was considered as a perfect and desirable role model to follow, the Riffians were only allies given the circumstances and a shared enemy.

The Triple Alliance of 1923:
An International Insurrection System against Colonialism

In the summer of 1923, Spain was experiencing a deep political, social and moral crisis and was using most of its resources to fight against Abd el-Krim's army. Spain could not have faced another war. Seeing the situation in Morocco and elsewhere in the peninsula, the Aberrianos knew that it was the right moment to act: Spain was on the verge of collapsing, and the Basques were not willing to sink with it. They had two options: 'to resign and die, or to rise up violently and to shake off the oppression, achieving the [nationalist] ideal'.[90] Basque radical nationalists would have been aware that they could not do this alone. With this in mind, and taking advantage of Spain's delicate situation, on 11 September 1923 Basque, Galician and Catalan nationalists met in Barcelona to sign a pluri-national alliance that aimed to achieve independence collectively from the Spanish state. Inspired by both the Irish and Riffian examples, Basque radicals were aware that 'in decisive situations, enslaved nations should give aid and warmth to each other in order to make sacrifice fruitful'.[91] The so-called Triple Alianza (Triple Alliance: henceforth TA) of 1923, which, to the dismay of Basque radicals, did not include the Riffian rebels, perfectly illustrates Basque radical anticolonial thought.

Before that summer, Basque radicals had barely established significant links with Galician nationalists, whilst contacts with Catalonia had mostly involved the CNV and the Lliga Regionalista.[92] This time, the contacts

90 Iker, '¡Alertas, mendigoxales!', p. 3.
91 Gudari, 'La guerra para la paz. Triple Alianza. Catalunya – Galicia – Euzkadi', *Aberri* (newspaper), 15 July 1923, p. 1.
92 For an extensive examination of Basque-Catalan relationships from 1890 to 1936 see Enric Ucelay-Da Cal, 'Política de fuera, política casera: Una valoración de la relación entre nacionalistas catalanes y vascos. 1923–1936', in Manuel Tuñón de Lara (ed.), *Gernika: 50 años después (1937–1987): nacionalismo, república, guerra civil: VI Cursos de Verano en San Sebastián=VI. Udako Ikastaroak Donostian*

were led mostly by the radical branches of each movement, all of which had experienced a period of maturation and radicalisation in recent years. Whilst in Euskadi, the PNV-*Aberri* represented the radical strand of Basque nationalism, two Catalonian parties emerged in 1922 that would establish important contacts with Basque nationalists in the following years. These were Acció Catalana (Catalan Action: henceforth AC), formed by young and recently radicalised sectors which split from the Lliga Regionalista in 1922, and the pro-arms and pro-independence party Estat Català (Catalan State: henceforth EC), founded by Catalan independentist leader Francesc Macià. On the other side of the country, the Galician nationalist movement also underwent a period of development and growth. After a period of paralysis, Galician regionalism reappeared when the first Irmandades da Fala (Language Brotherhoods), described by Helena Miguélez-Carballeira as 'a series of cultural associations with a political vocation' – were formed in 1916.[93] The same year that AC and EC were formed, a new nationalist association named the Irmandade Nazonalista Galega (Galician Nationalist Brotherhood) was established.

One of the biggest advocates of the alliance, Gallastegi, had already warned in an article published in June 1923 that 'either from the east or from the west, one day a breath of life will arrive'.[94] This 'breath of life', which was a subtle but revolutionary call against Spanish imperialism, materialised in September 1923, but the preparations for the meeting to sign the alliance had taken place during the summer of that same year. The first call for the formation of the Triple Alliance came from AC. On 8 July 1923, AC's newspaper *La Publicitat* (The Advert) launched this idea, calling for an international alliance that would take advantage of the favourable situation created by Spain's crisis.[95] *Aberri* newspaper immediately backed

---

(San Sebastián: Universidad del País Vasco, 1987), pp. 71–97; Ugalde, *La acción exterior del nacionalismo vasco*; José Luis de la Granja, 'Las alianzas políticas entre los nacionalismos periféricos en la España del siglo XX', *Studia historica. Historia contemporánea*, 18 (2000), pp. 149–75, which also considers the relationships with Galician nationalists; Ludger Mees, 'Tan lejos, tan cerca. El gobierno vasco en Barcelona y las complejas relaciones entre el nacionalismo vasco y el catalán', *Historia Contemporánea*, 37 (2008), pp. 557–91; Ugalde and Ucelay-Da Cal, 'Una alianza en potencia en un contexto más amplio'.

93 Helena Miguélez-Carballeira, *Galicia, A Sentimental Nation: Gender, Culture and Politics* (Cardiff: University of Wales Press, 2013), p. 61.

94 Gudari, 'El proceso de Berenguer', p. 1.

95 See original text by *La Publicitat* in Xosé Estévez, *De la Triple Alianza al pacto de San Sebastián (1923–1930): Antecedentes del Galeuzca* (San Sebastián: Universidad de Deusto, 1991), p. 365. Estévez's book is the most complete study of the Triple Alliance of 1923 to date.

La Publicitat's idea and reproduced the Catalan newspaper's call in its pages two days later. This text included an editor's note that confirmed the PNV-*Aberri*'s willingness to have a dialogue and form an alliance with Catalan (and Galician) separatists in order to 'find the way to reach a serious agreement that is able to bring forward the time of our liberation'.[96] From that moment, *Aberri* devoted daily articles to the TA and promoted AC's ideology by reproducing *La Publicitat*'s articles and by writing about Catalan radicalism.[97] *Aberri* was openly enthusiastic about the AC's petition to construct an organisation that sought to 'favour the aspirations of these three peoples subjected by the same oppressor'.[98]

Throughout the summer, other nationalist groups also joined the alliance, including EC and Unió Catalanista (Catalanist Union) in Catalonia, Irmandades da Fala and Irmandade Nazonalista Galega in Galicia, and groups of Valencian nationalists. *Aberri* welcomed this with enthusiasm and went further than the other members of the TA, advocating for the union of the Riffians to the alliance, an idea that as we will see was rejected by other members.[99] This enthusiasm was not unanimously shared in Euskadi and, unlike the PNV-*Aberri*, the CNV had reservations about the treaty. In fact, although the latter attended the meetings that preceded the alliance signing in Barcelona, it ultimately decided not to join. Indeed, like its Catalan counterpart, La Lliga Regionalista, the CNV did not share the radicalism of the alliance. This exposed, once again, the existing divisions between the two Basque organisations.[100]

After months of planning, representatives from Euskadi, Galicia and Catalonia met in September 1923 in Barcelona. The chosen date for the first meeting was highly symbolic, as the delegates of the three nationalities met on 11 September, Catalonia's National Day (commonly known as *La Diada*), which commemorates the fall of Barcelona during the War of the Spanish Succession in 1714 and the consequent move to a more centralised

---

96 Editor's Note, 'Noticias de la Península', *Aberri* (newspaper), 10 July 1923, p. 1.
97 Articles on Catalan nationalism were usually written by *Aberri*'s Catalan reporter, who wrote under the alias of C. de Sandazay.
98 Gudari, 'La guerra para la paz', p. 1.
99 *Aberri* also hinted a desire to integrate Portugal in the Triple Alliance: 'we all know that Spain borders with Euskadi in the north, with Catalonia in the east, with Morocco in the south and with Portugal in the west'. Editor's Note in 'Nacionalismos peninsulares. Camino del triunfo', *Aberri* (newspaper), 5 August 1923, p. 1.
100 De la Granja, 'Las alianzas políticas entre los nacionalismos periféricos en la España del siglo XX', p. 154. De la Granja argues that the differences between AC and EC also manifested during the signature of the alliance, as the moderate sector of AC did not embrace independentism.

political structure in Spain. That day, delegates from Basque, Galician and Catalan nationalist organisations paid tribute to the Catalan martyr Rafael Casanova, who had fought against the Spanish Bourbon forces during the War of the Spanish Succession.[101] During this homage, which had been planned for months, the Spanish police forces surprised the nationalists and attacked them brutally.

Despite this act of repression, which saw many nationalists injured and arrested, the representatives of the three nationalities were able to sign the TA. The meeting resulted in a text titled 'friendship pact and alliance between the patriots of Catalonia, Euskadi and Galicia', which was highly radical and contained allusions to armed struggle.[102] The pact aimed to create an 'alliance for the joint action and mutual assistance in the campaign for the national freedom of the three nations'.[103] The text also stated that the 'regime imposed by the Spanish state in Catalonia, Euskadi and Galicia, is a fruit of past violence and present extortions' and, alluding to the Wilsonian principles, protested that the three signatory nations were still not free despite the new situation created by a 'reconstructed Europe according to the principle of freedom of the large and small nations' following the First World War.[104] The outcome of this pact was, however, extremely brief. Two days after it was signed, Spanish nationalist Miguel Primo de Rivera led a coup d'état that resulted in a seven-year-long dictatorship. Indeed, as Xosé Estévez argues, the TA was the perfect pretext for Primo de Rivera's Spanish nationalist and anti-separatist coup, which was brought forward two days.[105]

The ephemeral experience of the first alliance that united the three peripheral nationalist movements in Spain, as well as its 'utopian' and 'purely symbolic' nature, has led scholars to downplay the importance of the TA.[106] Yet whether it was a complete or a partial failure, analysing how

---

101 This included the PNV-*Aberri* (with a delegation that included Gallastegi) and the CNV, *Irmandade Nazonalista Galega, Irmandes da Fala*, AC, EC, *Unió Catalanista*. Apart from the CNV, all these organisations signed the TA on 11 September.
102 La Triple Alianza, 'La Triple Alianza 11-9-1923', 1923, *Galeusca Historia* (in Catalan in the original).
103 La Triple Alianza, 'La Triple Alianza'.
104 La Triple Alianza, 'La Triple Alianza'.
105 Xosé Estévez, 'El Galeuzca histórico: la búsqueda trinacional de la soberanía (1923–1959)', *Hermes*, 29 (2009), pp. 72–83 (p. 73). See also Estévez, *De la Triple Alianza al pacto de San Sebastián*, pp. 339–443.
106 This vision was set by the first studies on contacts between peripheral nationalist movements in Spain. Scholars such as Anna Sallés and Ucelay-Da Cal present the pact negatively: as rushed, ill-thought-out and the product of blind enthusiasm. For instance, they classified the TA as a 'boastful' pact which, despite proclaiming self-determination as a goal, did not specify how to achieve

Basque radicals conceived of the alliance is essential to understanding the nature of Basque anticolonialism in the 1920s. The ideas that emerged in *Aberri* about the alliance serve to illustrate how Basque radicals imagined their struggle in a period of anticolonial upheaval, an imagining that was shaped by the international events that took place in the decade. These events led Basque radicals to imagine themselves as part of a global struggle against imperialism. In Basques' eyes, this struggle against imperialism could be won only through international cooperation and sacrifice. The fact that the Aberrianos attempted to transform what was originally conceived as a nationalist pact into an international anticolonial alliance by integrating the Riffians, as well as the violent allusions in *Aberri*'s texts (which were reflected in the TA's first draft), reinforces such a view. These ideas, I argue, would remain part of the Basque radical imagination.

It is no coincidence that the concept of an international multinational alliance appeared in a period of anticolonial upheaval around the globe. As mentioned above, during the late 1910s and early 1920s, Irish

---

it. Overall, they argue that connections between Basque and Catalan nationalism have always been superficial. Anna Sallés and Enric Ucelay-Da Cal, 'L'analogia falsa. El nacionalisme basc davant de la República Catalana i la Generalitat provisional, abril-juliol del 1931', in Manuel González Portilla, Jordi Maluquer de Motes and Borja de Riquer (eds), *Industrialización y nacionalismo: análisis comparativo: Actas del I Coloquio Vasco-Catalán de Historia* (Barcelona: Universidad Autónoma de Barcelona, 1985), pp. 443–70 (p. 445). Ucelay also described the pact as 'fanciful' or unrealistic. See Ucelay Da Cal, 'Política de fuera, política casera', p. 80. This vision coincides with that of de la Granja who has argued that the TA had no practical repercussions and that no one had interest in reviving the organisation after Primo de Rivera's dictatorship. See de la Granja, 'Las alianzas políticas entre los nacionalismos periféricos', p. 155. Mees is also of the opinion that the signature of the TA was mainly of a 'symbolic' nature because of its short life span. See Mees, 'Tan lejos, tan cerca', p. 564. Some scholars have been slightly more positive. In one of the first studies of the Triple Alliance, Margarita Otaegui recognised its legacy when pointing out that the TA meant the start of important relationships between sub-state nationalist movements and that similar pacts were established again after Primo's dictatorship. Yet the same author also claimed that it did not have any important political repercussions and that its nature was more 'testimonial' than 'political'. See Margarita Otaegui Arizmendi, 'La Triple Alianza de 1923', in González Portilla, Maluquer de Motes and de Riquer (eds), *Industrialización y nacionalismo*, pp. 431–42 (pp. 431–32 and p. 439). Despite its lack of political impact, Xosé Estévez agrees with Otaegui when suggesting that 1923 marked the start of formal contacts between Spain's peripheral nationalist movements. The TA became, as Estévez argues, a 'symbolic milestone' in the new contacts between Catalonia, Euskadi and Galicia. See Estévez, *De la Triple Alianza al pacto de San Sebastián*, p. 444 and Estévez, 'El Galeuzca histórico'. For a summary of the tri-national relationships that followed the TA see Estévez, *De la Triple Alianza al pacto de San Sebastián*, pp. 444–55 and p. 458.

nationalists had established direct contacts and united forces with other disaffected nationalist groups within the British Empire, seeking to form an international revolutionary movement of insurrection.[107] Nationalists across the British Empire had to put aside their differences to form part of this wider anticolonial movement, which united them against a common enemy. As an editorial of an Indian nationalist periodical based in San Francisco declared in 1920, 'the world must be made to feel that the struggle of Ireland is not isolated. The same tyranny and the same trampling of human rights are going on everywhere – in India, Egypt, Persia, China and other countries.'[108] Egypt and India were, as M. C. Rast argues, Ireland's sister nations.[109] Having seen the immense influence that Ireland had on the Basque movement and considering that the Aberrianos believed that like the Irish, Egyptians and Indians, the Basques were also victims of colonialism, one could assume that Basque radicals conceived of the Triple Alliance as an international organisation that sought to defeat Spanish colonialism collectively.[110]

Whilst less was said about the Egyptian and Indian struggles, the influence that the Irish international struggle had on the members of the Triple Alliance was significant. Ultimately, the Irish struggle had influenced and inspired all three nationalist movements that signed the TA separately and it is certain that the signatories were aware of Ireland's international insurrection. In August 1923, *Aberri* drew attention to a three-page article in the publication *Estat Català* devoted entirely to the TA. *Aberri* reported that this article reproduced a letter written by Galician nationalists that described their desire for freedom and argued that their 'sister' Ireland gave them a 'shining example'.[111] *Aberri* clearly had the Irish struggle in mind when imagining the future alliance. An article published in *Aberri* days before the signature of the alliance titled 'Ejemplos a seguir. Irlanda y nosotros' ('Examples to follow. Ireland and us') demonstrates this, as it claimed:

> We have to imitate the Irish ... England, despite its strength, is not able to defeat young Ireland. Do you believe that Spain, an inferior nation in every single way compared to England [note the residual Anglophilia],

---

107 M. C. Rast, '"Ireland's Sister Nations"', pp. 482–83.
108 Quoted in M. C. Rast, '"Ireland's Sister Nations"', p. 485.
109 M. C. Rast, '"Ireland's Sister Nations"'.
110 The international dimension of the TA has been stressed by most scholars. In particular, Ugalde recounts how Gallastegi appealed to the international nature of the treaty in *Aberri*. See Ugalde, *La acción exterior del nacionalismo vasco*, p. 310. AC also agreed with this international vision.
111 Anon., 'Nacionalismos peninsulares', *Aberri* (newspaper), 4 August 1923, p. 1.

would manage to defeat them [the Irish]? No way. Well then, if Spain could never defeat Ireland, let's be like that Ireland, let's imitate the Irish and the triumph will be ours. The Triple [Alliance] is a glimmer of hope which will be transformed in reality.[112]

The timing of this global insurrection against Spain could not be better. Gallastegi was aware of the advantages of the TA's formation in this context: considering 'the weakness and disorientation of Spain' caused by the war in Morocco, 'the strength of this growing international organisation could emerge'.[113] Indeed, given the timing, Abd el-Krim's struggle was also considered as an example to follow by the Aberrianos when envisaging the alliance. As Gallastegi argued in 1923, 'the Moors had proved their patriotism, their strength and their heroism again [when fighting against Spain], which we will make sure is going to be imitated by the Basque youth'.[114]

Certainly, this idea of emulating the Riffian (and of course the Irish) example, is what made *Aberri* conclude that the way to defeat Spain was through blood and sacrifice. This was expressed on many occasions in *Aberri*. As an article in Euskera in June 1923 said, 'we won't stop until we see our homeland free. There are two ways to achieve this: to trick our enemy or to leave aside the law and turn to arms.'[115] Another article advocated for the second option: 'the homeland will not be free until it is dyed red with the generous blood of the favoured sons of the homeland, the *mendigoxales*.'[116] These ideas expressed in *Aberri* were also reflected in the pact of the Triple Alliance. The first draft argued that considering the desperate situation, it was necessary 'to unite forces in the struggle and, if necessary, mix blood with sacrifice', although this was removed from the final version.[117] The (theoretical) embracement of violence implied a clear evolution and deviation from Sabino Arana's thought. As Watson argues, 'with much caution ... Basque nationalists had taken an important ideological step from Arana's pure imagining to a clear *aberriano* rhetoric of actual future struggle'.[118]

---

112 Bingen, 'Ejemplos a seguir. Irlanda y nosotros', *Aberri* (newspaper), 9 September 1923, p. 6.
113 Gudari, 'Ante la nueva tragedia. La primera preocupación de la Triple Alianza. ¡Abajo la guerra!', *Aberri* (newspaper), 31 July 1923, p. 1.
114 Gudari, 'Agitación. ¡Aunque no quede rastro de nuestro paso ... !', *Aberri* (newspaper), 23 August 1923, p. 1.
115 Bitxaña, '¿Azkatu lei Aberija?', *Aberri* (newspaper), 7 June 1923, p. 4. In Euskera in the original. Translated for the author by Echanojauregui Ripa.
116 S. Tar. I., 'Ideal y sacrificio', *Aberri* (newspaper), 22 July 1923, p. 8.
117 La Triple Alianza, 'La Triple Alianza'.
118 Watson, *Basque Nationalism and Political Violence*, p. 126.

Embracing armed resistance as a method to overcome oppression also brought together (at least rhetorically) the Riffian and the sub-state nationalist movements in Spain. Motivated by the Riffian example and convinced of the parallels between their movements, Basque radicals went further than their Catalan and Galician counterparts and advocated expanding the alliance to bring in a 'new and shining light from the most remote southern land'.[119] With this remark, Gallastegi was calling for the addition of the Riffians to form a 'Quadruple Alliance'.[120] The alliance, Basque radicals believed, had to go beyond peninsular borders and unite all the victims of Spanish colonialism. This proposition was not out of order considering that according to *Aberri*, the Basques – and therefore all the members of the TA – were suffering the same colonial oppression as the Riffians.

Although this proposition was ignored by the other members, the Riffian and the TA struggle became intertwined in *Aberri*. The newspaper claimed that one of the main priorities of the alliance was to end the Moroccan War: 'we [the nationalists of the TA] are enemies of every kind of occupation, protectorate or conquest, and we are even more opposed to a foreign war'.[121] In an article published a week before the signature of the TA, Gallastegi explained that despite the Spanish Protectorate of Morocco having less than half the population of Euskadi, it had managed to challenge Spain's power. After citing the respective numbers of Spanish and Riffian soldiers, he stated:

> if Morocco is able to do this with this army and this number of inhabitants, what can we expect from the Triple Alliance which will be constituted by three nations with eight million subjects? And [by nations] that have people who do not accept to live enslaved; people willing to give their lives for the freedom of the homeland.[122]

It is unsurprising that the Aberrianos assumed that if the Riffians, seen patronisingly as inhabitants of a 'poor and small nation', could cause problems for Spain, then an alliance of so-called advanced nations could deal a fatal blow to Spanish colonialism.[123] Indeed, the Riffians were only the perfect allies owing to the timing, and prejudice against them among

---

119 Gudari, 'La guerra para la paz', p. 1.
120 As it says at the end of the text: 'this way, the Quadruple Alliance would be created'. Gudari, 'La guerra para la paz', p. 1.
121 Gudari, 'Ante la nueva tragedia', p. 1.
122 Gudari, 'Un poder formidable. ¿Qué será la Triple Alianza?', *Aberri* (newspaper), 6 September 1923, p. 1.
123 Editor's Note, 'Información del extranjero. Marruecos', *Aberri* (newspaper), 15 July 1923, p. 1.

Basques did not disappear. Despite aiming to incorporate them into the alliance, the Aberrianos (much like their Catalan and Galician counterparts, who turned a blind eye to the idea of an extra-European alliance) regarded the Riffians as respectable but uncivilised (and therefore different to their western and civilised selves).[124]

All in all, *Aberri*'s idea of an alliance that united both European and extra-European movements marked a turning point in Basque anticolonialism. In fact, this project inspired the establishment of the Liga de las Naciones Oprimidas (League of the Oppressed Nations) of 1924, which tried to bring European and extra-European nations together to combat colonialism. Furthermore, despite the short-lived experience of the TA, it inaugurated the start of a series of direct links, agreements and alliances between the three main peripheral nationalist movements within the Spanish state. Indeed, the ideas that emerged through the alliance were never forgotten by Basque radical nationalists, who continually alluded to the TA and dreamed of a similar pact that would be able to destroy the Spanish state. Thus, the brief but intense history of the TA of 1923 cannot be cast as a complete failure. The alliance attempted to put into practice important doctrinal, rhetorical and theoretical aspects of Basque anticolonial nationalism, including ideas of violent sacrifice and international solidarity. These ideas were to have a deep and long-term effect on the imagination of Basque radicals.

Conclusion

The period of generalised euphoria and upheaval that different colonised and stateless peoples around the world experienced during the 1920s also affected Euskadi. Between 1921 and 1923, Basque radicals situated themselves within a global insurrection against colonialism, established contacts with other nations and appropriated ideas to their movement that had originally emerged in a colonial context. These ideas included allusions to violence and international solidarity, which were increasingly associated with forms of anticolonial resistance. The legacy of these ideas was never forgotten, and subsequent years saw the forging of different international alliances that sought to defeat colonialism.

Examining the anticolonial rhetoric that the Aberrianos used during this period confirms the shift that such ideas experienced during the

---

124 Interestingly, Dalmau briefly considers the rejection of a collaboration with Abd el-Krim by Catalan nationalists (which as he argued, had strong paternalistic views on the Riffians) as a final 'manifestation of the limits of internationalism'. See Dalmau, 'Catalans and Rifis during the Wilsonian Moment', p. 144.

Wilsonian moment. Unlike Sabino Arana and his immediate successors, this generation of radical nationalists portrayed colonialism as an inherently evil phenomenon regardless of who was the coloniser and who the colonised. This implied the end of the Anglophilia that had traditionally dominated the movement since its emergence. Yet despite Basque radicals' condemnation of all forms of colonialism and comparison of their struggle with those of non-European communities, this did not alter the racism and Orientalism that shaped their rhetoric. This suggests that the appropriation of a global anticolonial rhetoric was part of a political strategy rather than a colour-blind commitment to all national liberation struggles. Indeed, from the early 1920s Basque anticolonialism had two defined goals: the internationalisation of the movement and the legitimation of its own independence claims.

CHAPTER FIVE

Insurgency, Radicalism and Internationalism during Miguel Primo de Rivera's Dictatorship (1923–1930)

Between 1917 and 1923, the outdated Restoration system experienced one of its biggest crises since the '98 Disaster. The system was constantly challenged by social, military and political agitation, continual criticism from the public and increasing regionalist and nationalist demands. The humiliating defeat that Spain experienced after the Battle of Annual in 1921, as well as the crisis that the debate over those responsible generated, further positioned Spain as a state that desperately needed a military victory to prove its power both internally and internationally. As Julián Casanova and Carlos Gil Andrés have pointed out, 'the regime was in ruins, under attack from the outside and undermined from within, and nobody supported it when Primo de Rivera overthrew it in September 1923'.[1] Less than 48 hours after the signature of the Triple Alianza, Captain General Miguel Primo de Rivera issued a manifesto calling for a change of government. This marked the start of Spain's first dictatorship in the twentieth century.

Upon his arrival to power, the dictator proclaimed himself the 'saviour' of a nation that had been considered gravely ill since the Disaster of 1898. To 'cure' the nation, Primo believed, he had to eradicate two of the biggest perils of the state: colonial insurgency in Morocco and peripheral nationalist movements within Spain. At an international level, Primo was aware that the success of his regime partly depended on how he dealt with the Moroccan question.[2] Although Primo had initially advocated for a strategy of semi-abandonment in Morocco, he eventually led a successful campaign with France in 1925, which resulted in Abd el-Krim's surrender. Meanwhile at a national level, Primo needed to eradicate the nationalist threat. As Alejandro Quiroga points out, 'peripheral nationalism constituted the negative pole in the *primorriverista* conception of Spain', the "internal enemy"

---

1 Casanova and Gil Andrés, *Twentieth-Century Spain*, p. 78.
2 Alejandro Quiroga, *Miguel Primo de Rivera: Dictadura, populismo y nación* (Barcelona: Crítica, 2022), p. 119.

aiming to destroy the sacred union of Spain'.[3] Primo's obsession with the consolidation of a united Spain led him to carry out a harsh campaign based on the persecution of any sign of nationalism or regionalism, as well as a parallel one of 'Hispanicisation'. Although Primo's repression was much harsher in Catalonia than in Euskadi, the repression of Basque nationalism during the dictatorship forced Basques to move their activities abroad. This explains why this period has generated scarce attention in historiography and has been traditionally classified by some scholars, such as Ugalde, as 'years of transition' in terms of the Basque nationalist external activity from the previous dynamic years (1918–1923) to the proclamation of the Second Republic in 1931.[4]

This chapter seeks to contribute to the limited literature on Basque nationalism under Primo's dictatorship and argues that far from being a period of transition, the years between 1923 and 1930 were a period of activity and dynamism for Basque radicals who managed to go into exile. During Primo's dictatorship, Basque radicals reinforced and radicalised their anticolonial repertoire and established direct contacts with other groups from their new homes. Radical nationalists like Gallastegi, who spent some valuable time in France and Mexico, were able to experience firsthand the atmosphere lived in cities that became centres of anticolonial thought and intellectual exchange during the interwar period. The repression of an anti-separatist dictatorship that had forced many Basques out of their homes as well as the contacts established with both western and non-western movements in Paris, New York or Mexico taught Basques valuable experiences, which were never forgotten. Basques were part (or at least, so Basque radicals thought) of the many anticolonial movements that, disappointed with the outcomes of the First World War, conspired against empires both from the very centre of the metropole and beyond.

New Spaces, New Opportunities:
Basque Radical Nationalism during Spain's First Dictatorship

Before Primo's ascension to power, Spanish intellectuals such as Joaquín Costa, who believed that Spain was 'ill' and needed to be 'cured', had demanded an 'iron surgeon' who would lead the national revolution and

3 Alejandro Quiroga, *Making Spaniards: Primo de Rivera and the Nationalization of the Masses, 1923–30* (Basingstoke: Palgrave Macmillan, 2007), p. 49.

4 Ugalde, *La acción exterior del nacionalismo vasco*, p. 378. Quiroga argues that despite the great advances in the field in the last years, Primo de Rivera's dictatorship remains (as of 2022) the least studied period of twentieth-century Spain. Quiroga, *Miguel Primo de Rivera*, p. 12.

operate on the 'sick body' of Spain from above.⁵ Upon taking power in September 1923, Primo portrayed himself as the iron surgeon Costa had demanded. One of the ways to cure Spain was by eradicating its 'internal enemy'. The urgency of eradication is evidenced in the 'Real Decreto sobre el separatismo' ('Royal Decree about separatism'), issued on 18 September 1923, only five days after Primo's coup. Using medicalised metaphors and engaging with late nineteenth-century 'regenerationist' discourse, this decree referred to separatism as a 'virus'.⁶ According to the decree, only the Spanish flag could be flown and the only language to be spoken in official events was Spanish. Furthermore, prison sentences would also be imposed for disseminating separatist ideas.⁷ Thus, most existing cultural or nationalist associations, as well as newsletters, were closed or banned.

Amongst Primo's 'internal enemies', Catalonia was a serious preoccupation. As such, his regime led an indiscriminate campaign against Catalan nationalists in the months following his arrival to power. In contrast, in Euskadi the regime was usually 'lenient and pragmatic' as far as the use of regional languages was concerned and during the dictatorship certain publications in Euskera and moderate Basque nationalist activities were allowed.⁸ For instance, the moderate Basque publication *Euzkadi* was able to carry on publishing under Primo's dictatorship. Quiroga attributes one of the main reasons for this approach towards the Basque provinces to the 'relative willingness of the Basque Church to co-operate with the Dictatorship', which contrasted with that of the Catalan Church.⁹ This led to the radicalisation of sectors of the Catalan population, including its clergy.

This is not to say that the Basques were not punished by Primo. Despite being able to carry on publishing, *Euzkadi* was subject to censorship and, like any other pro-nationalist publication of the period, had to adapt its content and omit any references to national politics or any nationalist activity in Spain.¹⁰ Additionally, the CNV had to distance itself from political activity

---

5 Quiroga, *Making Spaniards*, pp. 16–17.
6 Miguel Primo de Rivera, 'Real decreto dictando medidas y sanciones contra el separatismo', 18 September 1923.
7 Primo de Rivera, 'Real decreto dictando medidas y sanciones contra el separatismo'.
8 Quiroga, *Making Spaniards*, p. 136.
9 Quiroga, *Making Spaniards*, p. 136 and Quiroga, *Miguel Primo de Rivera*, p. 225.
10 Óscar Álvarez Gila and José María Tápiz argue that owing to the new situation, the 'pseudo-nationalist' publications that were able to survive were forced to replace their content with articles that informed readers of the activities that nationalists were undertaking from America. See Óscar Álvarez Gila and José María Tápiz

and focused on religious and cultural activities instead.[11] The dictatorship was significantly harsher with Basque radical nationalists owing to both their radicalism and their direct opposition to the dictatorship: the PNV-*Aberri* was outlawed, and its centres and organisations were forced to close their doors. This included the closure of the main organisation within the PNV-*Aberri*: the JVB, which during the mid-1910s had managed to become Bilbao's most important political-cultural centre.[12] Whilst in 1923 the JVB had over 1,000 members, in 1930 it only had 348 'loyal members' left.[13] Organisations that were born out of the JVB, such as the EAB, were also closed. Repression also affected the Basque radical press. The newspaper *Aberri* published its final issue days after Primo's coup and its successor *Diario Vasco* (Basque Newspaper) was only able to survive for a month (from October to November 1923). The fact that unlike *Aberri*, its successor *Diario Vasco* had a Spanish name reveals an already noticeable fear of censorship and repression in the early months of the dictatorship.

Imprisonment was also a threat to Basque nationalists, and the source of many 'martyrs'. It is difficult to estimate how many Basque nationalists were imprisoned during Primo's dictatorship, although some Aberriano sources suggest that in 1925 around 50 Basques were in Spanish prisons for their 'rebellious offences' and that by 1928 around 100 Basques had experienced 'persecution, exile or jail'.[14] Whilst it is impossible to know if this number is reliable or was exaggerated, what is certain is that the new dictatorial regime changed the conditions for the development of Basque nationalism.

Those who stayed in Euskadi had to find ways to resume their activities without raising suspicion. The *mendigoxales*, supposedly mountaineers who went on long treks, were the perfect candidates to do this and continued their propaganda activities in rural areas, celebrating clandestine reunions and gatherings. Others were able to go into exile. For instance, Gallastegi – who had been arrested during his stag party, which had turned into a nationalist and anti-Primo event – had to take refuge first in France and later in Mexico, where he arrived in early 1927. Other radical leaders found refuge in Paris

Fernández, 'Prensa nacionalista vasca y emigración a América (1900–1936)', *Anuario de Estudios Americanos*, 1 (1996), pp. 233–60 (p. 243).

11 For instance, the yearly masses and events that commemorated Sabino Arana's death became a popular place where nationalists convened.

12 De Pablo and Mees suggest that despite the closure of the JVB, it seems that the organisation managed to have some activity during the dictatorship. The authors claim that this limited activity probably consisted of meetings in cafés in Bilbao. De Pablo and Mees, *El péndulo patriótico*, p. 99.

13 De Pablo and Mees, *El péndulo patriótico*, p. 99.

14 De Pablo and Mees, *El péndulo patriótico*, p. 99.

and other parts of France, the US and different countries in Latin America, where well-established communities of Basque nationalists had existed before 1923. From their new homes, Basque nationalists established direct contacts with other groups of Catalan, Irish and Latin American nationalists and resumed their propagandistic activity, evidenced by the New York-based newsletter *Aberri* (1925–1928) and the Mexican-based magazine *Patria Vasca* ('Basque Homeland', coordinated by Gallastegi from Torreón in 1928–1930).[15]

As I demonstrate in this chapter, Basque radicals were able to internationalise their struggle and gain visibility whilst in exile. International recognition was one of the main aims of the Comité Pro-Independencia Vasca (Basque Pro-Independence Committee), created by Gallastegi in San Juan de la Luz, a town in the French Basque Country. This new organisation, which aimed to promote the Basque separatist cause internationally, successfully established delegations in France, Catalonia and the US. The Comité was associated with Gallastegi's Ejército de Voluntarios Vascos (Basque Volunteer Army), created in 1925 and influenced directly by his role models, Sinn Féin and the IRA.[16]

Furthermore, from exile, the Aberrianos were able to conspire directly against the dictatorship. This differed much from the CNV's stance, which underwent a period of passivity and crisis during Primo's dictatorship. The Aberrianos conspired alongside Catalan radicals such as Macià and EC co-founder Daniel Cardona (also known as 'el irlandés', the Irish, owing to his devotion to the Irish struggle), both of whom also found refuge in the French capital.[17] Macià, who was the main head of these complots, discussed his plans with the Aberrianos directly and sought their support. This collaboration resulted in the Pacto de la Libre Alianza (Agreement of the Free Alliance), signed in Paris in January 1925.[18] This pact, brought together the

---

15 *Patria Vasca* published a total of six issues. Whilst the first five (1928–1930) were published from Mexico, the sixth issue was published in 1932 from Bilbao, as Gallastegi had already returned to Euskadi.

16 The only practical effect of this 'army' was the publication of violent texts in its own periodical, *Lenago il* (Rather Death).

17 Despite their radicalism, Macià and Cardona had important ideological differences. In fact, Macià – who was wary of his power being dismissed by Cardona – managed to isolate Cardona and consolidate his power in exile. See Ugalde and Ucelay, 'Una alianza en potencia en un contexto más amplio', p. 404.

18 Macià was not only the intellectual head of the complot, but he was also in charge of finding funding for the plan. Fernández Soldevilla, who claims that the Basque participation in the conspiracies organised by Macià was mostly from the sidelines, argues that whilst Catalan radicals were preparing an insurrection against the dictator, a PNV-*Aberri* delegate offered them a contribution of 300 men to lead an insurrectional movement against Primo. Pretending to make a pilgrimage to Lourdes, these men would cross the French border to acquire weapons and would

PNV-*Aberri*, the EC and Spain's anarchist union the Confederación Nacional del Trabajo (National Confederation of Labour) and established that the agreed method against Spain's regime was an 'armed and violent uprising ... [which was the] only worthy method against those used so far in politics'.[19] This new alliance had no practical success but Macià, convinced of the feasibility of a joint armed uprising, did not give up and travelled to Moscow personally to negotiate a new agreement with the Soviets. Macià was able to sign a pact with the Communists known as the Pacto de Moscú (Moscow Agreement) of November 1925, with the hope the Basque radicals would also join in. Yet the PNV-*Aberri* opted out: the pact had the approval of the Third International and this time the ideological differences went too far. Indeed, unlike Macià, who considered that all groups who wanted to take down the Spanish state were potential allies, Basque radicals were more reticent to form alliances with non-nationalist groups.

Aside from establishing contacts with the Catalans, Basque radicals were also exposed to new ideas in their new homes. During the interwar period, cities such as Paris, New York and Mexico City hosted many exiles across the world, creating a perfect space for intellectual exchange and radicalism. In the case of interwar Paris, where different Basque and Catalan radical nationalists settled, Michael Goebel goes as far as arguing that 'many of those who later took leading roles in the political and intellectual lives of their home countries became politicized during their stay in imperial centers, not before'.[20] This ideological change was facilitated by these individuals' experiences as migrants in the metropole and the networks and contacts they established with other nationalist and anti-imperialist actors, which made 'imperialism no longer look like a series of isolated injustices, but a larger system that had to be addressed as such'.[21] Like Paris and New York, Mexico City was also home to many exiles and refugees across the world. As Thomas Lindner has recently shown, the city became a hub or a laboratory of anti-imperialism in the 1920s

---

return to Bilbao to start the armed insurrection. However, these promises were never taken seriously or fulfilled. Fernández Soldevilla, 'De *Aberri* a ETA', p. 223. For a detailed exploration of these alliances see Estévez, *De la Triple Alianza al pacto de San Sebastián*.

19 Original in Josep Carner-Ribalta and Ramón Fabregat (eds), *Macià: la seva actuació a l'estranger* (México: Edicions Catalanes de Mèxic, 1952), p. 55. In Catalan in the original. The objectives of this pact mixed social and national claims including the defeat of the dictatorship, the freedom of Euskadi and Catalonia, and the improvement of the situation of the working classes.

20 Goebel, *Anti-Imperial Metropolis*, p. 4.

21 Goebel, *Anti-Imperial Metropolis*, pp. 5–6.

(especially between 1925 and 1927).²² Mexico City was recognised as a hub of anti-imperialism internationally: the Communist-sponsored and inspired Liga Antiimperialista de las Américas (also known as the Anti-Imperialist League of the Americas) was founded in Mexico City two years before Gallastegi's arrival in Mexico, combining both international nationalism and anti-imperialism.

Thanks to ideological exchange, the ideas that emerged both in the metropole and the peripheries certainly facilitated the creation of global leagues such as the League Against Imperialism (LAI), created in 1927 as a counter-organisation to the LN. The LAI was formed in Brussels following the convergence of activists (including representatives of communist, socialists and radical nationalist movements) from all over the world in what has been labelled 'the most important anticolonial congress of the interwar period'.²³ The congress brought together 174 delegates from 31 states, colonies or regions and 134 organisations and lasted five days.²⁴ At the end of the conference, the delegates decided to continue their work through a new organisation, the LAI, which would exist for ten years and be based in Berlin. Finding common ground amongst such a diverse list of participants from both metropoles and peripheries was not easy: but certainly, apart from a commitment to fight imperialism (whatever that meant), most delegates shared a similar critical view of the LN.²⁵ As I demonstrate below, Basque radicals developed similar ideas to the LAI.

---

22 Lindner, *A City Against Empire*.

23 Daniel Brückenhaus, *Policing Transnational Protest: Liberal Imperialism and the Surveillance of Anticolonialists in Europe, 1905–1945* (New York: Oxford University Press, 2017), p. 139.

24 Michele Louro, Carolien Stolte, Heather Streets-Salter and Sana Tannoury-Karam, 'The League Against Imperialism: Lives and Afterlives', in Louro, Stolte, Streets-Salter and Tannoury-Karam (eds), *The League Against Imperialism: Lives and Afterlives* (Leiden: Leiden University Press, 2020), pp. 17–51 (p. 17).

25 Lindner recounts how some attendees, like German writer Ernst Toller, ended their speech hoping that Brussels would lead to the creation of a 'real League of Nations, without masters and servants'. See Lindner, *A City Against Empire*, p. 165. It is worth pointing out that Latin Americans were an exception to the opposition to the LN in the Global South. In fact, unlike other stateless nations, Latin American nations were able to join the LN and they initially did so enthusiastically, hoping that the new organisation would limit or prevent US intervention in the region. These hopes would fizzle out in the next decade, when Latin Americans realised that the LN had ignored their claims. As Alan McPherson claims, 'the LN's failure to address Latin American concerns about occupation spoke to its largely Eurocentric orientation which doomed it as a truly global organization.' See Alan L. McPherson, 'Anti-Imperialism and the Failure of the League of Nations', in Alan L. McPherson and Yannick Wehrli (eds), *Beyond Geopolitics: New Histories of Latin America at the League of Nations* (Albuquerque: University of New Mexico Press, 2015), pp. 21–32 (p. 26).

Indeed, not only non-European exiles benefited from the transmission of ideas in these global cities. The fact that Basque radicals no longer had to fear Spanish censorship in their new homes abroad, alongside the direct influence they received from nationalists and anticolonial leaders, resulted in the development of a highly radical language with constant allusions to armed struggle. Anticolonialism remained an essential element of this rhetoric and continued having the same two aims as before 1923: the defence of independence and the internationalisation of the Basque cause. Indeed, the new dictatorial and repressive context gave Euskadi a more colonial feel to it, which the Aberrianos exploited from abroad when painting the Basque Country as a colony.

Prompted by the national and international context, Basques placed themselves once again in an international war against colonialism in which the oppressed (small nationalities) fought the oppressor (world empires) together, and in which violence and sacrifice were increasingly seen as legitimate methods. As in the period before, this implied that the situation of European movements was equated to that of extra-European ones. *Patria Vasca* stated in its introductory article that it was addressed to 'all the nations of the world, big or small, white or coloured, from one continent to another, that have been able to wake up and free their nation from slavery'.[26] Another article endorsed a definition of nationalism that resonated with the anticolonial liberation movements that dominated the interwar period: 'nationalism is an idea that has emerged in all countries across the globe with a need to end imperialism and strengthen the nationality and respect for every community.'[27]

The increased association with non-western movements saw a progressive rise of explicit anti-racist texts in Basque radical periodicals: 'men, white in Europe, black in Africa, reddish in America' – argued a text by *Aberri* New York – are the same men, coloured, so to speak, by the climate'.[28] Without a doubt, this timid change of attitude can also be explained by their experiences in global cities such as Paris or New York, where for the first time Basques shared spaces with people of all races, ethnicities and religions, who were united in a fraternal struggle against colonialism. As in the previous periods, however, this did not entail the complete abandonment of Orientalist, patronising and racist views. Rather, as this chapter demonstrates, such views were still very much ingrained in the Basque anticolonial corpus; an anticolonialism that continued to be more practical than heartfelt.

26 Patria Vasca, 'Saludo. Invitación. Recuerdo', *Patria Vasca*, May 1928, p. 1.
27 Anon., 'De todo un poco', *Patria Vasca*, June–July 1928, p. 28.
28 Anon., 'Pensamientos', *Aberri* New York, January 1928, p. 8.

Enemies or Allies? The Struggle for International Recognition and the League of Nations

During the 1920s, internationalism became a priority for Basque radicals. Whether through the establishment of direct contacts with similar national liberation groups or the appeal to international organisations such as the LN – which, as we will see, was not exempt from contradictions – Basque radicals aimed to make their movement visible internationally. Basque radicals paid attention to how other movements operated in the interwar period and used every opportunity offered by the new national and international situation. As Núñez Seixas claims, during the interwar period 'most nationalist émigrés searched for support abroad and acted out of strategic pragmatism during their exile'.[29] Basques radicals were no exception.

Forging Direct Contacts: La Liga de las Naciones Oprimidas (1924)

Establishing direct contacts with other nationalist movements had already been a priority in the previous period, as demonstrated by the signature of the 'international' Triple Alianza in September 1923. As Cullen and McCreanor suggest, although the TA never achieved its main aim, 'it was an important precursor for radical Basque–Catalan cooperation in the near future'.[30] Thanks to these previous contacts, during Primo's dictatorship, Basque and Catalan radicals plotted against a common enemy and celebrated many joint acts in exile.[31] Furthermore, the new circumstances in exile allowed Basque radicals to forge links with other movements from outside the peninsula. Núñez Seixas explains how in the interwar period, new groups of ethno-nationalist exiles from Spain, Italy and Ireland appeared and frequently interacted with nationalist activists from India, Vietnam and Indonesia.[32]

As shown above, the French capital became an ideal place to establish networks and exchange ideas. There, Basque and Catalan radicals were able to forge personal contacts with anti-Treaty Irish republicans, who also found a temporary home in Paris during the early 1920s. Among the Irish republicans who were in regular contact with Basques and Catalans in Paris, the figure of Ambrose Victor Martin stands out. Martin resumed

---

29 Xosé Manoel Núñez Seixas, 'Unholy Alliances? Nationalist Exiles, Minorities and Anti-Fascism in Interwar Europe', *Contemporary European History*, 25.4 (2016), pp. 597–617 (p. 616).
30 Cullen and McCreanor, 'Dangerous Friends', p. 1199.
31 The TA was remembered with admiration by exiled Basques. See, for instance, Anay Bat, 'El 11 de Septiembre de 1923', *Aberri* New York, October 1925, p. 1.
32 Núñez Seixas, 'Unholy Alliances?', p. 598.

the contacts he had established with the Aberrianos in the mid-1920s and encouraged Basques and Catalans to lead a violent insurrection against Spain.[33] Naturally, direct contacts were accompanied by words of praise and devotion to the Irish republican struggle and that of other nationalists against the British Empire. The words of emblematic anticolonial leaders such as Roger Casement or Mahatma Gandhi featured in Basque newsletters published in exile.[34] Once again, the will to overcome imperial oppression surpassed national allegiance.

Without a doubt, the Liga de las Naciones Oprimidas (League of the Oppressed Nations: henceforth LdNO) epitomises the Basque radical desire to forge transnational networks with other movements. This new project was originally developed by Basque Youth leader and Aberriano representative Telesforo Uribe-Echevarría, who sent a letter to Macià in February 1924 containing a draft of this new ambitious international alliance.[35] This organisation, which sought to counteract the influence of the LN, brought together nations that had either been subjected or were currently under Spanish and British control including Ireland, India, Egypt, Catalonia, the

33 For an examination of Basque–Catalan–Irish relationships during the dictatorship and the potential Irish involvement in plots to invade Spain see Cullen and McCreanor, 'Dangerous Friends', pp. 1201–03. The authors suggest that some Irish republicans in Paris were aware of the plots to invade Spain, which put the Irish in a tricky situation. Cullen and McCreanor, 'Dangerous Friends', p. 1204. See also Cullen, *Radical Basque Nationalist-Irish Republican Relations*, pp. 56–61.

34 For Ireland see articles such as Tio, 'Instituciones baskas. Su carácter', *Aberri* New York, November 1925, pp. 1–2; Bizkargi, 'Irlanda. Al voltear de las campanas. Pascua Dublinescas de 1916', *Patria Vasca*, May 1928, p. 3 and Roger Casement's quotes in *Patria Vasca* issues 1 (May 1928) and 4 (November–December 1928). For India see Crítica, 'Las grandes inquietudes de los pueblos. La marcha heróica de Mahatma Gandhi', *Patria Vasca*, April 1930, p. 5 and quotes of Mahatma Gandhi in *Patria Vasca* issue 1 and Gandhi's picture in issue 5 (April 1930).

35 Originally, Carner-Ribalta and Fabregat attributed the creation of this international league to Macià. Carner-Ribalta and Fabregat (eds), *Macià: la seva actuació a l'estranger*, p. 51. This idea was later disputed by Estévez, who argued that the LdNO was originally developed by Uribe-Echevarría and that Macià merely appropriated the former's idea. See Estévez, *De la Triple Alianza al pacto de San Sebastián*, p. 469. See also Ugalde and Ucelay-Da Cal, 'Una alianza en potencia en un contexto más amplio', p. 401. I agree with the latter view, as there are articles in *Aberri* before 1923 that already posited the idea of an organisation that resembled the LdNO. For instance, an Editor's Note in *Aberri* (1923) briefly proposed the creation of a 'League of Enslaved Nations' that involved 'all the oppressed peoples', including 'the Triple Alliance and Morocco, Algeria, Egypt, India, Ireland, etc.' to face 'this infernal League of Enslaving Nations'. See Editor's Note, 'Nacionalismos peninsulares. La "Triple Alianza" significa la "alianza de la libertad"', *Aberri* (newspaper), 28 August 1923, p. 1.

Philippines, the Rif Republic and of course, Euskadi.[36] Its delegates were to have occasional meetings in Paris, demonstrating an awareness of the French capital being a hub of anticolonialism where different colonial subjects plotted against empires. Uribe-Echevarría commissioned Macià to contact the rest of the delegates in the French capital. Eventually, it was Basque radical Francisco Gaztañaga who went to Dublin months later to deliver the invitation to join the League, an invitation that de Valera himself considered with sympathy, although he was later advised by the republican diplomat in Paris to decline it.[37]

In the letter, Uribe-Echevarría announced that this project had already been proposed to the Independence Committee of the Philippine Senate, suggesting that there was already a relationship between the Basque and the Philippine anticolonial projects. He also explained that the objectives of this new league were two-fold: mutual help to achieve freedom and to internationalise the claims of the members of the league.[38] Macià stressed these two objectives when he stated that 'this League's objective would be to bring our national struggles to the international sphere to achieve freedom and independence from our respective homelands'.[39]

Uribe-Echevarría also stressed that this new alliance did not invalidate the Triple Alliance but instead aimed to strengthen it, indicating that the project was an explicit continuation of the latter. Whilst the inclusion of the Philippines – as well as the exclusion of Cuba – was perhaps unprecedented and surprising, the inclusion of the other members signals the continuation of how the Aberrianos had envisioned the TA.[40] Given that the LdNO was

36 Although the letter did not directly mention Galicia, according to Estévez, it is possible that this was due to a 'lapsus memoriae'. See Estévez, *De la Triple Alianza al pacto de San Sebastián*, pp. 469–70. Carner-Ribalta and Fabregat mention Galicia as a member, but this does not seem to be part of the original document. Carner-Ribalta and Fabregat (eds), *Macià. La seva actuació a l'estranger*, p. 51.

37 Cullen and McCreanor, 'Dangerous Friends', p. 1200.

38 See letter and draft analysed in Estévez, *De la Triple Alianza al pacto de San Sebastián*, pp. 469–72. For a copy of the original draft written by Uribe-Echevarría see Estévez, *De la Triple Alianza al pacto de San Sebastián*, pp. 657–61.

39 Translated from Ugalde and Ucelay-Da Cal, 'Una alianza en potencia en un contexto más amplio', p. 401.

40 Having said this, it is worth noting that Basques and Filipinos have shared a long and complex history of connections. Basque nationalists were able to spread their movement in the archipelago and in 1909, the first Basque nationalist organisation in the Philippines (Euzkeldun Batzokija) was created. Basques also showed sporadic signs of solidarity with Filipinos and occasionally reproduced José Rizal's texts in their newsletters. The creation of the LdNO and the integration of the Philippines confirm a shift between the symbolic and the real. For a complete

an Aberriano project, it is hardly surprising that the new project sought to integrate the Riffians into the alliance, thus fulfilling the desires of Gallastegi when he had proposed a Quadruple Alliance a year earlier. Nor it is surprising that Uribe-Echevarría included in the league Britain's enemies – Ireland, India and Egypt – whose networks to challenge the Empire in the early 1920s had been a source of inspiration for the Aberrianos when imagining the TA. Indeed, both the TA and the LdNO aimed to foster cooperation with other nations that suffered a similar kind of (colonial, or at least in Basque eyes) oppression. Yet the 1924 project was far more ambitious as it involved extra-peninsular movements: Uribe-Echevarría imagined an international alliance against global colonialism, embodied, in his view, by the LN.

Basques were right to be wary about the recently formed LN. Established in 1919, the LN was a product of the Paris Peace Conference and was directly inspired by Wilson's Fourteen Points (although interestingly, the US never joined the league).[41] Although Wilson had acknowledged that the peace negotiations were not able to deal with colonial claims, he was confident that these had laid the 'institutional groundwork' for handling them.[42] Yet as Manela argues, 'it is hard to imagine that the league, controlled as it was by the major imperial powers, would have been sympathetic to colonial demands for self-determination'.[43] This was reflected in the Covenant of the League itself which stated in its Article 22 that instead of granting the colonised people independence, 'the best method of giving practical effect to [the principle of self-determination] is that the tutelage of such peoples should be entrusted to advanced nations ...'.[44] Indeed, as Vijay Prashad notes, the LN and the Wilsonian principles of self-determination, 'did not mean the end to colonialism, rather for the League of Nations it meant paternalistic imperialism'.[45]

Basque radicals were clearly aware of the imperialist nature of the LN, which had ignored the claims of colonial and stateless peoples, this being a key reason for the formation of the new Aberriano league. These ideas were

---

account of the Basque diaspora in the Philippines, see Marciano R. de Borja, *Los vascos en Filipinas* (Vitoria-Gasteiz: Servicio Central de Publicaciones del Gobierno Vasco, 2014).
41 Although Spain did not take part in the First World War or in the peace conferences, it was able to join as a non-permanent member of the LN in August 1919.
42 Manela, *The Wilsonian Moment*, p. 222.
43 Manela, *The Wilsonian Moment*, p. 222.
44 Quoted from Prashad, *The Darker Nations*, p. 21.
45 Prashad, *The Darker Nations*, p. 21.

present in the Basque radical corpus before 1924. An article published in 1923 by the *Aberri* newsletter argued: 'as long as there are oppressors and oppressed, victims and tormentors, as long as justice keeps being violated and the law keeps being trampled and as long as those who are bigger swallow the smaller ... peace cannot exist.'[46] '*ABERRI* already said it' – the article read – "we do not believe in the League of Nations". Neither do I.'[47] Like many other colonial subjects who soon realised that the post-war promises of self-determination did not apply to them, Basque radicals – who imagined themselves as colonised peoples and therefore also unheard by the new order – were aware that the LN, formed 'by a group of imperialist and amoral states', would not solve their grievances.[48]

The draft of the LdNO summed up the Aberrianos' anti-LN stance and their desire to be part of a global anticolonial struggle. The LdNO, as stated in its draft, aimed to overcome the lack of representation of small and marginalised minorities and to put an end to an unequal world divided into empires and vulnerable nations.[49] It also put into question the myth that placed Wilson and the US as protectors of the small and weak nationalities. According to the draft, the US had forgotten its oppressed past and had become the oppressor:

[the US] was a British colony a century and a half ago and today is the strongest nation in the world, and despite having intervened decisively in the World War as a champion of democracy and as protector of the small nationalities, [it] refused to recognise the independence of the Philippines, trampling over all its glorious history and the memory of its great men – Washington, Jefferson, Madison, Lincoln, etc.[50]

---

46 Ángel de Munain, 'Desde Alemania. La Sociedad de las Naciones', *Aberri* (newspaper), 23 August 1923, p. 6. See also Editor's Note, 'Nacionalismos peninsulares. La "Triple Alianza" significa la "alianza de la libertad"'.

47 Ángel de Munain, 'Desde Alemania', p. 6.

48 Editor's Note, 'Nacionalismos peninsulares', p. 1. This was also stated in the original draft of the LdNO found in Estévez, *De la Triple Alianza al pacto de San Sebastián*, p. 657.

49 The exclusionary character of the LN was mentioned in the draft of the LdNO, which argued that in the LN, 'not all nationalities are able to join in and the issues or problems that affect the nations that are oppressed by the states or governments that are members of the organisation are not discussed'. Quoted and translated from original LdNO draft in Estévez, *De la Triple Alianza al pacto de San Sebastián*, pp. 657–58.

50 Translated from original LdNO draft in Estévez, *De la Triple Alianza al pacto de San Sebastián*, p. 658.

It continued, 'the fact that almost half of the world is dominated, against all justice, by half-a-dozen imperial powers' without any material or moral links to those who advocate for the freedom of the oppressed nations, provided 'more than enough reasons for those who lead these popular nationalist movements in the five parts of the globe, to communicate with each other, with the aim of agreeing a more practical and united way of action in favour of the respective aspirations of freedom and independence'.[51] This indicates how Basque radicals believed that Euskadi formed part of a global struggle that affected all continents and as such, the new League stated that would not discriminate against any 'nationalities or races'.[52] 'The most viable way to achieve this task [independence]', the draft continued, 'would be through the immediate organisation of a LEAGUE OF THE OPPRESSED NATIONS' (capitals in the original).[53]

Ultimately, like the TA, the ambitious and hopeful draft that Uribe-Echevarría imagined had limited practical success. Possibly because of its utopian character and its lack of success, scholars have tended to skim over the LdNO.[54] However, this new alliance should not be overlooked. Aside from illustrating perfectly the use and nature of Basque radical anticolonialism, it allows us to link the Basque radical cause with that of other movements that operated in the 1920s. The LdNO had strong similarities with other projects that denounced the LN equally and envisioned an organisation to counter its influence. Some scholars such as Núñez Seixas have already noted the similarities between the LdNO and other organisations such as the so-called Lega di Fiume (League of Fiume), created in 1919 by Italian ultra-nationalist Gabriele d'Annunzio as an 'anti-League of Nations'.[55] But much more relevant

---

51 Translated from original LdNO draft in Estévez, *De la Triple Alianza al pacto de San Sebastián*, p. 658.

52 Translated from original LdNO draft in Estévez, *De la Triple Alianza al pacto de San Sebastián*, p. 659.

53 Translated from original LdNO draft in Estévez, *De la Triple Alianza al pacto de San Sebastián*, p. 658.

54 Although academics usually mention the LdNO, it is only named in passing and has not yet been analysed in any depth. See, for instance, Núñez Seixas, '¿Protodiplomacia exterior o ilusiones ópticas?', pp. 259–60; Ugalde, *La acción exterior del nacionalismo vasco*; de Pablo and Mees, *El péndulo patriótico*; Ugalde and Ucelay-Da Cal, 'Una alianza en potencia en un contexto más amplio'. One of the only scholars who has explored the League in detail is Xosé Estévez, although his book focuses mostly on other international alliances created during the rest of the 1920s and his approach is mostly descriptive. See Estévez, *De la Triple Alianza al pacto de San Sebastián*.

55 Núñez Seixas, '¿Protodiplomacia exterior o ilusiones ópticas?', p. 260. Núñez Seixas has also suggested that the LdNO had certain similarities with the previously

and influential than the Lega di Fiume, was the previously mentioned League Against Imperialism (LAI). As Prashad points out, the choice of the word 'league' in the title of the LAI was deliberate: 'the League against Imperialism was a direct attack on the League of Nation's preservation of imperialism in its mandate system.'[56]

Although Basque radicals probably did not agree with the Communist tone that the LAI acquired later (the LAI was indeed sponsored by the Comintern, although it brought together activists from different ideologies), the new league was everything that the Aberrianos had dreamed of: an organisation that counteracted the influence of the LN, that targeted several empires and facilitated contacts and networks between colonised and oppressed people around the globe. This is not to suggest in the slightest that the founders of the LAI were inspired by the LdNO – which probably never reached the ears of the LAI's architects – but rather that Basque radicals were aware of the anti-LN discourses that preceded the formation of the LAI and, like the founders of the Brussels-born league, they saw themselves as part of the unintended and ignored audiences of the Wilsonian moment. In sum, Basque nationalism should not be studied as an isolated phenomenon but as one that had evolved according to the local and international developments of the period.

Seeking the Enemy's Help: Basque Appeals to the LN

Whilst establishing direct contacts with other movements and operating outside Wilsonian and imperialist organisations was the preferred method of internationalising the Basque cause, on some occasions Basque radicals chose to appeal directly to the LN. Of course, this meant a complete change

---

mentioned Union des Nationalités (1912–1919). Although Núñez Seixas has not elaborated on these similarities in his article, they are particularly significant when it comes to those with the Lega di Fiume: like the LdNO, d'Annunzio's league emerged as an alternative to the LN. D'Annuzio had occupied the city of Fiume as a response of the negotiations at the Paris Peace Conference and its detrimental effects against the losing countries. Given d'Annunzio's strong resentment of the Allies, he proposed the creation of an 'anti-League of Nations', directed especially against Britain to hinder its influence in the Balkans. D'Annunzio's league would unite stateless nations, minorities and nations whose rights had been violated by the victors in the war and by the LN, considered as an organism in the service of imperialism. The list of included countries can be found in Marcel A. Farinelli, 'Irredentas y centauros de Fiume. Del congreso de Roma a las propuestas de D'Annunzio', in Ucelay-Da Cal, Núñez Seixas, Gonzàlez i Vilalta (eds), *Patrias diversas ¿misma lucha?*, pp. 249–69 (pp. 262–63).

56 Prashad, *The Darker Nations*, p. 21. See also Gopal, *Insurgent Empire*, pp. 265–66; Louro, Stolte, Streets-Salter, Tannoury-Karam, 'The League Against Imperialism', p. 34.

of rhetoric from the anti-LN words we have seen so far: when addressing the international organisation directly or when protesting about Spain being a member of the organisation, the LN was framed as a defender of the minorities. As a letter from AC to Primo reproduced by *Aberri* New York stated: Spain should not be part of the LN, 'because it is not compatible to act as a defender of the minorities in the east, whilst being an oppressor of the minorities in the west and in the territory of its own state'.[57] In another letter sent to the LN directly that will be analysed later, the organisation was labelled as an 'honourable society which aims to ensure that the rights of the small nations are respected'.[58] This highlights the opportunist nature of the Aberrianos, whose opinions and actions were modified depending on their aims. Furthermore, the texts sent to the LN had the clear intention of damaging the international reputation of the Spanish state, which constantly attempted to silence and deny the existence of national minorities within Spain.

Basque nationalists were not the only ones who sought the protection of the LN during the 1920s. Instead, many other western and non-western movements – blinded by the false hopes of the new order – including Riffian leader Abd el-Krim, resorted to the LN in the early 1920s.[59] The fact that most (if not all) of those petitions were ignored contributed to the radicalisation of anticolonial movements, which increasingly became convinced that the only possible form of cooperation was between the oppressed and anti-imperial peoples, as evidenced by the LAI.

The first letter that the Aberrianos directed to the LN came slightly late in comparison to that of other moments. It was not until 1926 that the Comité Pro-Independencia Vasca wrote a letter to the LN petitioning the organisation to force 'Spain to leave the Basque Country in the name of international law'.[60] The letter also listed the other aspirations of the Comité; the first of which was not to allow Spain to send Basques to fight in an 'unjust, abhorrent and barbaric' war in Morocco.[61] The allusion to Morocco's war in a document directed to the LN presents some striking similarities with other petitions sent from other parts of the world, such as that of the Federation of Colored

---

57 Letter from M. Massó Llorens to M. Primo de Rivera, 'Sección Pro-Cataluña. La verdadera razón porque España no es admitida en el consejo de la Liga de Naciones', *Aberri* New York, June 1926, p. 7.
58 See Comité Pro-Independencia Vasca, 'Del Comité Pro-Independencia Vasca a la Sociedad de Naciones', *Patria Vasca*, April 1930, pp. 13–14 (p. 13).
59 See Dalmau, 'Catalans and Rifis during the Wilsonian Moment'.
60 See original in 'Comité Pro-Independencia Vasca, 'A la Sociedad de las Naciones', *Aberri* New York, June 1926, p. 5.
61 Comité Pro-Independencia Vasca, 'A la Sociedad de las Naciones'.

Women's Clubs in the US (home of many Aberrianos and the *Aberri* New York), which sent a telegram to Geneva in 1925 denouncing the Rif War.[62] More importantly, perhaps, is the language used in the final point of the document, which asked the LN to not grant Spain a place in the organisation given the country's backwardness and lack of progress. According to the letter, Spain's backwardness was illustrated by its high illiteracy, mortality and criminality rates – higher than those of other European states – as well as its lack of hygiene and communications infrastructure.[63] The fact that the Comité considered Spain's alleged backwardness as the main reason why the country should not be part of the LN suggests that Basque radicals were re-appropriating the language of the Great Powers reunited in Versailles, who portrayed themselves as the guardians of progress and civilisation.[64]

Perhaps the most emblematic attempt to achieve international visibility through the LN took place in the summer of 1929 when Madrid became the centre of global geopolitics during the celebration of an LN meeting.[65] During that summer, and despite Primo's efforts to silence domestic problems, LN delegates were exposed to the unresolved sub-state nationalist problems within Spain. In fact, the alleged declarations that German foreign minister Gustav Stresemann made about the Catalan and Basque problem nearly caused a diplomatic conflict with Primo's government, which was trying to promote an external image of a diverse but united country.[66] Taking advantage of the chaos generated, a group of Aberrianos

---

62 Dalmau, 'Catalans and Rifis during the Wilsonian Moment', p. 141.

63 Comité Pro-Independencia Vasca, 'A la Sociedad de las Naciones'.

64 As Dalmau shows, Abd el-Krim used this language too when appealing to the LN, who in 1922 wrote an open letter titled 'To the Civilised Nations' denouncing Spanish oppression. Dalmau, 'Catalans and Rifis during the Wilsonian Moment', p. 138.

65 According to Núñez Seixas, the Aberrianos in America also attempted to get the attention of the Peruvian delegation of the LN so they could bring Basque claims to Geneva. The Peruvian government, however, ignored the petition and reported it to the Spanish government. See Núñez Seixas, '¿Protodiplomacia exterior o ilusiones ópticas?', p. 260.

66 Stresemann visited San Sebastian before making his way to Madrid. In San Sebastian, Stresemann allegedly made some declarations in which he located the unresolved nationalist question of both Catalonia and the Basque Country within the 'minorities problem' that originated after the First World War. To the benefit of Basque nationalists, the Spanish newspaper *La Voz* (The Voice) published Stresemann's allegations. Primo's government, which attempted to provide a vision of stability to the international community in any way it could, rapidly issued an official note that denied the existence of any nationalist problem within a firmly united nation. This episode has been explained in detail by scholars such as Ugalde. See Ugalde, *La acción exterior del nacionalismo vasco*, pp. 359–63.

approached Stresemann himself, as well as the LN. Ugalde argues that the Comité de Independencia Vasca sent 100 copies of a memorandum entitled 'El problema nacionalista vasco' ('The Basque nationalist problem') to Geneva, together with a letter written by Gallastegi (signed in name of the American delegation of the Comité).[67] The documents exposed the Basque case to the LN and claimed that despite Primo's attempt to silence the Basque nationalist problem, it was very much alive.

With these documents, the Aberrianos placed Euskadi in the unresolved problem of national minorities in order to encourage the LN to take the Basque situation into account. Yet Basques seemed convinced that if the LN were to ignore their claims, they would have to use their own methods. This was expressed in one of the documents, which, with a threatening tone, suggested that if the LN did not act accordingly, Basques would have to take some action: '[to achieve freedom] today or tomorrow, the Basque race will make all the sacrifices that a dignified and conscious nation can be able of.'[68] The desperation was palpable in the document.

As proved above, during the 1920s, Basque radicals followed the same steps as anticolonial nationalists around the world to give international visibility to their cause. Whilst some decided to appeal directly to the Great Powers who had won the Great War, others – more sceptical – decided that direct contacts should only be made with those who shared the same oppression. Certainly, both options seemed plausible and not contradictory in the views of Basque radicals themselves. For instance, *Aberri* New York's June 1926 issue included two pro-LN articles and one written by LN-sceptic Ángel de Munain. The latter labelled the organisation as a 'vile farse of the representatives of the imperialist states, which have nothing to say in this case [the Rif War]. They are meant to work towards peace, but for the peace and tranquillity of the thieves and usurpers.'[69] Once Munain's suspicions were confirmed and colonial subjects realised that their petitions would be repeatedly ignored, the second option gained more ground in the colonised world. Unsurprisingly, in the next decade, Basque radicals aligned their international strategy with contemporary anticolonial movements and were harsher than ever towards the LN and the interwar order.

---

67 Ugalde, *La acción exterior del nacionalismo vasco*, p. 365. Both documents were reproduced in *Patria Vasca*. See Comité Pro-Independencia Vasca, 'Del Comité Pro-Independencia Vasca a la Sociedad de Naciones', pp. 13–14 and Comité Pro-Independencia Vasca, 'El Problema Nacionalista Vasco. A los Representantes de los Estados en la Sociedad de Naciones', *Patria Vasca*, April 1930, pp. 15–19.
68 Comité Pro-Independencia Vasca, 'El Problema Nacionalista Vasco', p. 19.
69 Ángel de Munain, 'La tragedia de Marruecos', *Aberri* New York, June 1926, p. 6.

'To Arms!' Anticolonialism, Independence and Violence against Spanish 'Barbarism'

As the Aberrianos became increasingly convinced that collaboration with the oppressor was not feasible, Basque radicals found the possibilities of a violent insurrection more plausible than ever. During Primo's dictatorship, the Aberrianos experienced a period of radicalisation without precedent. This radicalisation was twofold, affecting not only those who were forced to leave Euskadi and establish direct contacts with nationalists and activists of all sorts but also those who stayed at home and directly experienced years of repression and silence. Certainly, the dictatorship of Primo fired the imagination of Basque radical nationalists, as the imposition of Spanish values, language and culture made Euskadi's colonial nature seem more real than ever. In Basque radical eyes, Euskadi was a possession of Spain and France, just as the Moroccan Protectorate was.[70] Furthermore, Primo's dictatorship and his actions in Morocco would allow Basque radicals to validate their claims of Spain as an obscure, backwards and repressive country that was outside of European modernity. The idea of Spain as the epitome of barbarism with whom it was impossible to dialogue, came to justify Basque radicals' calls for violence in pursuit of independence. This section shows how Basque anticolonial discourses in Morocco continued having strong analogies with those developed by Sabino Arana years before. The main difference is that during the 1920s Basque radicals used these discourses to legitimise not only the need for independence, but also the need to take up arms.

The situation in Morocco was crucial for the stability of the new regime as upon Primo's arrival to power in 1923, three-quarters of the Spanish protectorate was under Abd el-Krim's control.[71] Although at first, Primo advocated for a semi-abandonment strategy in Morocco, the radicalisation and expansion of the Riffian movement (which spread to the French Protectorate) and the pressure from the young Africanist army (to which Francisco Franco, amongst others, belonged) to intervene in the Protectorate led him to join forces with France in 1925.[72] This proved to be a success for Primo, whose troops led a decisive victory against Abd el-Krim in the Alhucemas Bay that

---

70 The analogies between the Rif and Euskadi were constant in *Aberri* New York, which was published during the last phase of the Rif War. These became less constant in *Patria Vasca*, in which Euskadi was mostly compared to the Latin American republics.
71 Quiroga, *Miguel Primo de Rivera*, p. 121.
72 For a concise but comprehensive account of Primo's actions in Morocco see, for instance, Shannon E. Fleming and Ann K. Fleming, 'Primo de Rivera and Spain's

same year. Shortly after Alhucemas, considered the first aeronaval landing in history, Abd el-Krim had no choice but to surrender to the Spanish and the French, putting an end to the long and deadly Rif War. As Rocío Velasco de Castro argues, if Primo's dictatorship was a consequence of the escalation of the Moroccan problem, this eventually became its solution.[73]

Whilst the Battle of Annual of 1921 had confirmed Spain's decay as a world power, after Alhucemas and Abd el-Krim's surrender, the Spaniards could redeem their international (and national) image. The French were not exactly fond of the Spanish – whom they saw as 'big children', bad and inept colonisers incapable of bringing 'civilisation' to other countries – but after the pacification of Morocco they had no choice but to admit that Spain had managed to improve its colonial military force.[74] Naturally, the Basques' vision of the Spaniards did not change after Abd el-Krim's surrender but instead, they echoed and amplified the vision that European chancelleries had of them. The violent and 'inhumane' colonial campaigns held in Morocco, alongside the traits of Primo's military dictatorship – which, in Basque eyes, perfectly illustrated the character of the Spaniards – were constantly stressed to delve into this vision.

Far from praising the 'heroic' actions of the Spaniards (and the French) in Morocco following the Alhucemas landing of 1925, *Aberri* New York included different articles questioning their alleged civilisation and stressed the atrocities that the Spaniards had committed against the Riffians.[75] In June

Moroccan Problem, 1923-27', *Journal of Contemporary History*, 12.1 (1977), pp. 85-99. For a more detailed and complete account see Balfour, *Deadly Embrace*, pp. 83-120.

73 Rocío Velasco de Castro, 'España y Marruecos: del desastre de Annual a la dictadura de Primo de Rivera (1921-1930). Introducción', *Hispania Nova. Revista de Historia Contemporánea*, 20 (2021), pp. 661-91 (p. 679).

74 For the Orientalist vision that the French diplomacy had of Spain and Primo de Rivera see: Quiroga, *Miguel Primo de Rivera*, pp. 121-22; Ángel Herrerín López and Susana Sueiro Seoane, '¿Quantité négligeable o rival terrible?: la imagen francesa de la España primorriverista', *Pasado y Memoria*, 16 (2017), pp. 17-45. For a general view of how European diplomacy saw Primo's dictatorship, see the different articles compiled in Herreín López and Sueiro Seoane (eds), 'La imagen de la Dictadura de Primo de Rivera en las cancillerías europeas', *Pasado y Memoria*, 16 (2017). The article that explores the British conception of the Spaniards during the dictatorship is particularly relevant for this study: see José Luis Neila Hernández, '"Entre el palco y la butaca": el apaciguamiento británico y el regeneracionismo internacional de la España de Primo de Rivera', *Pasado y Memoria*, 16 (2017), pp. 47-67.

75 See, amongst many others, R. de Artoolazabal, 'No hay vergüenza', *Aberri* New York, October 1925, p. 4, which condemned patriotic news coming from Spain and labelled its actions in Morocco as macabre. It is worth pointing out that Primo's operation in Morocco was the object of patriotic propaganda imposed by the regime. See Alfonso Iglesias Amorín, 'Imaginarios y conmemoración del fin del 'problema'

1926, *Aberri* New York published an issue that contained various articles condemning the total conquest of the Rif by Spain and France. An article titled 'La tragedia de Marruecos' ('the Moroccan tragedy') commented:

> the news [of the conquest of Morocco] could not be more unpleasant and distressing ... to invade a country like Morocco, to kill, steal and conquest are not actions worthy of being praised, but instead, this war demonstrates, once again, the savagery of our so-called civilisation and the false conception that Europe has of other's rights.[76]

Whilst in this article Spain seemed to be part of imperial Europe, Basque radicals continued 'de-westernising' Spaniards to justify their separatist claims. The front page of the June 1926 issue included graphic photographs – allegedly published in Spain – of Spanish soldiers holding the heads of beheaded Riffians as if they were trophies. These explicit images, which appealed directly to the so-called Black Legend, questioned 'the "humanitarian" way in which Spain treated the Riffians, who were guilty of the grave crime of defending their nation'.[77] Hispanic cruelty was reinforced with words and stereotypes that resonated with the European imaginary, such as the 'inquisitorial' abuses of the Spanish.[78] In fact, this very same word was used in a highly Orientalist article written in English and included in the same June 1926 issue in *Aberri* New York. Drawing from common European stereotypes about both Spain and France, this article denounced the repression that Basques suffered at the hands of 'the illiterate drunkards who rule Spain and the luminously

---

de Marruecos durante la dictadura de Primo de Rivera', *Hispania Nova. Revista de Historia Contemporánea*, 20 (2021), pp. 857–88. Iglesias Amorín argues that without a doubt, the Alhucemas landing (attributed mostly to the dictator) was key for the glorification of Primo. Iglesias Amorín, 'Imaginarios y conmemoración del fin del "problema"', p. 870.

76 Ángel de Munain, 'La tragedia de Marruecos', p. 6.
77 Anon., 'Fragmentos', *Aberri* New York, June 1926, p. 1.
78 The word 'inquisitorial' was used on different occasions across the newsletter to describe Spanish actions throughout history: see Gastelu, 'Basque and not Spanish', *Aberri* New York, June 1926, p. 2, which alludes to the 'inquisitorial prisons' of Sabino Arana's period, and 'Sección Pro-Cataluña', *Aberri* New York, July 1926, pp. 5–7, which offers a chronicle of a meeting in France against the 'inquisitorial abuses of Spanish militarism', p. 5. Other articles such as 'Arriba' talked about the re-implementation of the 'black inquisition' to allude to the repression of Primo's regime. See Inunzi, 'Arriba', *Aberri* New York, May 1926, p. 2. See also a reference to the first Inquisitor, Tomás de Torquemada, in an article denouncing the repression experienced during Primo de Rivera's dictatorship: Kaloka, 'Euzkaro bajo el imperialismo español', *Aberri* New York, April 1928, p. 2.

civilised France'.⁷⁹ If the French, who deprived Euskadi of its 'liberty', were 'the banner-bearers of Progress and the torch-carriers of Civilization', the Spanish, who 'savagely chased' Basques, were 'the African dogs of Europe'.⁸⁰

Indeed, Primo's repressive dictatorship (which according to the Aberrianos suited the Spanish character) and its actions in Morocco only reinforced the stereotypes and the view that Basques had of the Spanish: Spain was the 'most backwards of all the Latin countries which were in a state of decadence'; an illiterate country full of irrational and lazy people, as the dictatorship evidenced.⁸¹ Using medical language characteristic of the 'regenerationist' discourse and inverting the binaries of civilisation and barbarism, *Aberri* New York described Spain as a 'sickly, crumbling and discredited' nation that dominated a 'superior, free, moral and noble race' (the Basques), who 'always walked next to the most civilised peoples'.⁸² Without a doubt, for Basque radicals the US was an example of the civilised countries that aligned with the Basque appreciation for 'freedom', as Basques seemed to brag.⁸³ This romanticised vision of the US as a land of freedom, which recalled Sabino Arana's discourses, was supported by the iconography of the *Aberri* New York, which from its fourth issue featured a drawing of the Statue of Liberty on its front page. Unlike Spain, the US was referred as a 'great and free nation'.⁸⁴

This characterisation of the Spaniards as the antithesis of what the west was supposed to represent, alongside Euskadi's colonial analogies, served

79 Gastelu, 'Basque and not Spanish', p. 2.
80 Gastelu, 'Basque and not Spanish', p. 2. It is worth pointing out that the word in Euskera for dog, *txakurra*, was used frequently by ETA activists to refer to the security forces. It seems like in this case the word 'dog' acquires the same meaning. ETA also used the word *cipayo* ('sipahi') – note the colonial tone – to refer to the Basque police, although I have not observed this word in the chronology studied.
81 Karakatza, 'Cuestión de vida o muerte', *Aberri* New York, July 1926, p. 1. The image that Basques had of Spain, aligns with the view that the rest of Europeans had of the country in the first decades of the twentieth century. As Ucelay-Da Cal claims, during that period, Spain was considered in European culture as the prime example of decline. See Enric Ucelay-Da Cal, 'La imagen internacional de España en el periodo de entreguerras: reminiscencias, estereotipos, dramatización neorromántica y sus consecuencias historiográficas', *Spagna contemporanea*, 15 (1999), pp. 23–52 (p. 32). See also Chapter 1 for the origin of the debates on Spanish decline.
82 Un obrero vasco, 'Queremos y basta', *Aberri* New York, April 1926, pp. 3–4 and Anon., '25 Octubre de 1839', *Aberri* New York, September 1926, p. 3.
83 For an example of the love of freedom as an innate Basque trait, see Un obrero vasco, 'Ultrajes a la nación', *Aberri* New York, February 1926, p. 3.
84 Gudari, 'Los Estados Unidos y la independencia de Cuba. España y la Esclavitud de Euzkadi', *Aberri* New York, March 1926, p. 2. This article reminded *Aberri*'s readers of the telegram Arana had sent to Roosevelt congratulating him on Cuba's liberation, stirring a sense of pride and nostalgia.

Basque radicals to promote the necessary use of violence as the only possible tool of liberation. Following the Riffian example, negotiating with what Basques labelled as a Quixotic regime of imperialist dreamers was presented as impossible: 'we have no choice but to get ready for war, like honourable men, or to be pariah and slaves ... when dealing with irrational people the answer can only be one: to arms!'[85] This was not an isolated article in *Aberri* New York. References to a violent struggle to achieve independence were recurrent throughout.[86] An article entitled 'Fines y medios' ('Ends and means'), which bragged about the international relations that Basques had with other movements, stated: 'independence ... is not going to be granted by Spain, as some deluded have dreamed. Independence can only be conquered with blood and money. In one word: with sacrifice.'[87] The Aberrianos dreamed about what these relationships with other movements could mean: 'sooner or later the block of Catalans, Basques and Moroccans will sever the head of this fierce Spanish lion (a circus lion) and all together will sing the liberation hymn.'[88] After a brief publishing hiatus, in 1928 *Aberri* New York assured that the day on which 'we leave the pen and take up the liberation riffle' was getting closer.[89]

In sum, as one of the last articles of *Aberri* New York assured, collaboration with the oppressor was unfeasible: 'we can't expect solutions from Madrid.'[90] As I show in the next chapter, this claim was repeatedly made by Basque radicals during the 1930s to reject a statue of autonomy with Spain. Although the scarce scholarship on the topic has overlooked the inflammatory and violent language used by Basque radicals during this period, this is key to understanding the future development of Basque radicalism.[91] Years later,

---

85 Ángel de Munain, 'Momentos actuales', *Aberri* New York, April 1926, pp. 5–6 (p. 6).
86 Interestingly, although *Patria Vasca* was not exempt from making violent references, they were less frequent. An article published on April 1930 (shortly after the death of Primo), praised Gandhi's peaceful struggle against the British Empire. See Crítica, 'Las grandes inquietudes de los pueblos', p. 5.
87 Kara-Katza, 'Fines y medios', *Aberri* New York, 10 April 1926, pp. 4–5.
88 Gudari Bat, '¡Visca Catalunya!', *Aberri* New York, January 1928, p. 6.
89 Anon., 'Happy New Year', *Aberri* New York, January 1928, p. 1.
90 Tximbo, 'Un solo lema', *Aberri* New York, April 1928, p. 1.
91 In his monograph about the intellectual origins of ETA, Watson omits Primo de Rivera's period, jumping from 1923 to 1930. See Watson, *Basque Nationalism and Political Violence*. Instead of considering this language, scholars have tended to pay attention to the failed Catalan and Basque radical attempts to plot against the dictatorship during the 1920s. Their failure has made scholars classify the plots as isolated attempts that were purely rhetorical and never actioned. See, among others, Fernández Soldevilla, 'De *Aberri* a ETA', p. 223; José Luis de la Granja, 'Una

ETA – also radicalised by the experiences of Franco's dictatorship – came to posit arguments that had been advanced previously by the Aberrianos of the 1920s: to enter dialogue with repressive forces was impossible and instead, it was necessary to take up arms.

Hispanismo vs Basqueness: Basque Radicalism and the Latin American Struggle for Independence

As this chapter has demonstrated, the time that Basque radicals spent in exile led to an important degree of radicalisation as well as new opportunities to internationalise the Basque cause. Not only was this facilitated through the direct contacts that Basques established with other groups in western cities such as Paris and New York, but the experiences the Aberrianos had in Latin America also brought apparent changes to the Basque rhetoric. Whilst up until Abd el-Krim's defeat Basque radicals continued to follow the Riffian struggle with interest, the former struggles for independence in Latin America became a new source of influence in the Mexican-based newsletter *Patria Vasca*. Abd el-Krim may have been defeated, but the nineteenth-century Latin American wars for independence reinforced the belief that independence from Spain could be achieved through violent struggle. Yet as we will see, the sympathies that Basque radicals showed for the Latin American liberation movements were not entirely genuine.

Before the dictatorship, articles on Latin America in the two *Aberris* had been limited. Like later examples in *Patria Vasca*, the few articles found in *Aberri* criticised the positive vision of the conquest that Spain was imposing through festivities such as the so-called Fiesta de la Raza (Festival of the [Hispanic] race – today known as Día de la Hispanidad), which celebrated the day on which Spaniards first reached the Americas (12 October 1492). For instance, in an article published on 15 October 1921, the *Aberri* newsletter challenged the traditional civilisation discourse used to justify the conquest. The article claimed that this date did not mark the beginning of 'Christian civilisation in America' but instead 'initiated first the enslavement, and then the extermination, of all the indigenous American races'.[92] After criticising the 'conquest and colonisation' or 'the extermination of the indigenous people', *Aberri* condemned the celebration

---

autocrítica del nacionalismo vasco tras la dictadura de Primo de Rivera: el manifiesto del Comité Pro-Resurgimiento Vasco (1930)', *Bilduma: Revista del Servicio del Archivo del Ayuntamiento de Errenteria*, 3 (1989), pp. 185–209 (p. 188).

92 Dorkaitz, 'La fiesta de la raza', *Aberri* (newsletter), 15 October 1921, p. 1. For similar texts see Idara, 'Entremeses', *Aberri* (newsletter), 12 October 1918, p. 3.

of the Fiesta de la Raza, and relabelled it as 'the holiday of the enslaved and exterminated race'.[93] Another article acknowledged the contribution of the Basques in 'the atrocious crimes of conquest, slavery and extermination of the American "Indian"'.[94] The Basque contribution to colonialism was used to underscore the colonial subjugation that Euskadi was experiencing as a penalty of past crimes; as the article suggested, 'Providence, as a punishment for those [colonising] crimes [in America], had reduced the Basques to the condition of Indians'.[95]

Whilst these articles were an exception in the pre-dictatorship years, Latin America and its struggles for independence became the centre of attention for *Patria Vasca*. This is hardly surprising not only because the magazine was published in Mexico, but also because, like the Riffian example, the Basque romanticisation of Latin American independence struggles served to attack Primo's pro-colonial discourses, inspired by the principle of *Hispanismo*. By stressing the transmission of knowledge, language and culture from the metropole to the former colonies, *Hispanismo* promoted a positive and benign vision of the Spanish conquest or a White Legend in contrast to the negative and demonising Black Legend which had surrounded the Spanish Empire since the sixteenth century.[96] Determined to promote a benign conception of the Empire, the Fiesta de la Raza acquired special importance during Primo's dictatorship. Despite having been declared a national holiday in 1918 to bring Spain closer to the new Spanish-American republics, the Fiesta de la Raza gained little popular support until Primo seized power. Primo made great efforts to popularise the Fiesta de la Raza, the celebration of which was a perfect opportunity to promote the White Legend and to underscore the supremacy and legacy of the Spanish language and culture in Latin America.[97] His efforts to promote the festival paid off. Not only did hundreds of villages celebrate the holiday for the first time during the dictatorship but by 1928, cities such as Madrid saw about 30,000 children marching in the streets on 12 October.

Naturally, Basque radicals took every opportunity to challenge Primo's patriotic efforts to promote a positive vision of the conquest through their

---

93 Dorkaitz, 'La fiesta de la raza', p. 1. This same view was expressed in an article about the festivity published a year later. See: Arkaitz, 'La fiesta de la "razzia"', *Aberri* (newsletter), 7 October 1922, p. 2.
94 Arkaitz, 'La "razzia" de los vascos', *Aberri* (newsletter), 14 October 1922, p. 2.
95 Arkaitz, 'La "razzia" de los vascos', p. 2.
96 See Jessaca Leinaweaver, 'Transatlantic Unity on Display: the "White Legend" and the "Pact of Silence" in Madrid's Museum of the Americas', *History and Anthropology*, 28.1 (2017), pp. 39–57 (p. 40).
97 See Quiroga, *Making Spaniards*, p. 174.

publications. Most of these writings stressed the leading role that Basques had played in the independence of Latin America (a strategy to overcome the role that Basques played in the conquest) and reversed the discourses of *Hispanidad* to the benefit of the Basques: whilst Spaniards had brought misery and violence to their former colonies, Basques had brought nothing but virtue to the Americas.[98]

The alleged Basque influence in the Americas was the object of many articles in *Patria Vasca*. An article entitled 'Nuestra raza en Colombia. Su influencia en Colombia' ('Our race in Colombia. Its influence in Colombia') described the Basque influence in the Colombian region of Antioquia and collected testimonies of Colombians who agreed with this view: 'we are Basques and that is why we are how we are', a man from Antioquia reportedly told the author of the article.[99] In addition, Colombian politician José Joaquín Casas had allegedly claimed that 'Colombia is the work of the Basques'.[100] According to *Patria Vasca*, the influence of the Basques in Latin America was felt on a continental scale. As the magazine boasted, quoting a book published by the Basque-Argentine doctor Tomás Otaegui, 'the Basques brought to America what they had: their racial, social and political idiosyncrasies, their love for freedom, democracy and equality'.[101]

Unlike the Spanish, the Basques were not portrayed as *conquistadores* but instead, as a people who respected other nations and had a passion for freedom. Such differences in behaviour between Spanish and Basques were, according to *Patria Vasca*, determined by one's race, nation and culture. As Gallastegi claimed, 'the Basques that have stood out in the history of America are those who rose against the Spanish spirit, those who turned away from their imperialist action'.[102] Another article on the Basque influence in Mexico argued, 'the Basque race, a melting pot of free men, has always stood out

---

98 Núñez Seixas has pointed out that these types of discourses were also expounded by Catalans and Galician nationalists in Latin America who wanted to escape from and reject Spain's colonial past and establish links with nationalists of former colonies. See Xosé Manoel Núñez Seixas, '¿Negar o reescribir la Hispanidad? Los nacionalismos subestatales ibéricos y América Latina, 1898–1936', *Historia Mexicana*, 67.1 (2017), pp. 401–58 (p. 418).

99 Mendizabal' darr Errapel, 'Nuestra raza en América. Su influencia en Colombia', *Patria Vasca*, November–December 1928, pp. 25–26 (p. 26).

100 Mendizabal, 'Nuestra raza en América', p. 26.

101 Anon., 'República Vasca', *Patria Vasca*, June–July 1928, p. 5.

102 Gudari, 'Los vascos libertadores. De cómo el espíritu individualista produjo en América libertadores, en contraste con los pueblos feudalistas que engendraron dominadores', *Patria Vasca*, September–October 1928, pp. 9–12 (p. 10).

for its fierce love of independence and for its hatred towards every kind of servitude'.[103]

To stress the Basque influence on Latin America, *Patria Vasca* argued that most of the national leaders who had freed their respective countries from Spanish rule were Basque in origin. Unsurprisingly, most if not all the leaders claimed as Basques were *criollos*, and therefore white. Simón Bolívar was perhaps the most acclaimed Basque leader. Sabino Arana himself had already presented Bolívar as the main exponent of the Basque desire for freedom, and so did the *Aberri* newspaper.[104] But *Patria Vasca* went much further, as it claimed not only that figures such as Bolívar had Basque blood, but also that most of the fathers of Latin American independence – especially from Mexico – were Basque.

In the first issue of *Patria Vasca*, an article called 'Los vascos y la independencia de México' ('The Basques and the Mexican independence') narrated the epic fight that Mexicans led to achieve their long-awaited independence and stressed the Basque origin of many of those who fought for freedom in Mexico.[105] Among the many patriots who 'gave their blood for Mexican independence', this article asserted that Miguel Hidalgo Costilla, who called for independence, and Agustín de Iturbide, who 'achieved emancipation', had Basque blood.[106] As *Patria Vasca* claimed repeatedly, 'the Basques fought for Mexican independence with sacrifice'.[107] Months later, another article in *Patria Vasca* stressed the Basque origins of Hidalgo and stated that the Navarran-born martyr Francisco Xavier Mina was also originally from Euskadi.[108] Besides his love for freedom, Mina had two other Basque traits: his warrior character and his sense of dignity, 'which made him prefer death to dishonour'.[109] As the article stated, after his death he was remembered as a hero of the fight for independence. Alongside Sabino Arana, Bolívar, Iturbide, Hidalgo and Mina were Basque martyrs who gave their lives for independence.[110]

---

103 Anon., 'Los vascos y la independencia de México', *Patria Vasca*, May 1928, p. 8.
104 Núñez Seixas, '¿Negar o reescribir la Hispanidad?', p. 421. As Núñez Seixas recounts, these discourses continued after the 1930s. For instance, during the Spanish Civil War, a battalion of Basque nationalists was called Simón Bolívar. See Núñez Seixas, '¿Negar o reescribir la Hispanidad?', p. 421.
105 Anon., 'Los vascos y la independencia de México', p. 8.
106 Anon., 'Los vascos y la independencia de México', p. 8.
107 Anon., 'Los vascos y la independencia de México', p. 8.
108 See Anon., 'Arte vasco. Nuestros grabados', *Patria Vasca*, September–October 1928, pp. 13–14.
109 Anon., 'Arte vasco', p. 14.
110 Arana was considered a martyr even if, unlike other nationalist figures who died fighting for their nation, he died in his bed owing to illness. An article

With these texts, Basque radicals attempted to justify the extensive Basque involvement of the Basques in the colonisation of the Americas, whilst directly challenging the assumptions of a shared culture and heritage between Spaniards and Latin Americans. Basque radicals instead claimed that there was a strong shared culture and heritage between Basques and Latin Americans. Furthermore, these texts linked the two struggles and presented the Basque fight as a direct continuation of the nineteenth-century Latin American battles for independence (allegedly led by *criollos* of Basque descent). The same article that talked about the Basque role in Mexico's independence did this explicitly: whilst in 1811 'Mexico recovered its freedom', 'the same Basques that knew how to push Mexico forward in its emancipation campaign, fell in 1839 after an exhausting war, by the same Empire that had subjected Mexico'.[111] This drew the same parallel that Sabino Arana had established decades before: in the same century in which the Latin American republics achieved freedom, the Basques lost theirs. The Basques, who had contributed to the liberation of the Americas, were colonised in 1839 by the same enemy that had oppressed Latin America for centuries.[112]

Patria Vasca hoped that by stressing these continuities and parallels in the Basque and Latin American struggles the Basque cause would be taken seriously in America. As an article published in 1928 called 'Hacia la independencia' ('Towards independence') claimed, the Basques' desire for freedom was going to be favourably listened to in the Americas as 'our [Basque] problem is a reflection of their [the Latin American republics] own life'.[113] Another article equated the two struggles and called for solidarity. After talking about Augusto Sandino's anti-imperial resistance to the US occupation of Nicaragua and the wave of solidarity that his campaign had generated in America, the author stated, 'if the American Republics find a reason to defend generously the threatened or intervened free nations, they must surely feel sympathy for a nation such as Euskadi which lost its sovereignty last century'.[114]

Indeed, comparisons between non-western nations and Euskadi were, as at earlier moments, a way of gaining international visibility and

---

published in 1928 attempted to excuse his non-violent death. See Anon., 'Muertes heroicas. Pensamientos luminosos', *Patria Vasca*, November–December 1928, pp. 1–2.
111 Anon., 'Los vascos y la independencia de México', p. 8.
112 See Anon., 'Los vascos y la independencia de México', p. 8 and Anon., 'Paz y guerra', *Patria Vasca*, September–October 1928, pp. 1–2.
113 Garaya' tar Ander, 'Hacia la independencia', *Patria Vasca*, September–October 1928, pp. 25–26 (p. 25).
114 Comité Pro-Independencia Vasca, 'Del Comité Pro-Independencia Vasca. Queremos ser libres', *Patria Vasca*, May 1928, pp. 12–14 (p. 13).

underscoring the Basque colonial situation to justify independence. As seen in this section, the shift of attention to Latin America did not translate into innocent claims of praise towards the 'new' Latin American states. Instead, anticolonial claims against Spain were tainted with paternalistic and imperialist comments, which instead of recognising the agency of Latin American newly founded republics, ascribed independence to the white west, represented by the Basques. This demonstrates that Basques were not necessarily concerned with Latin American struggles but rather, that their romanticisation offered a great rhetorical advantage.

Conclusion

Primo de Rivera's dictatorship was a short and less intense preview of what separatism in Spain would experience during Francisco Franco's dictatorship: repression of peripheral identities, silence and exile. Yet at least when examining Basque nationalism and its development in exile, it would be misleading to reduce the seven years of Spain's first dictatorship in the twentieth century to a period of crisis, failure and immobility. If anything, Primo's repression of separatism had the opposite effect. It led to the radicalisation of Basque radical nationalists, as well as the enrichment of the Basque anticolonial repertoire, which continued obeying two well-defined aims.

Basque radicals wrote violent texts in this period as part of the process of profound radicalisation. Primo's Hispanisation campaign across the peninsula, as well as the parallel campaigns he led in the Rif, made the idea of Euskadi being a Spanish colony – which had been in the mind of Basque nationalists for a while – seem more real than ever. To face this impossible and repressive situation and to finally reach freedom, Basque radicals were increasingly convinced that violence was the only option. Basque radical allusions to violence should not be overlooked as they were a prelude to the ideas that led young Basque radicals to take arms from the 1960s.

The experience of exile also contributed to the radicalisation of Basque radicals. From their new homes, Basque radicals were able to establish new contacts and consolidate others, leading them to bring Latin American affairs into the spotlight for the first time. Furthermore, Basque radicals were able to observe and learn from the strategies that other movements followed to internationalise their movement. These varied, leading Basques to seek the attention of the LN or to contest the 'imperialist' organisation by seeking networks with other movements; two strategies that were put in place not only by Basques but by other anticolonial agents and movements across the globe. This demonstrates that Basques imagined themselves (or at least wanted to project themselves) as part of wider anticolonial movements that emerged following widespread disappointment with the new Wilsonian order. The desire to be part of this wider movement led Basque radicals to upgrade their anticolonial claims, although as we have seen, this did not imply a total eradication of paternalistic and imperialist views. Once again, anticolonial claims were not necessarily genuine, but rather strategic.

CHAPTER SIX

'Oppressed Peoples of the World, Unite!' Anticolonialism with a Purpose: Independence and Internationalism (1931–1936)

During his time in power, Miguel Primo de Rivera attempted to reverse Spain's fortunes by winning colonial wars in Africa, modernising the country and boosting the Spanish economy.[1] Nevertheless, by the late 1920s, the repressive state he had built started to show signs of disintegration, and many of those who had welcomed his dictatorship as a short parenthesis began to oppose it. As William D. Phillips and Carla Rahn Phillips argue, 'despite the outward appearance of success, the regime had merely papered over some of the widest cracks in Spanish life', and Spaniards were not willing to live in a permanent repressive state.[2] After both King Alfonso XIII and the army indicated their withdrawal of support for the dictatorship, Primo had no choice but to resign. Primo finally abandoned power on 28 January 1930 and retired to Paris, where he died a month and a half later.

Following Primo's fall, Dámaso Berenguer – a general known for his role in the Rif War and the Annual Disaster – was asked by the king to form a new government. Yet King Alfonso's temporary solution was to prove flawed, as Berenguer's *dictablanda* lasted only a year, and the Second Spanish Republic (1931–1936) was proclaimed shortly after the Spanish monarch installed another army man in office. The new Republican regime, proclaimed on 14 April 1931, promised changes that would bury the structures of the old Restoration system.

Amongst other things, the Republic opened a new world of possibilities for Spain's peripheral nationalist movements. A few hours after the Spanish Republic had been proclaimed, Macià announced the creation of a Catalan Republic and after months of negotiations, Catalonia was granted its first Statute of Autonomy in 1932. The same day the Spanish Republic was

---

1 A previous version of this chapter has been published in the *Journal of Contemporary History* (Volume 58, 2023, Issue 4).
2 William D. Phillips, Jr and Carla Rahn Phillips, *A Concise History of Spain* (Cambridge: Cambridge University Press, 2010), p. 243.

declared, the council of the Biscayan town of Getxo, presided over by the young Basque nationalist leader José Antonio Aguirre, imitated Macià and proclaimed the 'Basque Republic linked in federation with the Spanish Republic'.[3] Achieving autonomy, however, was not as smooth for the Basques as it was for the Catalans and took until October 1936 to obtain it. Although the Basque city of Eibar was the first to proclaim the Republic in Spain, the strong Catholic and conservative ideas of the PNV (which had brought together both sectors of Basque nationalism in 1930) initially clashed with the new secular and progressive Republican regime. Furthermore, not all sectors of Basque nationalism agreed with the pro-autonomy programme of the PNV. Instead, like the PNV-*Aberri*, the Basque radical newsletter and organisation *Jagi-Jagi* (Arise-Arise) believed that collaboration with the 'enemy' was not feasible, and that independence was the only way to go forward. Like its radical predecessors, *Jagi-Jagi* reinforced this belief by drawing parallels between the situation of the Basque Country and that of other colonised nations, positing that Euskadi was a colony within Spain.

Various scholars have studied *Jagi-Jagi*'s ideology and its long-term influence within the Basque liberation movement.[4] Nevertheless, scholars have failed to acknowledge and analyse *Jagi-Jagi*'s explicit anticolonial ideas, which were an essential part of its ideological core. For instance, Eduardo Renobales – whose monograph *Jagi-Jagi: Historia del independentismo radical* is one of the few academic studies that analyses *Jagi-Jagi* in depth – has argued that *Jagi-Jagi*'s doctrine can be summarised as follows: strong independentism, opposition to any kind of agreement with the Spanish state, and anti-fascist and anti-capitalist traits.[5] Although Renobales's summary is a good representation of *Jagi-Jagi*'s radicalism, the blatant and aggressive anticolonial language of the newsletter should be added to this list. Anticolonialism is one of the most important aspects of *Jagi-Jagi*'s radical thought. Like the different Basque radical publications of the 1920s, *Jagi-Jagi* proclaimed itself an anti-imperial newsletter that advocated the freedom of the oppressed nations and positioned Euskadi as part of a global anticolonial struggle.

This chapter examines in detail *Jagi-Jagi*'s appropriation of anticolonial language through an analysis of both its national and international dimension. It shows how *Jagi-Jagi* refashioned Sabino Arana's anticolonialism

---

3 Translated from de Pablo and Mees, *El péndulo patriótico*, p. 121.

4 See among others Antonio Elorza, *Ideologías del nacionalismo vasco 1876–1937 (De los 'euskaros' a Jagi-Jagi)* (San Sebastián: Haranburu, 1978); Lorenzo Espinosa, *Gudari*; Watson, *Basque Nationalism and Political Violence*; Eduardo Renobales, *Jagi-Jagi: Historia del independentismo radical* (Bilbao: Imprenta Luna, 2010); Fernández Soldevilla, 'De Aberri a ETA'.

5 Renobales, *Jagi-Jagi*, p. 96.

to suit the period and relates how anticolonial claims responded to two main objectives. On the one hand, *Jagi-Jagi* painted Euskadi as a colony within Spain suffering multifaceted economic, cultural and political domination. This was used to reject the PNV's pro-autonomy strategy and to present Basque independence as the next logical and necessary step. The belief that Euskadi was a colony and that collaboration with Spain was unfeasible also prompted *Jagi-Jagi* to consider different extra-parliamentary strategies used in colonial settings to achieve independence. On the other hand, *Jagi-Jagi* also used its anticolonial discourse to internationalise and make visible the Basque cause. In a period in which *Jagi-Jagi* was unable to establish significant international connections and direct links with other nations, the newsletter proclaimed its solidarity with colonised nations and decried global colonialism. In sum, *Jagi-Jagi*'s anticolonialism had two clear aims in service of the movement: to stress the need for independence and to internationalise the Basque cause.

The 'strategic' use of anticolonialism by Basque radicals during the Second Republic suggests that like its predecessors, *Jagi-Jagi*'s anticolonial claims did not necessarily mean that its members were driven by a genuine hatred for colonialism. Rather, we need to consider *Jagi-Jagi*'s anticolonialism as a rhetorical strategy that was adapted to the needs of the movement. In that way, it is hardly surprising to observe that *Jagi-Jagi*'s language still portrayed some problematic views on race. As this chapter shows, *Jagi-Jagi*'s anticolonialism entailed two contradictory visions of race in the newsletter. When condemning Spain's rule and advocating independence, *Jagi-Jagi* used the classic racial arguments against the Spanish that had characterised Basque nationalism since its emergence. Contrarily, when decrying global colonialism, *Jagi-Jagi* directly attacked the structures of colonial rule, including racism. In other words, discourses of race responded to the two main objectives of Basque anticolonialism. By unpacking the set of complex and often contradictory ideas that existed within *Jagi-Jagi*, this final chapter serves as a summary of the wider complexities of the Basque anticolonial discourse that this book has sought to analyse.

Basque Nationalism during the Second Spanish Republic: Autonomy vs Independence

In November 1930, after nine years of internal divisions, the PNV reunified in the Basque town of Bergara, bringing the PNV-*Aberri* and the CNV together into a single party. The reunification had to overcome a major disagreement amongst Basque nationalists over whether the new party should alter Sabino Arana's pro-independence doctrines (the stance of the revisionists), a position opposed by the Aberrianos. Eventually, the reunified PNV committed to a programme that respected the values and political demands articulated by Sabino Arana, including the definition of the party as a strictly Catholic one.[6]

Although the two branches found points in common that allowed them to merge into a single party, the subsequent years demonstrated that the differences between radicals and moderates were as considerable as they had been in 1921. This was caused partly by the fact that with the arrival of the Republic, the PNV's main goal became the achievement of autonomy. Without abandoning the cause of independence, the PNV thought that it should take advantage of the new republican and democratic climate to advance Basque self-determination claims. This led to the drafting of the autonomy statutes of Estella (1931) and Gestoras (1932), which unlike the Catalan Statute were rejected, and to the participation of the PNV in the Republic's political life.[7] Naturally, this was accompanied by a process of moderation in the PNV's discourse. In fact, during the Republican years, the PNV evolved from a 'right-wing, Catholic, and xenophobic movement into

---

6 See Mees, *The Basque Contention*, p. 70. The stance that the reunified PNV took was not universally welcomed. A new nationalist party (Acción Nacionalista Vasca: Basque Nationalist Action, henceforth ANV) emerged shortly after the reunification to protest the terms of the 1930 agreement. The founders of the ANV belonged to the 'reformist' sectors of the party, which wanted to update Sabino Arana's fundamentalist programme. Thus, the new group –formed mainly by old members of the CNV – defended a non-Aranist form of nationalism and a programme based on liberalism, non-confessionalism, anti-racism, republicanism and pro-autonomy. In addition, the ANV did not share Arana's views on race and did not believe that it should be an essential element in defining the Basque nation. See de Pablo and Mees, *El péndulo patriótico*, p. 116 and Diego Muro, *Ethnicity and Violence*, p. 83. To understand the foundation of the ANV and the tensions and interactions with the other Basque nationalist groups during the Second Republic see José Luis de la Granja, *Nacionalismo y II República en el País Vasco: Estatutos de autonomía, partidos y elecciones. Historia de Acción Nacionalista Vasca: 1930–1936* (Madrid: Siglo XXI, 1986). See pp. 337–46 for a concise summary of the differences between the ANV, the PNV and *Jagi-Jagi*.

7 The statute of Estella was a strongly Foralist, Catholic and nationalist text due to the PNV's alliance with the right-wing and traditionalist Carlist forces and therefore, unacceptable for the Republic. In contrast, the statute of the Gestoras was more adapted to the Republican regime and its ideology. This was voted for by the Alavese, Biscayan and Gipuzkoan town halls, but rejected by Navarrese town halls, which meant the separation of Navarra from the autonomy process. To understand the Basque autonomic process in the Second Spanish Republic see: Juan Pablo Fusi, *El País Vasco, 1931–1937: Autonomía, Revolución, Guerra Civil* (Madrid: Biblioteca Nueva, 2002); de la Granja, *Nacionalismo y II República en el País Vasco*; José Luis de la Granja, 'Cinco años de República en Euskadi', *Historia Contemporánea*, 1 (1988), pp. 95–108.

a social-Christian, moderate and, of course, nationalist party'.[8] This shift explained the period of growth and expansion that the party experienced during the Second Republic.[9]

Not everyone within the PNV agreed with the new direction of the party. This time, opposition to the PNV's pro-autonomy programme came from a new radical group formed around the newsletter *Jagi-Jagi* (composed mostly of former members of the PNV-*Aberri*, like Gallastegi), which during the first years of the Second Spanish Republic was part of the PNV. Although for the PNV achieving autonomy did not imply abandoning independence as a main objective but taking a first step towards national liberation, *Jagi-Jagi* believed that this represented a clear deviation from Sabino Arana's fundamentalist ideas and believed that collaboration with Spain was unfeasible. With such major disagreements, a second split within the movement seemed inevitable. This took place between December 1933 and January 1934, when a group of radical dissidents – including Gallastegi, who had been sceptical about the reunification since his return from exile – left the PNV, and *Jagi-Jagi* separated from the main party.[10]

Jagi-Jagi published its first issue in September 1932, a year and a half after the proclamation of the Second Spanish Republic. The newsletter emerged as the press organ of the Federación de Mendigoxales de Bizcaya (Biscayan Federation of Mendigoxales). Although *Jagi-Jagi* had a strong and well-established competitor, the PNV's official newspaper *Euzkadi*, the radical newsletter had significant success during the Second Republic. Lorenzo Espinosa goes as far as to claim that *Jagi-Jagi* became the most widely read Basque periodical by young nationalists during the pre-war

---

8 Muro, *Ethnicity and Violence*, p. 85.

9 The electoral results of the PNV are illustrative of this growth. In the elections of 1933 the party achieved its best electoral results since its formation, with 12 MPs (50 per cent of those who could be elected between the four Basque provinces). In contrast, in the 1936 elections the PNV experienced an electoral decline, although the PNV continued being the party with more votes in the province of Biscay and in Gipuzkoa. Although the PNV continued to have its centre in Biscay (where it had around 13,470 members in 1933, around 50 per cent of its total members), the party also experienced a growth in popularity in other Basque-Spanish provinces. See de Pablo and Mees, *El péndulo patriótico*, pp. 134–35, p. 153 and p. 165.

10 Compared to the dissidents that joined the PNV-*Aberri* in 1921, this new rupture was very small: some *mendigoxales* followed Gallastegi (although most of these were not part of the PNV), but others stayed to defend independence from within the party. Furthermore, unlike the PNV-*Aberri*, *Jagi-Jagi* was not a political party and could not compete electorally against the PNV. Yet the new rupture was testament that the divisions between radicals and moderates were far from resolved.

period.[11] Whilst this claim is perhaps exaggerated, *Jagi-Jagi*'s popularity among Basque youths was undeniable; a fact that should not be overlooked, as the PNV was a 'young' party of which 60 per cent of its members in Biscay had been born after 1900.[12] In its strongest periods, *Jagi-Jagi* was able to print more than 22,000 copies per issue. Whilst between September 1932 and January 1934 *Jagi-Jagi* published an issue every Saturday, from 1934 to 1936 it published fewer and fewer issues, mostly owing to problems relating to printing access once the newsletter was separated from the PNV. On 18 July 1936, the day on which the Spanish Civil War started, *Jagi-Jagi* published its 110th issue, which would be its last.

Like previous Basque radical newsletters, *Jagi-Jagi* was the object of constant repression and censorship. On occasions, the Republic suspended the publication of nationalist periodicals and accused them of rebellion against the regime. In addition, many *Jagi-Jagi* members were harshly fined or imprisoned owing to direct violent confrontations between nationalists and republicans.[13] Indeed, the pronounced differences between the wider Basque nationalist movement (strongly Catholic, conservative and fearful of a possible social revolution) and the Republic (which had imposed restrictions on religious practice such as the suspension of confessional education) caused considerable friction, tension and direct confrontation between them in the early years. Furthermore, whilst the aim of achieving autonomy implied a process of moderation in the PNV's discourse and doctrine, *Jagi-Jagi* continued experiencing a process of radicalisation during the Republican years. As a result, the differences between the Republic and *Jagi-Jagi* became increasingly prominent. The climate of social tension, violence and repression during the Republic turned into a propitious strategy for *Jagi-Jagi* to sustain an anti-collaborationist and anti-statute campaign.

Indeed, *Jagi-Jagi* promoted a more extreme version of Basque nationalism than the official party. Unlike the PNV, and like its predecessors the Aberrianos, *Jagi-Jagi* advocated the use of extra-parliamentary methods (from civil disobedience to political violence) to achieve independence. In fact, as Fernández Soldevilla suggests, *Jagi-Jagi* was practically a paramilitary organisation – many of its members were armed, and they practised shooting and received military training.[14] As *Jagi-Jagi* claimed on many occasions, its

11 Lorenzo Espinosa, *Gudari*, p. 160.
12 De Pablo and Mees, *El péndulo patriótico*, p. 135. Despite the growth of the radicals and *Jagi-Jagi*, their influence did not surpass that of the PNV and the radical newsletter was limited mainly to Biscay and Bilbao.
13 De Pablo and Mees, *El péndulo patriótico*, p. 126.
14 See Gaizka Fernández Soldevilla, 'Ecos de la Guerra Civil. La glorificación del

members, the *mendigoxales*, were 'soldiers of the motherland'.[15] In its second issue, *Jagi-Jagi* stated: 'Let me tell you this in secret, *mendigoxale*, you are not a sportsman. Listen properly: you are a soldier of the motherland ... Yes, you are a soldier ... a soldier of a state that does not exist, but whose future existence depends largely on you.'[16]

Furthermore, the PNV fought vigorously to achieve independence whilst participating in Spain's political life, whereas *Jagi-Jagi* advocated the complete independence of Euskadi, criticised the Republican government daily and rejected any collaboration with Spanish forces.[17] *Jagi-Jagi* defended its fervent separatism by constantly quoting the radical thought of Sabino Arana, who they considered an unquestionable and almost messianic authority. The newsletter considered itself the real defender of Arana's ideology: as *Jagi-Jagi* claimed, 'Sabino Arana y Goiri is a dead man who is still alive'.[18] As the following sections of the chapter demonstrate, during the Second Republic *Jagi-Jagi* inherited and adapted Arana's anticolonialism to the needs of Basque radicalism.

'We Refuse to Talk with the Oppressor': Anticolonialism and Independence

Jagi-Jagi interpreted the Basque problem in the same way as Sabino Arana: Euskadi had been a free and independent nation until the nineteenth century, when it was forcefully colonised. According to *Jagi-Jagi*, 'Spanish monarchical imperialism' – inherited by the Republic – had established a formal dominion in the Basque Country in the previous century and since then, Basques had been forcibly subjugated and enslaved.[19] Thus the relationship between colony and metropole that had shaped the modern

---

gudari en la génesis de la violencia de ETA (1936–1968)', *Bulletin d'histoire contemporaine de l'Espagne*, 49 (2014), pp. 247–61 (p. 250).

15 Urduri, 'La labor de los mendigoxales', *Jagi-Jagi*, 24 September 1932, p. 2. Some of the page numbers in *Jagi-Jagi* are blurry, so the pagination may be slightly inaccurate in places.

16 M.S., '¡Quietas las makilas!', *Jagi-Jagi*, 24 September 1932, p. 3.

17 In fact, *Jagi-Jagi* advocated the establishment of a Frente Nacional Vasco (Basque National Front) which, inspired by the Irish example, united the most prominent Basque nationalist forces, including the PNV and the recently founded ANV. However, both PNV and ANV rejected *Jagi-Jagi*'s initiative. As de la Granja says, for *Jagi-Jagi* the main struggle in Spain was not one of class (left vs right) but one of race (Spain vs Euskadi). De la Granja, *Nacionalismo y II República en el País Vasco*, p. 527.

18 Translated from Fernández Soldevilla, 'De *Aberri* a ETA', p. 224.

19 See EMB (signed by different nationalist women), 'Carta abierta a don José María de Amilibia', *Jagi-Jagi*, 21 January 1933, p. 6.

history of Euskadi made the collaboration between coloniser and colonised unbearable: independence was the only option. As this section demonstrates, anticolonialism became a recurrent strategy for legitimising *Jagi-Jagi*'s separatist and anti-collaborationist claims.

Euskadi: A Colony in the West

Jagi-Jagi devoted many articles to analysing and critiquing Euskadi's alleged colonial situation from every angle. The economic consequences of colonial rule were analysed from a profoundly anti-capitalist perspective. For *Jagi-Jagi*, capitalism was the most substantial consequence of colonialism.[20] In 1934, Basque radical nationalist Trifón Etxebarria (also known as Etarte), who was in charge of writing about Euskadi's social problems in *Jagi-Jagi*, summarised the anti-capitalist doctrine of Basque radicalism: 'we hate capitalism, because similarly to imperialism, it enslaves nations – the latter enslaved men and the former enslaves workers.'[21] Another text claimed: 'imperialism aims to have small nationalities in its claws, and its ally, capitalism, aspires to do the same with humble men.'[22] Basques were doubly exploited and oppressed by imperialism and capitalism. Therefore, it was necessary to eradicate these 'ills' from Euskadi.[23]

Although *Jagi-Jagi*'s claims sometimes resembled those made by Lenin in *Imperialism, the Highest Stage of Capitalism* (1917), its anti-capitalist conceptions did not emanate from socialism. In fact, whilst it is true that some radicals were deeply influenced by the ideas of Irish socialist James Connolly, *Jagi-Jagi*'s anti-capitalism came from the social doctrine of the Church.[24] Therefore, such anti-capitalist claims did not translate into a rapprochement between the left

---

20 Sabino Arana had already denounced the effects of industrialisation during his lifetime, when criticising the consequences of the industrial revolution in the Basque region of Biscay, seen as a direct result of the 'Spanish invasion'. *Jagi-Jagi* also attributed the practices of capitalism to Spaniards, who were accused of bringing it to Euskadi. However, unlike Arana, *Jagi-Jagi* denounced the consequences that capitalism brought for both the Spanish and Basque working classes settled in Bilbao. This issue had already been raised in the 1920s by Gallastegi, who became one of the most charismatic leaders of *Jagi-Jagi*. In the 1920s, Gallastegi had already advocated the solidarity of the working classes – and even collaboration with Spanish workers – and disassociated these from any 'racial' criteria. See Mees, *Nacionalismo vasco, movimiento obrero y cuestión social*, p. 335.
21 Etarte, 'Capitalismo y orden social', *Jagi-Jagi*, 14 July 1934, p. 6.
22 *Jagi-Jagi*, 14 March 1936, p. 2.
23 *Jagi-Jagi*, 14 March 1936, p. 2.
24 Fernández Soldevilla, 'De *Aberri* a ETA', p. 225; Watson, *Basque Nationalism and Political Violence*, p. 132.

'Oppressed Peoples of the World, Unite!' 173

and Basque radical nationalists. In fact, Basque radical nationalists believed that socialism had deep contradictions: Etarte, for instance, could not comprehend how socialism – which was allegedly an internationalist and anti-imperialist movement – denied rights to the oldest nation of Europe, Euskadi.[25]

Colonial rule also had many cultural and social dimensions. According to *Jagi-Jagi*, a foreign power had invaded Euskadi and had imposed its 'exotic' laws and its imperialist traditions, intending to suppress Basque identity, language and race. *Jagi-Jagi* believed that the Spanish tried to 'kill the traditional soul of our race' by imposing their educational system, which it considered 'the most powerful weapon that Hispanic imperialism has had in Euskadi'.[26] Through their invasion, Spaniards had imposed their violent practices and their 'militarist imperialism', corrupting the peaceful nature of the Basques.[27] This imperialism had 'taught [Basques] how to use weapons in order to usurp free nations' and had 'covered American and Moorish lands with young Basque blood, which Euskadi needs to cultivate a new life'.[28] As seen in these texts, like its predecessors, *Jagi-Jagi* justified the Basque involvement in past colonial activities by blaming Spanish influence on Euskadi.

As in other periods, Basque radicals also criticised the political consequences of imperial rule which, in their view, had led to the loss of Basque political sovereignty. 'WE BASQUES ARE NOT SPANISH', *Jagi-Jagi* stated in capital letters. 'TO FORCE A FOREIGN NATION ON US IS TO EXERCISE AN IMPERIALIST ACT.'[29] Basque radicals gave this direct form of control an explicit name: colonialism. *Jagi-Jagi* criticised 'the methods of colonisation of Spaniards in Euskadi', and wrote about the racial conflict between 'an imperialist race which has not resigned itself to ceasing to rule … over a traditionally unconquerable race that does not wish to be ruled by anyone with colonial pretensions'.[30] *Jagi-Jagi* argued that the 'violent domination' that Basques experienced was justified by the excuse of "civilising" the Basques.[31] Following their predecessors' thought, however, *Jagi-Jagi* argued that it was the coloniser (the Spanish), not the colonised (the Basques), who needed to be civilised. Like Sabino

---

25 See Lorenzo Espinosa, *Gudari*, p. 173.

26 Manuel de la Sota, 'Escuelas del pueblo', *Jagi-Jagi*, 1 April 1933, p. 3.

27 Anon., 'Del libro de *Gudari*. Por la libertad vasca. Fragmentos', *Jagi-Jagi*, 2 January 1934, p. 2.

28 E. de Umaran, 'Meditando. Servicio militar', *Jagi-Jagi*, 2 January 1934, p. 6 and '21-Julio-1876', *Jagi-Jagi*, 21 July 1934, p. 2.

29 *Jagi-Jagi*, 8 April 1933, p. 7. Note: 'Basques are not Spanish' and 'imperialist' are in bold in the original.

30 Anon., 'Naskaldija', *Jagi-Jagi*, 1 April 1933, p. 10 and M.S., 'Epistolario de la semana', *Jagi-Jagi*, 20 May 1933, p. 3.

31 Azke, 'España independentista', *Jagi-Jagi*, 19 August 1933, p. 3.

Arana or *Aberri*, the newsletter justified this idea by stressing the alleged barbaric customs of Spaniards, including bullfighting, alcoholism and their innate impulse to invade free nations, impose their culture and language and persecute indigenous peoples.[32]

Basque radicals were, however, optimistic about the end of colonial rule in Euskadi. Since Latin America was an important point of analogy to reinforce the idea of Euskadi as a colony, *Jagi-Jagi* thought that the independence of the Basque Country would also arrive soon.[33] For example, *Jagi-Jagi* noted when reminding its readers that Cuba was now independent from Spain: 'history repeats itself'.[34] Another article published in the same issue stated: 'Spain lost its American colonies because it cruelly persecuted [Latin] American nationalism. But Spanish governors have not learned their lesson. Do they intend that within 50 years Spain is reduced to the Castilian barren plain?'[35] *Jagi-Jagi* even compared the indigenous communities of America to Euskadi: 'those American lands are not American nor Spanish but instead indigenous, just like us, like Euskadi, which is Basque.'[36] The solution to this situation was simple: to fight for 'the recognition of our nation free of colonisers'.[37] 'Nationalism' – *Jagi-Jagi* stated – 'fights against those who impose their colonising desires in this Basque land.'[38] The struggle for national liberation and for the end of colonial rule were two compatible and complementary struggles.

32 For a general criticism of Spanish culture and bullfighting see Gaztelumendi'tar L, 'Cultura Española', *Jagi-Jagi*, 2 June 1934, p. 2. For a criticism of the 'barbaric customs' that Spaniards brought to the Basque Country, including alcoholism, see Doctor Lazpita, 'Por la raza vasca. El alcohol no es alimento, es un veneno', *Jagi-Jagi*, 24 September 1932, p. 5 or Beti Aldage, '¿Civilización o barbarie?', *Jagi-Jagi*, 30 June 1934, p. 4.

33 For texts that make explicit comparisons between Euskadi and the former Latin American colonies see for instance: Gogo-Ituna, 'De corazón a corazón. ¡Escucha, enemigo! Y quizás mañana me llames hermano', *Jagi-Jagi*, 9 June 1934, p. 5; Azke, 'España independentista'. Many other nations were used as a mirror to stress Euskadi's colonial situation. For instance, when talking about Ireland and India, *Jagi-Jagi* argued that they were Euskadi's 'sisters of slavery'. See Gudari, 'A ti, mendigoxale. ¿Y nosotros, los vascos … ?', *Jagi-Jagi*, 24 September 1932, p. 3.

34 Anon., 'Los grandes libertadores. La República española ante la revolución cubana de José Martí', *Jagi-Jagi*, 5 November 1932, p. 7. This text is reproduced before an original text by José Martí written during the First Spanish Republic, in 1873. According to *Jagi-Jagi*, Martí's text could have been written in Euskadi in 1932.

35 Anon., 'Consideraciones', *Jagi-Jagi*, 5 November 1932, p. 6. See also, Txanka, 'Epistolario de la semana', *Jagi-Jagi*, 15 July 1933, p. 8 which explicitly says that Spain has already virtually lost its Basque colonies, the same way it lost its American colonies in the past.

36 P. de Agire, 'Aspectos. Libertad y opresión', *Jagi-Jagi*, 21 July 1934, p. 1.

37 *Jagi-Jagi*, 30 June 1934, p. 3.

38 Erotari, 'Cuartilla suelta. Nacionalismo', *Jagi-Jagi*, 5 May 1934, p. 6.

This anticolonial rhetoric that constantly condemned the colonial situation of Euskadi and stressed its consequences turned independence from the 'metropole' into something logical. Thus, the collaboration between coloniser and colonised (autonomy) seemed unbearable and the only plausible solution was independence. As *Jagi-Jagi* stated in capital letters:

[WE] BASQUES ARE NOT SPANISH AND WE AIM TO RECOVER THE INDEPENDENCE THAT THE SPANISH MONARCHY TOOK AWAY FROM US AND THAT THE REPUBLIC DENIES US ... THEREFORE, [WE] BASQUE NATIONALISTS ARE INDEPENDENTISTS AND SEPARATISTS.[39]

Another text that adapted Connolly's thought to the Basque cause argued: 'the conquest of Euskadi has entailed the social and political slavery of the Basque nation. Therefore, the liberation of Euskadi needs to entail the social and political independence of the Basques.'[40]

Indeed, whilst the PNV saw great opportunities to achieve self-determination within the new political framework, *Jagi-Jagi* believed that the Republic would never grant independence to Euskadi since Spain was 'the imperialist country par excellence'.[41] Despite the great efforts that the republican and socialist government of Manuel Azaña (1931–1933) had made to disassociate the new regime from Primo's imperialist and paternalist regime, Basque radicals continuously argued that the Republic had inherited the imperialist nature of monarchical and Catholic Spain, morphing into a type of 'imperialist modernism'.[42] This was because for *Jagi-Jagi*, Spain's imperialist essence was grounded in its blood and race, and was therefore unchangeable. As an article published in 1933 maintained, the racial characteristics of Spain had not changed despite its changing form of government: 'the Spanish people are used to ruling with the sword throughout history and they will keep ruling that way, whether their government is a republic, a monarchy or a socialist regime.'[43] Spanish people were not prepared to govern Basques democratically and through a republic because of the 'imperialism' that was inherent in the Spanish core.[44] As

39 *Jagi-Jagi*, 29 April 1933, p. 4.
40 *Jagi-Jagi*, 15 February 1936, p. 3.
41 Gudari, 'Anti-imperialismo socialista', *Jagi-Jagi*, 7 January 1933, p. 5.
42 Gudari, 'Ante la situación. Aún es hora ... ¿para qué?', *Jagi-Jagi*, 15 April 1933, pp. 6–7 (p. 7).
43 Ramón de Madariaga, 'La forma de gobierno', *Jagi-Jagi*, 11 March 1933, p. 8.
44 de Madariaga, 'La forma de gobierno', p. 8.

another article stated, it was a characteristic of the Spanish race to 'persecute other people and races'.[45]

The direct confrontations with republicans and the repression Basques experienced during the Republic served as proof of this. Furthermore, the colonial operation that the Republican government conducted in Morocco in 1934 strengthened *Jagi-Jagi*'s conviction regarding the imperialist nature of the new regime. During that year, the Republican government completed the occupation of the Moroccan territory of Ifni, attempting to finish a long colonial endeavour that began in the nineteenth century and was continued by Primo de Rivera. *Jagi-Jagi* did not take long to comment on the operation and use it for political gain.[46] As *Jagi-Jagi* claimed, 'those who rule Spain today are just as imperialist and enemies to the freedom of peoples as those who came before, as the recent occupation of Ifni demonstrates'.[47] *Jagi-Jagi* had plenty of reasons to refuse to engage with the Republic. As one issue stated, 'we don't want to hear anything else about the Statute. We refuse to talk with the oppressor'.[48]

Anticolonialism, Civil Disobedience and Violence

Since collaboration with the Republic was not a possibility, sacrifice and martyrdom were unanimously praised as the way forward. *Jagi-Jagi*'s believed that the oppression of Euskadi was akin to that of other colonies around the world, which made Basque radicals consider anticolonial forms of resistance in the Basque Country, much like their predecessors in the 1920s. These included extra-parliamentary methods, both violent and non-violent, which were directly copied and adapted from the struggle of other nations. Whether advocating for violence or not, it was clear that Basque radicals

45 Gudari, 'Del momento. Comentarios', *Jagi-Jagi*, 25 February 1933, p. 3.
46 *Jagi-Jagi* launched an anticolonial campaign against the occupation of Ifni. This included multiple texts comparing the situation of Basques and Moroccans and others condemning the occupation and the Republican regime. For instance, an article written by *Jagi-Jagi*'s ideologue and leader Gallastegi devoted some sarcastic lines to the Republic while stressing its colonial nature: 'Ifni is now part of the empire of the new Spanish Republic, which was born to the cry of justice, democracy and freedom! In order to bury, so they said, the old imperialist politics of the Monarchy.' Gudari, 'Pacifismo y desarme. Vuelo sobre Ifni', *Jagi-Jagi*, 5 May 1934, pp. 4–5 (p. 4). The newsletter also criticised the fact that only one Spanish MP had denounced the invasion while the rest of the Parliament, including the PNV, remained silent. *Jagi-Jagi* could not understand the silence of the PNV since they believed that Ifni and Euskadi shared the same oppression and the same enemy.
47 Mentxaka eta Basare tar Iñaki, 'En el crisol del Patriotismo', *Jagi-Jagi*, 10 May 1934, p. 1.
48 *Jagi-Jagi*, 26 August 1933, p. 5.

had concluded that achieving freedom through parliamentary means was no longer an option. Similarly to what *Aberri* New York had advanced some years before, *Jagi-Jagi* was increasingly convinced that an agreement with Madrid was not going to grant Basques their freedom. *Jagi-Jagi* agreed unanimously that when promises were broken: 'what cannot be solved via a legal path, can be resolved – and it has always been this way in nationalist redemptions – with sacrifice.'[49] 'Sacrifice to win', the article continued. 'There is no other way.'[50]

On the one hand, civil disobedience methods such as those put in practice in former British territories such as Ireland and colonies such as India were regarded by Basque radicals with enthusiasm, with both countries being the most frequent international references of the newsletter.[51] In particular, the sacrifices of Gandhi or Terence MacSwiney, who had died in 1920 in Brixton prison after 74 days fasting, were romanticised and praised by the radical newsletter with the intention of inspiring its readers.[52] As an article in *Jagi-Jagi* stated, Basques should walk 'steadily towards the path that the Irish marked for us, where the mayor of Cork [Terence MacSwiney] with his 60 days of agony was admired globally; admiration which will hopefully become imitation'; Basques had to go 'to where Gandhi is today ... challenging powerful England'; Basques had to 'walk, to imitate our Master Sabino, an example who must endure in

---

49 Pedro de Basaldua, 'Apuntes. Desvergüenzas de rapazuelo', *Jagi-Jagi*, 7 January 1933, p. 8. Sacrifice and martyrdom remained a fixation in *Jagi-Jagi*: there are references to these values in virtually most, if not all, of its 110 issues.

50 Pedro de Basaldua, 'Apuntes', p. 8.

51 Ireland was without a doubt the strongest international reference of *Jagi-Jagi*, with up to four references in four different articles in some issues. Furthermore, the Irish example was continuously praised in Gallastegi's book *Por la libertad vasca* ('For Basque Freedom'), published in 1933, which contained several pieces devoted to Ireland and its struggle for independence as an example to imitate for the Basques. See Gallastegi, *Por la libertad vasca* (Bilbao: Talleres E. Verdes, 1933). This interest was not reciprocal. Instead, Basque nationalism was not very present in Irish public opinion. As Núñez Seixas argues, only the Catalan autonomy question and the confessional tendencies of the Catalan movement were issues that attracted some Irish newspapers. See Núñez Seixas, 'Ecos de Pascua', p. 472.

52 Both Gandhi and MacSwiney had already been praised by Basque radicals in the previous period. For instance, *Patria Vasca* devoted some articles to Gandhi's Salt March. See Crítica, 'Las grandes inquietudes de los pueblos', p. 5. MacSwiney had perhaps received more coverage in the Basque radical press, as he became an international (and of course national) martyr symbolising the Irish struggle for independence and the power of sacrifice. See, for instance, Anon., 'Del movimiento nacionalista irlandés', *Aberri* (newsletter), 15 April 1922, p. 2.

our minds'.⁵³ The fact that Basque nationalists believed themselves to be involved in a struggle against colonialism, like India was and Ireland had been, facilitated these comparisons. As another article claimed, quoting *Jagi-Jagi*'s ideologue Manuel de la Sota (who usually wrote under the pseudonym Txanka), 'there are two kinds of freedom: "one that can be achieved through a few votes and one which costs blood". Those who are settled, who don't want to suffer, should follow the first option; we [Basques] should be like Gandhi.'⁵⁴

The desire to imitate both MacSwiney and Gandhi's struggles had material consequences. In September 1931, a year before *Jagi-Jagi* issued its first number, a group of Basque nationalists led by Gallastegi went on hunger strike in prison. The strike took place after 14 nationalists were arrested following a pro-nationalist demonstration in Bilbao, which was severely repressed by the Spanish authorities and left one person dead. The strike lasted only two days since, as soon as the strike began, the civil governor ordered the release of the prisoners. As Lorenzo Espinosa points out, 'a new rebellion and another strategy – with prison as a reference – began to take theoretical shape in Gallastegi's mind. A year after the strike, this found a suitable vehicle of expression: the weekly newsletter *Jagi-Jagi*.'⁵⁵ The first issue of *Jagi-Jagi*, published exactly a year after the hunger strike began, reproduced the original document calling for the strike of 1931 and praised the sacrifice of the Basque martyrs who had been prepared to give their lives for the Basque cause.⁵⁶

Furthermore, influenced directly by Gandhi, *Jagi-Jagi* activists developed a new civil disobedience method that was based on reversing the effects of repression by benefiting from them. For Basque radicals, prison was not something to fear but instead a positive experience. As *Jagi-Jagi* quoted from Gandhi:

> The imprisonment of innocent people under an unfair government must be considered a consequence as natural as getting ill when living in an unhealthy atmosphere. Government will stop imprisoning us when we stop fearing imprisonments.⁵⁷

---

53 Goi, 'Desespañolización y patriotismo', *Jagi-Jagi*, 27 January 1934, p. 7.
54 Polixene T. De Mandaluniz, 'Soy revolucionaria', *Jagi-Jagi*, 13 January 1934, p. 6. Note: Only the text within two quotation marks was a direct quote from de la Sota.
55 Translated from Lorenzo Espinosa, *Gudari*, p. 193.
56 See 'El juramento de la cárcel de Larinaga', *Jagi-Jagi*, 17 September 1932, p. 2.
57 Mahatma Gandhi, *Jagi-Jagi*, 25 March 1933, p. 1. The original is in Spanish, not in English.

Jagi-Jagi stated confidently that the biggest achievement of the PNV after the proclamation of the Republic was to defeat prison.[58] *Jagi-Jagi*'s passive resistance strategies should not be underestimated: for the first time, Basque radicals put into practice strategies that would be later developed by ETA, including hunger strikes and the exaltation of 'martyrs'.

On the other hand, some of the nationalists writing in *Jagi-Jagi* went further and believed that sacrifice implied violence. As we have seen, this was not a novelty but a continuation of the Basque radical trend which, during the Irish Revolution, had reinterpreted Sabino Arana's rhetoric as an explicit defence of armed struggle. After *Jagi-Jagi* became an organisation independent from the PNV, references to violence became even more substantial than before. An article published in 1934 by Etarte seemed convinced of the advantages of the use of violence: 'before dying, kill! We can help the Homeland more by killing our enemies than by letting us be killed by them ... let's not be – we can't be, anyway – the first to kill but the last to die.'[59]

With the embrace of anticolonial forms of resistance (either civil resistance or violence), *Jagi-Jagi* had found a practical way to defend its non-collaborationist strategy. In 1934, de la Sota stated that 'real freedom cannot be achieved by talking with the oppressor, but by confronting him'.[60] In 1936, another article in *Jagi-Jagi* reiterated de la Sota's point: 'Basque patriots: the oppressed nations that have freedom have never achieved this by negotiating with the enemy, but by fighting incessantly against him.'[61] Following this line, an extremely aggressive article published in one of the last issues of *Jagi-Jagi*, declared the end of peace with Spain:

> it is time! ... our patience has been abused and once more events of history need to be repeated ... our patience is exhausted, our spirit has awakened, disenchanted by fake promises, the soul of our grandparents has revived in our soul. WE DO NOT ACCEPT PEACE! (capitals in the original)[62]

Ironically, soon after that article was published, the end of peace came for the whole of Spain, including the Basque Country. On July 18, the same day

---

58 Lorenzo Espinosa, *Gudari*, p. 196.
59 Etarte, 'Odio de pueblos. ¡Bastante!', *Jagi-Jagi*, 4 August 1934, p. 6.
60 Manuel de la Sota, 'Rumbo y designio de las huellas sabinianas', *Jagi-Jagi*, 6 January 1934, pp. 4–5 (p. 5).
61 Begitasuna, 'Luchemos sin claudicar', *Jagi-Jagi*, 6 June 1936, p. 4. Similar points were made in the penultimate issue of *Jagi-Jagi*. See Anon., 'Tomemos nota', *Jagi-Jagi*, 11 July 1936, p. 4.
62 Keamti, '¡En pie raza vasca!', *Jagi-Jagi*, 13 June 1936, p. 3.

that *Jagi-Jagi* published its last issue, the coup that had begun in Morocco to end the democratically elected Republic spread to different parts of the peninsula. With it, the most tragic event in recent Spanish history began. The experiences of Basque nationalists during the Spanish Civil War would be essential for the future of the movement. As Watson points out,

> where previously Basque nationalism conceptualized its cause in terms of a symbolic recourse to resistance and heroism, during the Civil War, Basque nationalists experienced firsthand many of the thoughts and emotions that, until that time, had remained limited to metaphor and allusion.[63]

These new experiences, alongside the harsh repression Basque nationalists experienced during Francoism and the emergence of a new wave of anticolonial nationalism during the 1950s, would be essential for the formation of ETA in 1959. As this book has shown, ETA activists were not the first generation of Basque nationalists who advocated for violence and sacrifice when parliamentary methods were, at least in their view, exhausted.

Jagi-Jagi's Internationalism in a Period of Anticolonial Convergence: Direct Contacts and the Occupation of Abyssinia

Apart from using strong anticolonial language to legitimise independence and promote a non-collaborationist strategy, *Jagi-Jagi*'s anticolonialism also had a clear internationalising goal. Since the merging of the two branches of Basque nationalism in 1930, the movement aimed to publicise and internationalise its cause to gain international visibility and forge alliances with other movements. In the first years of the Republic, PNV leaders already exposed the need to internationalise the movement and make the Basque cause known to 'other peoples and States of Europe'.[64] This became a priority for the PNV during the Second Republic, as exemplified by its presence in conferences held by the Congress of European Nationalities (CEN) or the Europeanist subtitle (Euskadi-Europe) that the celebrations of Aberri Eguna carried in 1933.[65] Indeed, the quest for autonomy led the PNV to include

---

63 Watson, *Basque Nationalism and Political Violence*, p. 145.
64 Translated from Núñez Seixas, '¿Protodiplomacia exterior o ilusiones ópticas?', p. 264.
65 Despite some reservations, the PNV had entered the CEN organisation in 1930. The CEN was created in 1925 with the aim of bringing the different western national minorities (especially those in central-Europe) together and acting as a mediator with the LN to solve the minorities question. See Xosé Manoel Núñez Seixas,

Euskadi's struggle among the small European nationalities that had not achieved self-determination after the Great War but hoped to be protected by the Wilsonian order.

Unsurprisingly, the strictly separatist programme of *Jagi-Jagi* did not fit with this Europeanist and collaborationist vision and the organisation sought to establish direct links, alliances and solidarity networks with other anticolonial movements. Once again, this presented an important continuity with the previous period. But if in the previous decade, the Aberrianos had appealed to Wilsonian institutions such as the LN to internationalise their cause, by the 1930s the scepticism that Basque radicals felt towards the Great Powers was too strong to consider their help. *Jagi-Jagi* seemed to firmly believe that the LN and the Great Powers would once again ignore the Basque question, as they had done with other colonised nations in the 1920s.

Jagi-Jagi fully engaged with the period of transnational solidarity and anticolonial upheaval that characterised the decade in which it operated. In the late 1920s and the early 1930s, anticolonial organisations such as the LAI – which became openly communist in the late 1920s – continued operating and holding congresses in major European cities. Despite internal disagreements, the organisation kept active and led initiatives such as the organisation of a global 'anti-exposition' to the 1931 International Colonial Exposition in Paris, which aimed to demonstrate 'the blessings of colonial rule'.[66] In the meantime, anticolonial forms of resistance such as those that emerged in India or Abyssinia (present-day Ethiopia) became leading examples in fighting colonial rule.

The anticolonial upheaval and international solidarity that characterised the interwar period solidified the Basque radical belief that the only way to defeat colonialism was through the union of oppressed nations. *Jagi-Jagi* altered the internationalist motto of 'workers of the world, unite!' to 'enslaved countries of the world, unite!'.[67] According to *Jagi-Jagi*, both non-western and western movements had to unite in a transcontinental struggle against imperialism: 'this ray of justice ... will cast a threatening glow across the sinister skies of the globe ... uniting every man from east to west, a rainbow of harmony between redeemed countries.'[68] Like the LAI, the union of the oppressed countries transcended any difference of race, religion

---

'¿Autodeterminación o autonomía cultural? Debates ideológicos en el Congreso de Nacionalidades Europeas (1925–1939)', *Hispania: Revista española de historia*, 58.200 (1998) pp. 1113–51 and Núñez Seixas, '¿Protodiplomacia exterior o ilusiones ópticas?'.

66 Brückenhaus, *Policing Transnational Protest*, p. 161.
67 Gudari, 'Ante la situación', p. 6.
68 M.S., 'Sabino denunciado', *Jagi-Jagi*, 8 October 1932, p. 1.

or culture. As Gallastegi wrote in 1933 when talking about the contacts and alliances forged between Basques, Catalans and Galicians in the last decade,

> it is enough if they [Catalans and Galicians] call themselves nationalists, if they recognise themselves as sons of an enslaved nation, if they manifest their desire for freedom. And we feel the same or more sympathy and attachment when we talk about the Irish or Macedonian movement; the Syrian or Nicaraguan, the Egyptian or Philippine, the African or Hindu, regardless of the differences in lifestyle, religion or other pillars of our movements.[69]

Despite these claims of union, *Jagi-Jagi* had little success when establishing direct contacts with other nations and movements. At the end of the day, unlike the PNV-*Aberri* of the 1920s, *Jagi-Jagi* was not a political party and therefore had little agency to form its own contacts and alliances. Thus, when in July 1933 the PNV signed a new pluri-national pact called GALEUZCA – which united the same stateless nations as the Triple Alliance of 1923 with the intention of fomenting the relationship between Galicia, Euskadi and Catalonia – *Jagi-Jagi* opted out.[70] Indeed, unlike the Triple Alianza, GALEUZCA's goal was not independence but the autonomy of the three nationalities.[71] Despite this, *Jagi-Jagi* was able to establish contacts with organisations that also refused to join GALEUZCA, such as the Catalan radical organisation Nosaltres Sols (whose name was a Catalan translation of Sinn Féin: 'Ourselves Only'). Yet, unlike the previous period when the Aberrianos had managed to establish direct contacts with Irish republicans in exile, this time there was little contact with movements based outside the peninsula. In fact, most of the contacts with Ireland took place before *Jagi-Jagi* was formed, although evidence suggests that these were facilitated by Basque radicals.[72]

---

69 Gudari, 'Canalización nacional. El primer eslabón a forjar', *Jagi-Jagi*, 5 August 1933, pp. 4-5.

70 This was initially signed by representatives of the PNV and five Galician and Catalan parties and organisations. Later, the ANV, Esquerra Republicana de Catalunya and the Lliga Catalana also signed.

71 See de la Granja, *Nacionalismo y II República en el País Vasco*, p. 364; de Pablo and Mees, *El péndulo patriótico*, p. 146; Mees, 'Tan lejos, tan cerca', pp. 564-65.

72 Some of these contacts include Ambrose Martin's visit to Bilbao in summer 1932, which symbolised a continuation with the Aberriano policy. During his visit, he inaugurated a new EAB office and gave lectures which insisted on the value of sacrifice. See Núñez Seixas, 'Ecos de Pascua', pp. 470-71. Coinciding with Martin's visit, a nationalist delegation of the PNV left Euskadi for a 'strange political-sporting mission' in Dublin. In Ireland, Basque nationalists were warmly received with cries of 'Gora Euzkadi' ('long live Euskadi'), and were able to meet leading figures of

When direct contacts were scarce, anticolonial and solidarity statements symbolically united the Basque struggle with others. As *Jagi-Jagi* stated: 'we should show solidarity with those who suffer and die for independence, because this way we can demonstrate to the world, and ourselves, our rights.'[73] Another article read: 'we are enemies of every war of conquest, every despotism, every oppression. We are enemies of this selfish imperialism which subjects other nations to its despotic power.'[74] This later article strongly resonated with how the Aberrianos had introduced themselves in 1923: 'fundamentally anti-imperialists and enemies of all wars of conquest'.[75]

The most remarkable example of Basque radical transnational solidarity during this period is that of Abyssinia. Between 1935 and 1936, *Jagi-Jagi* united its voice with those who condemned the unprecedented occupation of Abyssinia. This had begun in October 1935 when Benito Mussolini invaded the free nation of Abyssinia without any previous declaration of war. Mussolini justified this occupation by claiming that it would guarantee the security of eastern Africa and would provide land for the growing Italian population. The occupation of Abyssinia confirmed both the LAI and Basque radicals' suspicions about the LN's lack of interest in protecting extra-European nations from colonial rule. Indeed, although Abyssinia was a member of the LN, this had not been enough to stop Mussolini's invasion. As José María Tápiz suggests, this dispute tested the LN's capacity for action and diminished its authority.[76] This was the perfect opportunity for *Jagi-Jagi* to strengthen its anticolonial and anti-LN claims.

Jagi-Jagi was neither the only nor the first organisation to protest the occupation of Abyssinia. The invasion of one of the only territories in Africa that had remained free from colonial rule saw a moment of convergence in which many anti-imperial voices around the world emerged and united against the occupation. Protests took place both before and during the occupation. Black people across the Americas including the United States,

Irish nationalism such as De Valera and Mary MacSwiney, the sister of the globally praised martyr Terence MacSwiney. See Ugalde, *La acción exterior del nacionalismo vasco*, pp. 415–16; Kyle McCreanor, 'Ireland and the Basque Country: Nationalisms in Contact, 1895–1939' (unpublished Master's thesis, Concordia University, 2019), pp. 56–58; Cullen, *Radical Basque Nationalist-Irish Republican Relations*, p. 64. Perhaps the only significant direct contact between Irish and Basque radicals during *Jagi-Jagi*'s time was the establishment of an Irish-Basque trading initiative led by Martin and Gallastegi. See Cullen, *Radical Basque Nationalist-Irish Republican Relations*, p. 67.

73 Beti-Aldage, '¡Gora Etiopía Azkatuta!', *Jagi-Jagi*, 18 April 1936, p. 1.
74 *Jagi-Jagi*, 4 April 1936, p. 2.
75 See Chapter 4: Anon., 'El árbol malato', *Aberri* (newsletter), 10 March 1923, p. 3.
76 José María Tápiz, 'El Partido Nacionalista Vasco ante la guerra de Abisinia (1935–1936)', *Journal of Inquiry and Research*, 79 (2004), pp. 95–110 (p. 95).

parts of the Caribbean and Uruguay protested forcefully against the war.[77] Europe also saw the formation of different alliances and anti-imperial organisations. For instance, prior to the invasion, the threat of the occupation prompted an alliance between Black activists, left-wing French intellectuals and Italian anti-fascists in Paris. This led to the formation of the International Committee for the Defence of the Ethiopian People in 1935, which sent petitions against the invasion to the LN and united about 250 political groups from around the globe.[78] The protests at the invasion during 1935 and 1936 transcended class and race.[79]

The Black community in London also raised its voice against the occupation by establishing ties with their Parisian counterparts through Pan-African leader George Padmore and forming organisations such as the International African Friends of Ethiopia, founded in 1935. As Minkah Makalani points out, 'London-based black radicals agreed on the importance of Ethiopia to their liberation and the future of the British empire'.[80] Other thinkers felt similarly, as proved by Jawaharlal Nehru's ties to London-based Pan-African leaders such as Padmore and by his energetic anticolonial claims against both Italy and the LN. Abyssinia became the focus of Nehru's anti-imperial campaign. He united both the Indian and the Abyssinian struggle by claiming that they shared a 'common bond' as 'victims of imperialist greed and exploitation'.[81] As shown below, *Jagi-Jagi* developed a very similar rhetoric.

This considerable confluence of anticolonial thinkers and groups against the occupation of Abyssinia should not go unremarked. As Goebel has pointed out, 'the convergence around singular moments [in this case, the invasion of Abyssinia] entrenched the perception that anticolonialism in

---

77 Goebel, *Anti-Imperial Metropolis*, p. 166.
78 Goebel, *Anti-Imperial Metropolis*, p. 167.
79 See also Joseph Fronczak, 'Local People's Global Politics: A Transnational History of the Hands Off Ethiopia Movement of 1935', *Diplomatic History*, 39.2 (2015), pp. 245–74.
80 Minkah Makalani, *In the Cause of Freedom: Radical Black Internationalism from Harlem to London, 1917–1939* (Chapel Hill: University of North Carolina Press, 2011), p. 163.
81 Michele L. Louro, *Comrades Against Imperialism: Nehru, India, and Interwar Internationalism* (Cambridge: Cambridge University Press, 2018), p. 204. When the Spanish Civil War broke out in July 1936, both the Indian Nationalist Congress and Nehru showed solidarity with the Spanish republicans. Nehru even went to Spain in 1938, where he witnessed the war for himself. See Louro, *Comrades Against Imperialism*, pp. 214–55. See also Michael P. Ortiz, 'Spain! Why? Jawaharlal Nehru, Non-Intervention, and the Spanish Civil War', *European History Quarterly*, 49 (2019), pp. 445–66.

any one place was part of a more global struggle against imperialism, which also affected other regions and countries'.[82] This was the perfect occasion for Euskadi to be integrated in this anticolonial global struggle.

Jagi-Jagi did not take long to join the transcontinental protests at the occupation. The PNV and its newsletter *Euzkadi* also added themselves to the voices that condemned the war and defended the Abyssinian's right to independence. Both *Euzkadi* and *Jagi-Jagi* used the Abyssinian example strategically to defend their own principles and goals. Through the colonial analogy of Euskadi and Abyssinia, the PNV and *Euzkadi* used the occupation to promote Basque autonomy claims: if the Abyssinians could regain control of their own destiny, so too could the Basques who were fighting for the approval of their Statute of Autonomy.[83] In contrast, *Jagi-Jagi* used the war to endorse the independence of Euskadi. Ultimately, both branches of Basque nationalism had shared a similar goal through multiple generations: to internationalise the Basque cause. Furthermore, for *Jagi-Jagi* this was a unique chance to stress the evil and selfish character of both imperial powers and imperial organisations such as the LN and to underscore the rationale behind its anti-collaborationist posture.

Jagi-Jagi began to publish about Abyssinia as soon as it was able to publish again, having been unable to print any issues between September 1934 and November 1935. On the first page of the first issue published after this hiatus, *Jagi-Jagi* informed readers of the re-emergence of the newsletter. This was followed by a brief but clear line on the Abyssinian struggle: 'Abyssinia fights bravely for its independence. Let's admire this nation and let's follow the example of its great heroism.'[84] From that moment until the last issue of *Jagi-Jagi* on 18 July 1936, the newsletter wrote about Abyssinia in most of its issues and supported the Abyssinians in their struggle 'against this new barbaric act'.[85]

Jagi-Jagi also used this opportunity to denounce the colonial nature of western powers such as France and Britain that had remained 'passive' in this situation. They were labelled as opportunist, selfish and imperialist nations that did not stop the invasion because they were more concerned with their own interests.[86] An article in *Jagi-Jagi* argued that the situation of all the oppressed nations of the world would improve considerably if Britain

82 Goebel, *Anti-Imperial Metropolis*, p. 174.
83 Adapted translation from de Pablo, '¡Grita Libertad!', p. 272.
84 *Jagi-Jagi*, 30 November 1935, p. 1. The same issue included more references to the Abyssinian conflict.
85 *Jagi-Jagi*, 11 January 1936, p. 2. In another article, *Jagi-Jagi* spoke about the 'brutal imperialism' of Italian fascists. E., 'Los invasores', *Jagi-Jagi*, 25 January 1936, p. 2.
86 For criticism of international passivity, see A., 'Dos medidas', *Jagi-Jagi*, 14 March

was defenceless (literally, naked).[87] *Jagi-Jagi* also criticised the passive and imperialistic attitude of the LN, which had already been the object of critique by Basque radicals during the 1920s.[88]

Like its predecessors had done with the Rif War, *Jagi-Jagi* used the occupation of Abyssinia as a point of comparison for the oppression to which the Basques were subjected. The war in Abyssinia was seen as 'a war of conquest ... in which thousands and thousands of men are paying the price for their love for freedom, against the imperialism of one man'.[89] The situation of Abyssinia was described in the same way as that of Euskadi: like the Basques, Abyssinia nourished a heroic love for independence; Abyssinia had seen, like the Basques, how its land and home were invaded and robbed; Abyssinia was, like Euskadi, a victim of imperialism and therefore, both nations had a legitimate right to defend themselves against usurpation. In addition, both nations suffered the economic and political consequences imperialism: 'Abyssinia dies under Italian imperialism, whereas global capitalism applauds and waits to share the treasure of the poor Abyssinian'.[90] The fight against oppression united both nations:

> as if the sacred echoes of our ancestors – noble and generous warriors who split blood to defend the rights of our Euskadi – awoke within us, we have felt united in a close and fraternal embrace with these humble beings of colour who, with noble simplicity, bare their chests against cannons and bombs.[91]

When in May 1936 Mussolini's forces entered Addis Ababa and Italy annexed Abyssinia, *Jagi-Jagi* reported the end of freedom for the Abyssinians and concluded by advocating the union of the oppressed nations: 'Freedom for Ethiopia! Enslaved peoples of the world unite!'[92] Two months later, in July 1936, the start of the Spanish Civil War and then the occupation of Bilbao in 1937 by Francoist troops reinforced even more the parallels between Euskadi and Abyssinia.

1936, p. 4; Uarlia, 'El Carnaval Internacional', *Jagi-Jagi*, 21 March 1936, p. 4 and Gudari, 'Ante el caso de Etiopía. Indiferencia criminal', *Jagi-Jagi*, 11 April 1936, p. 1.
87 Uarlia, 'El Carnaval Internacional', p. 4.
88 See Beti-Aldage, '¡Gora Etiopía Azkatuta!'; A., 'Dos medidas'; and Gudari, 'Ante el caso de Etiopía'.
89 Beti-Aldage, 'Inquietud. Siguiendo la ruta', *Jagi-Jagi*, 28 March 1936, p. 2.
90 'Gran mítin de afirmación nacionalista en Sodupe', *Jagi-Jagi*, 25 April 1936, p. 1.
91 Beti-Aldage, 'Arriba los pueblos oprimidos', *Jagi-Jagi*, 2 May 1936, p. 1.
92 'Solidaridad internacional de los pueblos oprimidos', *Jagi-Jagi*, 9 May 1936, p. 1.

Racists or Anti-Racists? *Jagi-Jagi* and Its Two Approaches to Race

As this chapter has demonstrated, anticolonialism was one of the main facets of *Jagi-Jagi*'s ideological core. *Jagi-Jagi* used strong anticolonial rhetoric to reject the possibility of any collaboration (autonomy) with the 'enemy' (Spain) and to establish transnational links of solidarity with other colonised nations. This led to two contradictory approaches competing within *Jagi-Jagi*: when talking about Spain, *Jagi-Jagi* stressed the racial inferiority and the inherently evil nature of their alleged colonisers. Conversely, when condemning global colonialism, *Jagi-Jagi* wrote explicitly anti-racist claims and denounced racial hierarchies. I argue that these two contradictory approaches to race within *Jagi-Jagi* respond to the different uses of Basque anticolonialism: racist claims against the Spanish were used to justify the need for independence whilst anti-racist statements aimed to bring Basques and other colonised nations together and ultimately internationalise the Basque cause.

The extent to which *Jagi-Jagi* was racist or anti-racist has generated disagreement amongst scholars. Whilst some scholars such as Lorenzo Espinosa have argued that *Jagi-Jagi*'s members did not use racial arguments against Spaniards and that racist accusations against Basque nationalism are clichés used by anti-nationalists, others like Fernández Soldevilla have argued that hatred of Spanish immigrants or *maketos* and hence 'race' were still crucial concepts for *Jagi-Jagi*.[93]

There is some truth in both interpretations. The reason why Lorenzo Espinosa has argued that *Jagi-Jagi* did not use racist arguments against the Spanish is that some Basque radical ideologues started challenging several well-established dogmas within Basque nationalism, such as racial hatred for *maketos*. For example, according to de la Sota, Basque nationalism should defend itself from Spain, not Spaniards.[94] *Jagi-Jagi* gave space to de la Sota's arguments in its newsletter. From there, he occasionally advocated a form of nationalism that rejected a biological conception of race: 'our nationalism has to be, above all, humanism.'[95] In another article, de la Sota stated: 'one man can be superior to another – the same way that generally an Englishman is superior to the Spaniard [note the residual Anglophilia] – but this is due to the stage of culture which its race has reached, and not because of

---

93 See Lorenzo Espinosa, *Gudari*, pp. 181–90; Fernández Soldevilla, 'De *Aberri* a ETA', p. 224.
94 Lorenzo Espinosa, *Gudari*, p. 184.
95 Translated from de la Sota in Lorenzo Espinosa, *Gudari*, p. 185.

the qualities of the race.'⁹⁶ He concluded the article: 'I would like to repeat endlessly those marvellous words by Mahatma Gandhi so they stay in the hearts of all Basque nationalists: "For me, patriotism and humanity are the same thing. I am a patriot, because I am a man and a human."'⁹⁷

De la Sota also argued that contrary to what happened 100 years before when racial purity existed (because a Spanish invasion had not happened yet), the *maketos* should not be evicted from Euskadi but rather should be welcomed.⁹⁸ In fact, he believed that it was necessary to choose Spaniards who had embraced Basque culture ahead of Basques who had embraced 'Spanishness'. For this reason, he even condemned the word *maketo* and argued that this was an 'insulting and anti-Christian' adjective that should no longer be used.⁹⁹

De la Sota was not alone, and other articles supported the rejection of anti-*maketismo*. For instance, an article written by the son of a German man and a Basque woman that commented on the acceptance of non-Basque members of the PNV, downplayed the importance of 'race' in the movement and rejected anti-*maketismo* and Sabino Arana's belief that Basqueness and purity were determined by one's last name. As the article posited, Irish nationalist leader de Valera had a Spanish last name but was undoubtably Irish.¹⁰⁰ The article continued: 'to attempt to categorise the Basque nation according to its blood purity ... is, in modern times, a truly ridiculous idea which would be the ruin and discrediting of our ideals'.¹⁰¹

Fernández Soldevilla has acknowledged de la Sota's challenges to Arana's dogmas.¹⁰² However, Fernández Soldevilla has downplayed de la Sota's arguments by stating that they were minoritarian and that his view was harshly criticised by *Jagi-Jagi*. There is, as I say above, also logic to this argument. My close analysis of *Jagi-Jagi* reveals that race was still an essential element in the newsletter and that the word 'race' was used in every issue analysed. As a text which openly disagreed with the examples above stated, 'race is Euskadi: it is its principle and its basis'.¹⁰³

---

96 Manuel de la Sota, 'Corrigiendo errores. Para el extraño inevitable', *Jagi-Jagi*, 24 September 1932, p. 2.
97 De la Sota, 'Corrigiendo errores', p. 2. Note: Only the text within double quotation marks is a quote by Gandhi.
98 De la Sota, 'Corrigiendo errores', p. 2.
99 Manuel de la Sota, 'Los "maketos" al servicio de Euzkadi', *Jagi-Jagi*, 25 February 1933, p. 5.
100 Julio Yankee Murua, 'Una opinión', *Jagi-Jagi*, 10 December 1932, p. 5.
101 Yankee Murua, 'Una opinión', p. 5.
102 Fernandez Soldevilla, 'De *Aberri* a ETA', p. 224.
103 Utarsusi, 'Raza vasca', *Jagi-Jagi*, 4 March 1933, p. 7.

Following Arana's line of thought, *Jagi-Jagi* also consistently stressed the purity of the Basque race – which contrasted with the mixed or *mestizo* nature of the Spaniard – through both new articles (interestingly, some of them written by de la Sota himself) and fragments of Arana's most radical texts that were reproduced in the newsletter.[104] As a *Jagi-Jagi* article written in 1934 stated, 'preserving racial purity is the preferred principle in those places in Euskadi where the foreign invasion has not managed to corrupt the vital essence'.[105] Another article – written by de la Sota himself – reinforced this view when stating that Basque nationalism should make an effort to 'resurrect the original soul of the race and clean it of the exoticism that deforms it'.[106] It is worth noting that these highly racist and xenophobic articles were developed in a period that coincided with the ascension of Adolf Hitler to power in 1933 and the configuration of the Nazi 'racial state'. An article published in 1933 even compared Hitler's project and the Basque case:

> it looks like Hitler wants to unite all Germans. On this point, at least, we agree. We also want the union of all the Basques: France in the north, and Spain in the south. And for wanting this union they call us separatists. Paradoxical concepts. Mediterranean lack of culture.[107]

Therefore, I argue for a middle ground between Lorenzo Espinosa and Fernández Soldevilla's positions. First, I agree with the latter that de la Sota's arguments were minoritarian. Furthermore, as we can see, whilst condemning anti-*maketismo*, de la Sota also wrote some radical texts that reproduced Arana's rhetoric. As in Arana's period, the struggle between Spaniards and Basques was read and interpreted by many nationalists as a struggle between two antagonistic races: one dominant (violent, savage and imperialist by nature) and one dominated (naturally peaceful, humane and

---

104 Arana's texts were reproduced under the subtitle 'la pureza de la raza' ('race purity'). See for instance, Sabino Arana, 'Páginas del maestro. La pureza de la raza', *Bizkaitarra* (1895), reproduced in *Jagi-Jagi*, 6 June 1936, p. 1 and Sabino Arana, 'Páginas del maestro. La pureza de la raza (continued)', *Bizkaitarra* (1895), reproduced in *Jagi-Jagi*, 13 June 1936, p. 1.
105 Errotari, 'Aspectos. El nacionalismo y las Encartaciones', *Jagi-Jagi*, 9 June 1934, p. 3.
106 Manuel de la Sota, 'Eskertarak eta Eskumataraz', *Jagi-Jagi*, 4 February 1933, p. 2.
107 Jym, 'Txa txar keriak', *Jagi-Jagi*, 11 March 1933, p. 9. Although in the early years of *Jagi-Jagi*, the newsletter seemed to express lukewarm sympathy for Hitler (and even on occasions condemned Spanish socialists and republicans for their anti-fascist opposition), from 1934 *Jagi-Jagi* included some articles that indicated direct opposition to him. For instance, an article published in 1934 stated that 'the current case of Hitler is sickening'. See Anon., 'Del momento. Dictadura y parlamentarismo', *Jagi-Jagi*, 30 June 1934, p. 3.

tolerant).[108] The intrinsic and innately imperialist nature of the Spanish race was used to stress the need for independence.

Second, more nuance is necessary when talking about race. None of the scholars mentioned recognise that *Jagi-Jagi* used differing discourses on race depending on the context and intentions behind each article. When talking about Spain, the majoritarian posture in the periodical was still to underscore the intrinsically evil and imperialist characteristics of the Spanish race. This heavily racialised and aggressive language was used to present independence as the next logical step. In contrast, when talking about other extra-European nations, *Jagi-Jagi* directly condemned racial hierarchies and wrote explicit anti-racist texts. As such, the newsletter was able to highlight the common cause of non-European anticolonial movements and Basque nationalism. Indeed, anticolonial nationalists were mainly people of colour who challenged the racist and paternalistic principles of imperialism. The LAI itself challenged the 'civilising' rhetoric traditionally used by western countries to justify the colonisation of non-western nations and question racial hierarchies.[109] The fervent desire to be part of this global anticolonial insurrection and movement prompted *Jagi-Jagi* to write anti-racist texts.

Different Basque radical writings exemplify this anti-racist posture when advocating the union of 'oppressed' peoples against imperialism. For instance, an article titled 'Humanismo' ('Humanism') – which was originally published in *Patria Vasca* (1932) and was reproduced in *Jagi-Jagi* in 1934 – advocated the solidarity and brotherhood of different nations and regions across the world. 'This way we become brothers,' the article claimed, 'through this great and deep sense of humanism, with people of opposing beliefs, of dissimilar thought, of distant latitudes, skin of different colour ...'[110] Referencing a text written by Cuban martyr José Martí, *Mi Raza* ('My Race', 1893) the text continued: 'because for Basque nationalists, like Martí, man is more than white, more than mulatto, more than black ...'[111] After this, the article condemned racist attacks against people of colour in

---

108 Like in the previous periods, stressing the imperialist nature of Spain was a way of differentiating the 'oppressor' from the 'oppressed'. As an article stated, 'the Basque Country has always hated practices grounded in strength and deceit and has been a model for free nations. This is very different to Spain with its imperialist and conquering monarchs'. See Makala, 'Con serenidad y alta la frente', *Jagi-Jagi*, 29 October 1932, p. 11.
109 Gopal, *Insurgent Empire*, pp. 272–73.
110 Gudari, 'Recuerdo. Haití, independiente', *Jagi-Jagi*, 25 August 1934, p. 1. See original in Baltzuri, 'Humanismo', *Patria Vasca*, January 1932, pp. 23–24.
111 Gudari, 'Recuerdo. Haití, independiente'.

'Oppressed Peoples of the World, Unite!'   191

Bilbao, and claimed that the Basque Youth of Bilbao opened its doors to them as if they were their 'brothers'.[112]

Another *Jagi-Jagi* article directly condemned racial hierarchies when talking about imperial oppression and compared Arana to influential anticolonial leaders:

> like Bolivar and Rizal [perhaps they mistook Rizal for Martí] in America, like Pearse in Ireland, like Gandhi in India, Sabino [Arana] is one of those great fighters who will be able to free Humanity from the evil imperialism of the states, helping to bring an era of Peace and Fraternity from the rotten ruins, making the men from free and equal nations equal and free themselves.[113]

Essentially, *Jagi-Jagi* adopted one posture or the other depending on the tactical intentions of the text. Discourses on race were adapted to the needs of Basque radicalism and were put at the service of *Jagi-Jagi*'s anticolonialism. For this reason, although racist and patronising attitudes when condemning international colonialism were substantially less apparent in comparison with the period in which Arana developed his ideas, it is hardly surprising to still observe some problematic thoughts in the Basque radical corpus. Amongst other things, and despite condemning the Spanish conquest of the Americas, *Jagi-Jagi* continued stressing the Basque contributions to the 'discovery' as well as their role as transmitters of the values of freedom to the region.[114] Other articles continued to display Orientalist attitudes when talking about non-western movements. For instance, a text that supported the Abyssinians against the Italian occupation referred to the former as 'peoples from a black

---

112 Gudari, 'Recuerdo. Haití, independiente'. To exemplify this interracial brotherhood, in the original article in *Patria Vasca*, an anti-racist poem by Afro-American poet Langston Hughes accompanied a picture of two black people (possibly a mother and her child) smiling at each other.

113 M.S., 'Sabino denunciado', p. 1.

114 For instance, an article in *Jagi-Jagi* written by Beti-Aldage (most likely a pseudonym used by Gallastegi) argued that Basques had historically fought in 'fair' causes and that their adventurous nature led them to participate 'in the greatest gestures of humanity and the discovery of America'. The same article also claimed that Basques powerfully influenced the life of these civilisations, as they conveyed their love of 'freedom' to them, which led in turn to independence. With a highly condescending tone, this article questioned and mocked the idea of the Spaniards civilising the Basques and claimed: 'Who can say to us that they [the Spaniards] have come to civilise us? ... We have not been like "Indian" Comanches or Bedouins, have we?' See Beti-Aldage, '¿Civilización o barbarie?', p. 4.

race, almost defenceless, of rudimentary civilisation but who possess a clear instinct for the freedom of their territory'.[115]

This reinforces the strategic nature of anticolonialism: it is impossible of course, to know whether Basque radical nationalists truly despised colonialism or if they believed that Euskadi was actually a colony within Spain. Nevertheless, what we do know is that anticolonialism served two important aims for Basque radical nationalists. As in the other periods this book has studied, anticolonialism was a key tactic used to the advantage of the movement.

Conclusion

This chapter has explored *Jagi-Jagi*'s anticolonial discourse, demonstrating how it used explicit anticolonial rhetoric on both a national and an international scale. In other words, *Jagi-Jagi* denounced not only the effects that Spanish colonialism had on its nation, but also decried the impact of global imperialism and its legacies across the world. *Jagi-Jagi*'s anticolonialism had two well-defined aims, which shows important continuities with the previous periods. First, Basque radicals insisted on the conception of Euskadi as a colony to legitimise their pro-independence agenda and to reject the PNV's autonomy project. As an anti-imperial organisation, collaboration with what was presented as an innately evil colonising country seemed implausible. As a result, *Jagi-Jagi* considered extra-parliamentary methods that were being applied in former and contemporary anticolonial struggles, namely civil disobedience and violence. Second, by condemning colonialism on a global level and establishing solidarity claims with other nations, Basque radicals attempted to internationalise their cause and become part of the global anticolonial context. This strategy was necessary in a period when direct contacts with other nationalist groups were scarce.

As this chapter has shown, these two well-defined aims and uses of anticolonialism entailed two contradictory views on race in the newsletter. Whilst *Jagi-Jagi* adopted an explicitly racist position when denouncing Euskadi's internal situation, the newsletter adopted a completely different stance when condemning global imperialism. The contradictory ideas that we observe in *Jagi-Jagi* were not new to this period but had been observed in the Basque anticolonial corpus for over 40 years. Whether it was genuine or not, anticolonialism had become a crucial part of the Basque radical agenda.

---

115 Beti-Aldage, '¡Gora Etiopía Azkatuta!', p. 1.

Conclusion

This book tells a very different story than I had initially expected. I started this research project in 2017 with the belief that there was an unexplored yet rich anticolonial tradition within Basque nationalism. This assumption was based on both personal and academic experiences. When I was in my late teens, I visited Belfast with my family and was surprised to see how the city was divided by numerous walls covered with colourful murals depicting the Irish struggle for independence and various western and non-western national liberation movements. One of these walls was dedicated to the Basque struggle for independence. This immediately made me wonder what it was that united Ireland, Euskadi and the struggles of so many other non-western nations, apart from the desire for national freedom. I found the answer to this question when I returned to Spain and, after doing some research on the subject, found that Basque nationalists, like the Irish, framed their struggle as one against colonialism. Having made this preliminary discovery, I started the project with certain expectations about what I was going to find in the archives. I expected to find continual words of support for anticolonial insurgents in the newspapers I studied, regardless of their race or country of origin. I also anticipated reading repeated anticolonial claims against all world empires. Much to my surprise, this was not exactly the case. Instead, as this book has shown, I observed that Basque anticolonial statements were often mixed with pro-colonial ones. But it is precisely these contradictions, or these connections and disconnections with anticolonial language, that make this story worth telling.

The connections between Basque nationalism and other anticolonial movements, which are what initially motivated me to carry out this research, are obvious. From its origins, Basque nationalists reappropriated ideas that emerged in a colonial setting to their own cause. The idea that Basques shared the same type of oppression with that of other territories or colonies fuelled the imagination of Basque nationalists and facilitated analogies or comparisons. Furthermore, Basque nationalists followed the events that took place in remote places closely and imagined what could happen in Euskadi if Basques imitated those examples. In fact, this book has demonstrated that Basque radical nationalism evolved according to the international developments in global anticolonialism, and the movement modified its rhetoric accordingly. For instance, it was not until the late 1910s and early 1920s that Basque radical nationalists began to condemn the imperialist actions of all global empires, and not just the Spanish Empire. This reflects a will to align with other anticolonial movements that were particularly active following the Wilsonian moment. Furthermore, like other anticolonial movements and agents, from the 1920s Basque radicals condemned the actions of the League of Nations, labelling it an association that represented the interests of global imperialism. The frustration Basque radicals felt when their demands for independence were ignored internationally clearly contributed to their radicalisation, the main manifestation of which was their frequent appeals to (violent) sacrifice and an armed insurrection.

Thus, this book has placed Basque nationalism within the global and wider context of anticolonial nationalism and has traced the direct connections and influences nationalist movements such as the Irish, Riffian or Indian had on the Basques. But, as I have mentioned, this is not only a book on the connections and entanglements between Basque nationalism and global anticolonialism. Instead, it is also a project about the disconnections and contradictions that existed within these two movements and ideas. As this book has shown, whilst anticolonialism proved to be a very effective and integral part of the Basque rhetoric, it was not always sincere. In other words: if Basque nationalists used strong anticolonial rhetoric from the start of the movements it is not, as I first believed, because they were fervent defenders of the colonised and the oppressed peoples, but because this rhetoric offered important advantages to the Basque nationalist discourse. Anticolonialism formed the core of a narrative that helped both to justify independence claims and internationalise the Basque cause.

With this, I do not seek to demonise the Basque nationalist movement but to understand how western nationalist movements operate. All nationalist movements need to use a rhetoric that appeals directly to the national community in order to mobilise the nation against a common enemy. In the Basque case, the notion that Euskadi had been colonised by what was considered by many the most despicable country in the world became a powerful rhetoric that contributed, without a doubt, to the mobilisation of the Basque nation. Proof of this was the constant use of this language to justify independence from the start of the movement, except for a brief parenthesis in the early twentieth century. Furthermore, as this book has shown, nationalist movements do not operate in a vacuum. Instead, they are directly inspired by other movements that have similar ideas and goals. The idea that Basque nationalists were not alone, but were part of a global struggle against colonialism, served to internationalise the movement. All nationalist movements use discursive elements to their benefit, and Basque nationalism was not the only western movement to develop similar anticolonial claims.

Stressing the 'strategic' nature of Basque anticolonialism has allowed me to delve into the movement's disconnections with anticolonialism, or the inherent contradictions in the corpus. As this book has repeatedly shown, despite their constant denunciation of colonial rule, Basque nationalists themselves expressed imperialist ideas. For instance, in the first 20 years of the movement, Basque nationalists engaged with ideas of British exceptionalism and considered the British Empire as the epitome of civilisation and benevolence. In contrast, the Spanish Empire was seen as the embodiment of decay and misrule. Basques constantly compared Spain to Africa to stress this idea and discredit Spain's imperial aspirations. Like the northern European powers, Basques situated Spain outside of European modernity, suggesting that it was Spain's hybrid identity (between Europe and Africa, between civilisation and barbarism) that prevented the country from being an adequate colonial power. In sum, according to early Basque nationalists, colonialism was not the problem, rather it depended on who practised it. Therefore, the Basque anticolonial discourse was not influenced only by discourses that emerged on the 'periphery' but also by others that emerged at the very core of imperial Europe.

These problematic ideas, which engaged directly with intellectual discourses that emerged in northern Europe, have tended to be overlooked. Yet without analysing them, we cannot get a full picture of the complexities of western nationalist movements in general, and of peripheral nationalist movements within Spain in particular. By exploring them, this book not only attempts to unpack Basque anticolonial ideas, but it offers a comprehensive view of the paradoxical case of modern Spain. Unlike other imperial states such as Britain or France, Spain was imagined by both its neighbours and inhabitants as a country that was Orientalised and Orientalising, self and other.[1]

Alongside anticolonial claims, race was another of the key discursive elements that Basques used from the start of the movement. Influenced by existing discourses of racial difference, the founder of Basque nationalism argued that Basques were part of a unique and sacred race, which differed significantly from the Spanish race. One of the reasons why Basques had to fight for their independence was precisely so they would not mix their blood

---

1 Martin-Márquez, *Disorientations*.

with that of the inferior Spanish race. This discourse of racial difference proved particularly useful in the incipient Basque movement. As this book has shown, on many occasions, Basque nationalists made explicit racist claims against the Spanish, whom they presented as mixed-race, tainted and impure. This does not necessarily mean that Basques believed this. Rather, this was part of a strong anti-Spanish discourse that, like anticolonialism, targeted everything Spanish.

Whilst this strong racist discourse proved helpful in justifying the necessity of independence, it created a strong barrier between Basques and the extra-European anticolonial movements with whom they aimed to establish networks. This is why, especially from the 1920s, we observe a timid increase in anti-racist texts. This led to contradictory ideas of race in the Basque nationalist corpus: whilst strongly racist texts against the Spaniards continued being common throughout the period studied, Basque radicals condemned racism when talking from an international point of view. These differing, contradictory ideas of race can be explained by assessing their intentions: racist statements against Spaniards were part of a strong anti-Spanish discourse. In contrast, anti-racist assertions reflected an attempt to align with anticolonial movements. In other words, discourses on race were adapted to the needs of the movement. Concepts of race acquired different meanings depending on the objectives and priorities of Basque nationalism. These contradictions were not overcome until after the Spanish Civil War, when Basque nationalists rejected Aranist theories of the Basque race and racial terms began to be eradicated from the nationalist language.

Whilst the idea of 'race' was eventually eradicated from Basque nationalism, allusions to violence became increasingly prevalent in the years that followed the Spanish Civil War. These ideas, as this book has proven, were not new. Following the Easter Rising of 1916, the ideas of national sacrifice that Sabino Arana had launched in the 1890s were interpreted as a call to arms. From the 1920s onwards, Basque radical nationalists seemed to believe that an armed revolution in Euskadi was on the cards. These allusions had barely any significant practical effects in the period studied. However, they should not be overlooked as they were never forgotten by subsequent generations of Basque radical nationalists. The experiences of a devastating civil war – interpreted by some as a veritable war of independence – and subsequent years of repression, state violence and silence were key to the emergence of a new generation of Basque nationalists who believed that when parliamentary methods were exhausted, violence was the only option. During the 1950s and 1960s, the Aranist belief that Euskadi was a colony within Spain was reinforced by both internal (a repressive dictatorship that made the occupation real) and international factors (following the new wave of anticolonial nationalism that emerged in Africa, Asia and Latin America). Both factors led a new generation of Basque radical nationalists to believe that every national liberation struggle had, without exception, followed a violent path. As this book has shown, they were not the first generation of Basque nationalists to make this argument.

Owing to the richness of the material analysed in the period this book has covered, I decided to end this book at the start of the Spanish Civil War, in July 1936. Other factors contributed to this decision, such as the fact that the Spanish Civil War marked the end of an era and the birth of a new generation of Basque nationalists. I hope that this book inspires subsequent research on the anticolonial ideas that emerged in Basque nationalism after 1936. I suspect that anticolonial language after this date would continue to be rich and extensive, considering that this language was developed mostly by those who managed to escape repression and go into exile. Many Basque radical newsletters were published from Latin America, where, as under Primo de Rivera's dictatorship, many nationalists became radicalised.[2] Radical groups in countries like Venezuela became the centre of a large Basque radical community that saw the creation of organisations and newsletters directly inspired by *Aberri* and *Jagi-Jagi*.

Writing this book has certainly taught me a valuable lesson: looks can be deceiving. I have learned that we need to be prepared to find in the archives uncomfortable truths that perhaps we did not want to find. What is more, I have learned that not only can these uncomfortable and unexpected findings change a whole project; they can make it more valuable. What started as an ambitious project that sought to establish connections between anticolonial ideas and Basque nationalism is now also a history of disconnections, a history of Basque (anti)colonial ideas. I hope that this book inspires subsequent studies into the global connections and disconnections that are a defining feature of western nationalist movements.

---

2 For a study of Basque radicalism in the Latin American exile, see Fernández Soldevilla, 'De *Aberri* a ETA', pp. 219–64.

Bibliography

Allen, Kieran. *1916: Ireland's Revolution Tradition* (London: Pluto Press, 2016).
Álvarez Cuartero, Izaskun. 'Lecturas de la independencia de Cuba en el discurso nacionalista de Sabino Arana' in Antonio Gutiérrez Escudero and María Luisa Laviana Cuetos (eds), *España y las Antillas: el 98 y más* (Sevilla: Diputación Provincial de Sevilla, 1999), pp. 199–214.
Álvarez Gila, Óscar and José María Tápiz Fernández. 'Prensa nacionalista vasca y emigración a América (1900–1936)', *Anuario de Estudios Americanos*, 1 (1996), pp. 233–60.
Álvarez-Junco, José. *Spanish Identity in the Age of Nations* (Manchester and New York: Manchester University Press, 2011).
Anderson, Benedict. *Under Three Flags: Anarchism and the Anti-Colonial Imagination* (London and New York: Verso, 2005).
Arana, Sabino. 'El discurso de Larazabal', Begoña, 3 June 1893, http://www.sabinoaranagoiri.eus/PDF/PDF145.pdf.
——. 'Obras Completas', see https://www.sabinoaranagoiri.eus/obra.php.
——. 'Telegrama a Roosevelt', 27 May 1902, http://www.sag150.eu/archivo.php.
——. *Bizkaya por su independencia* (Bilbao: Edn Verdes, 1932).
Arendt, Hannah. *On Violence* (New York: Harcourt Brace Jovanovich, 1970).
Aresti, Nerea. 'De heroínas viriles a madres de la patria. Las mujeres y el nacionalismo vasco (1893–1937)', *Historia y política*, 31 (2014), pp. 281–308.
——. 'El *gentleman* y el bárbaro. Masculinidad y civilización en el nacionalismo vasco (1893–1937), *Cuadernos de Historia Contemporánea*, 39 (2017), pp. 83–103.
Balcells, Albert. *El projecte d'autonomia de la Mancomunitat de Catalunya del 1919 i el seu context històric* (Barcelona: Parlament de Catalunya, 2010).
Balfour, Sebastian. *The End of the Spanish Empire, 1898–1923* (Oxford: Clarendon Press, 1997).
——. 'Spain and the Great Powers in the Aftermath of the Disaster of 1898', in Sebastian Balfour and Paul Preston (eds), *Spain and the Great Powers in the Twentieth Century* (New York: Routledge, 1999), pp. 13–32.
——. *Deadly Embrace: Morocco and the Road to the Spanish Civil War* (Oxford: Oxford University Press, 2002).
——. 'The Spanish Empire and its End: A Comparative View in Nineteenth and Twentieth Century Europe', in Alexei Miller and Alfred J. Rieber (eds), *Imperial Rule* (Budapest and New York: Central European University Press, 2004), pp. 151–60.

Beltza. *El nacionalismo vasco, 1876–1936* (San Sebastián: Txertoa, 1976).

Blanco, John D. 'Bastards of the Unfinished Revolution: Bolívar's Ismael and Rizal's Martí at the Turn of the Twentieth Century', *Radical History Review*, 89 (2004), pp. 92–114.

Bolorinos Allard, Elisabeth. *Spanish National Identity, Colonial Power, and the Portrayal of Muslims and Jews during the Rif War (1909–27)* (Woodbridge: Tamesis, 2021).

Borja, Marciano R. de. *Los vascos en Filipinas* (Vitoria-Gasteiz: Servicio Central de Publicaciones del Gobierno Vasco, 2014).

Brückenhaus, Daniel. *Policing Transnational Protest: Liberal Imperialism and the Surveillance of Anticolonialists in Europe, 1905–1945* (New York: Oxford University Press, 2017).

Camino, Íñigo and Luis de Guezala. *Juventud y nacionalismo vasco. Bilbao (1901–1937)* (Bilbao: Fundación Sabino Arana, 1991).

Carner-Ribalta, Josep and Ramón Fabregat (eds). *Macià: la seva actuació a l'estranger* (Mexico: Edicions Catalanes de Mèxic, 1952).

Casanova, Julián and Carlos Gil Andrés. *Twentieth-Century Spain: A History* (Cambridge: Cambridge University Press, 2014).

Castells, Luis. 'El nacionalismo vasco (1890–1923): ¿una ideología modernizadora?', *Ayer*, 28 (1997), pp. 127–62.

Comellas, José Luis. *Del 98 a la Semana Trágica, 1898–1909: Crisis de conciencia y renovación política* (Madrid: Biblioteca Nueva, 2002).

Conversi, Daniele. 'Domino Effect or International Developments? The Influences of International Events and Political Ideologies on Catalan and Basque Nationalism', *West European Politics*, 16.1 (1993), pp. 245–70.

——. *The Basques, the Catalans and Spain: Alternative Routes to Nationalist Mobilisation* (London: Hurst, 1997).

Corcuera Atienza, Javier. *La patria de los vascos: Orígenes, ideología y organización del nacionalismo vasco (1876–1903)* (Madrid: Taurus, 2001).

Chacón Delgado, Pedro José. 'El concepto de independencia vasca en Sabino Arana Goiri', *Historia Contemporánea*, 50 (2014), pp. 75–103.

Cullen, Niall. *Radical Basque Nationalist-Irish Republican Relations: A History* (Abingdon: Routledge, 2024).

Cullen, Niall and Kyle McCreanor. '"Dangerous Friends": Irish Republican Relations with Basque and Catalan Nationalists, 1916–26', *International History Review*, 44.6 (2022), pp. 1193–210.

Dalmau, Pol. 'Catalans and Rifis during the Wilsonian Moment: The Quest for Self-Determination in the Post-Versailles World', *Contemporary European History*, 32 (2023), pp. 131–45.

Díaz Noci, Javier. 'Historia del periodismo vasco (1600–2010)', *Mediatika: Cuadernos de Medios de Comunicación*, 13 (2012), pp. 1–261.

——. 'El recluta periodista: Manuel Aznar, cronista de la Guerra Mundial para el diario *Euzkadi*' in Xavier Pla and Francesc Montero (eds), *En el teatro de la guerra: cronistas hispánicos en la Primera Guerra Mundial* (Granada: Editorial Comares, 2020), pp. 351–56.

Díaz Noci, Javier and Koldobika Meso Ayerdi. 'Manuel Aznar Zubigaray: los inicios de la prensa nacionalista vasca. De Imanol a Gudalgai (1913–1914)', *Obra Periodística*, 1 (2010).

Douglass, William A. 'Sabino's Sin: Racism and the Founding of Basque Nationalism', in Daniele Conversi (ed.), *Ethnonationalism in the Contemporary World: Walker Connor and the Study of Nationalism* (London: Routledge, 2002), pp. 95-112.
Eleizalde, Luis de. *Países y razas. Las aspiraciones nacionalistas en diversos pueblos (1913-1914)* (Bilbao: Universidad del País Vasco, 1999).
Elorza, Antonio. *Ideologías del nacionalismo vasco 1876-1937 (De los 'euskaros' a Jagi-Jagi)* (San Sebastián: Haranburu, 1978).
English, Richard. *Irish Freedom: The History of Nationalism in Ireland* (London: Pan Books, 2008).
Estévez, Xosé. *De la Triple Alianza al pacto de San Sebastián (1923-1930): Antecedentes del Galeuzca* (San Sebastián: Universidad de Deusto, 1991).
——. 'El Galeuzca histórico: la búsqueda trinacional de la soberanía (1923-1959)', *Hermes*, 29 (2009), pp. 72-83.
ETA. 'La insurrección en Euskadi', *Fondo Documental Euskal Herriko Komunistak* (1964), pp. 1-33.
Farinelli, Marcel A. 'Irredentas y centauros de Fiume. Del congreso de Roma a las propuestas de D'Annunzio', in Enric Ucelay-Da Cal, Xosé Manoel Núñez Seixas, Arnau Gonzàlez i Vilalta (eds), *Patrias diversas ¿misma lucha? Alianzas transnacionalistas en el mundo de entreguerras (1912-1939)* (Barcelona: Edicions Bellaterra, 2020), pp. 249-69.
Fernández Soldevilla, Gaizka. 'Ecos de la Guerra Civil. La glorificación del gudari en la génesis de la violencia de ETA (1936-1968)', *Bulletin d'histoire contemporaine de l'Espagne*, 49 (2014), pp. 247-61.
——. 'El simple arte de matar. Orígenes de la violencia terrorista en el País Vasco', *Historia y Política*, 32 (2014), pp. 271-98.
——. 'De *Aberri* a ETA, pasando por Venezuela. Rupturas y continuidades en el nacionalismo vasco radical (1921-1977)', *Bulletin d'histoire contemporaine de l'Espagne*, 51 (2015), pp. 219-64.
——. 'Mitos que matan. La narrativa del "conflicto vasco"', *Ayer*, 98 (2015), pp. 213-40.
——. *La voluntad del gudari. Génesis y metástasis de la violencia de ETA* (Madrid: Tecnos, 2016).
Ferrera Cuesta, Carlos. 'Explicaciones de una política exterior: la crisis de Melilla de 1893-1894', *Ayer*, 54 (2004), pp. 305-26.
Fleming, Shannon E. and Ann K. Fleming. 'Primo de Rivera and Spain's Moroccan Problem, 1923-27', *Journal of Contemporary History*, 12.1 (1977), pp. 85-99.
Fronczak, Joseph. 'Local People's Global Politics: A Transnational History of the Hands Off Ethiopia Movement of 1935', *Diplomatic History*, 39.2 (2015), pp. 245-74.
Fuentes Codera, Maximiliano. 'Germanófilos y neutralistas: proyectos tradicionalistas y regeneracionistas para España (1914-1918)', *Ayer*, 91.3 (2013), pp. 63-95.
——. 'Imperialismos e iberismos en España: perspectivas regeneradoras frente a la Gran Guerra', *Historia y política: ideas, procesos y movimientos sociales*, 33 (2015), pp. 21-48.
Fusi, Juan Pablo. *El País Vasco, 1931-1937: Autonomía, Revolución, Guerra Civil* (Madrid: Biblioteca Nueva, 2002).

Gabilondo, Joseba. 'Imagining Basques: Dual Otherness from European Imperialism to American Globalization', *Rev. int. estud. vascos.*, 2 (2008), pp. 145-73.

Gallastegi, Eli. *Por la libertad vasca* (Bilbao: Talleres E. Verdes, 1933).

Garton, Stephen. 'The Dominions, Ireland, and India' in Robert Gerwarth and Erez Manela, *Empires at War: 1911-1923* (Oxford: Oxford University Press, 2014), pp. 152-79.

Ghosh, Durba and Dane Kennedy (eds). *Decentring Empire: Britain, India and the Transcolonial World* (New Delhi: Orient Longman, 2006).

Goebel, Michael. *Anti-Imperial Metropolis: Interwar Paris and the Seeds of Third-World Nationalism* (Cambridge: Cambridge University Press, 2015).

Goode, Joshua. *Impurity of Blood: Defining Race in Spain, 1870-1930* (Baton Rouge: Louisiana State University Press, 2009).

Gopal, Priyamvada. *Insurgent Empire: Anticolonial Resistance and British Dissent* (London and New York: Verso, 2019).

Granja, José Luis de la. *Nacionalismo y II República en el País Vasco: Estatutos de autonomía, partidos y elecciones. Historia de Acción Nacionalista Vasca: 1930-1936* (Madrid: Siglo XXI, 1986).

——. 'Cinco años de República en Euskadi', *Historia Contemporánea*, 1 (1988), pp. 95-108.

——. 'Una autocrítica del nacionalismo vasco tras la dictadura de Primo de Rivera: el manifiesto del Comité Pro-Resurgimiento Vasco (1930)', *Bilduma: Revista del Servicio del Archivo del Ayuntamiento de Errenteria*, 3 (1989), pp. 185-209.

——. *El nacionalismo vasco: (1876-1975)* (Madrid: Arco/Libros, 2000).

——. 'Las alianzas políticas entre los nacionalismos periféricos en la España del siglo XX', *Studia historica. Historia contemporánea*, 18 (2000), pp. 149-75.

——. 'El *Antimaketismo*: La visión de Sabino Arana sobre España y los españoles', *Norba. Revista de Historia*, 19 (2006), pp. 191-203.

——. 'Cronología de Sabino Arana (1865-1903)', *Sancho el Sabio*, 31 (2009), pp. 285-98.

——. 'Sabino Arana', in Santiago de Pablo, José Luis de la Granja, Ludger Mees and Jesús Casquete (eds), *Diccionario ilustrado de símbolos del nacionalismo vasco* (Madrid: Tecnos, 2012), pp. 118-43.

——. *Ángel o demonio: Sabino Arana. El patriarca del nacionalismo vasco* (Madrid: Tecnos, 2015).

——. 'La forja de un líder mesiánico: Sabino Arana (1865-1882), *Sancho el Sabio: Revista de cultura e investigación vasca*, Extra 3 (2020), pp. 159-80.

——. 'El nacionalismo vasco en el tiempo de las Irmandades da Fala: Moderados, radicales y heterodoxos (1916-1923)' in Ramón Villares Paz, Xosé Manoel Núñez Seixas and Ramón Máiz Suárez (eds), *Irmandades da Fala no seu tempo: perspectivas cruzadas* (Santiago de Compostela: Consello da Cultura Galega, 2021), pp. 273-95.

Grant, Kevin. 'The Transcolonial World of Hunger Strikes and Political Fasts, c. 1909-1935', in Durba Ghosh and Dane Kennedy (eds), *Decentring Empire: Britain, India and the Transcolonial World* (New Delhi: Orient Longman, 2006), pp. 243-69.

Hagimoto, Koichi. *Between Empires: Martí, Rizal, and the Intercolonial Alliance* (Basingstoke: Palgrave Macmillan, 2013).

Herrerín López, Ángel and Susana Sueiro Seoane. '¿Quantité négligeable o rival terrible?: la imagen francesa de la España primorriverista', *Pasado y Memoria*, 16 (2017), pp. 17-45.
Hobsbawm, Eric J. and Terence Ranger (eds). *The Invention of Tradition* (Cambridge: Cambridge University Press, 1983).
Hobson, John M. *The Eurocentric Conception of World Politics: Western International Theory, 1760-2010* (Cambridge and New York: Cambridge University Press, 2012).
Howe, Stephen. *Ireland and Empire: Colonial Legacies in Irish History and Culture* (Oxford: Oxford University Press, 2000).
Hugo, Victor. *Les Orientales: Les Feuilles d'Automne* (Paris: Librairie Hachette, 1872).
Iarocci, Michael P. *Properties of Modernity: Romantic Spain, Modern Europe, and the Legacies of Empire* (Nashville: Vanderbilt University Press, 2006).
Iglesias Amorín, Alfonso. 'Los intelectuales españoles y la Guerra del Rif (1909-1927)', *Revista Universitaria De Historia Militar*, 3.5 (2015), pp. 59-77.
——. 'The Hispano-Moroccan Wars (1859-1927) and the (De)nationalization of the Spanish People', *European History Quarterly*, 50.2 (2020), pp. 290-310.
——. 'Imaginarios y conmemoración del fin del "problema" de Marruecos durante la dictadura de Primo de Rivera', *Hispania Nova. Revista de Historia Contemporánea*, 20 (2021), pp. 857-88.
——. 'Sub-state nationalisms in Spain during the Moroccan War and the Rif War (1909-1927)', *Studies on National Movements*, 8 (2021), pp. 2-25.
Jackson, Alvin. 'Ireland, the Union, and the Empire, 1800-1960' in Kevin Kenny (ed.), *Ireland and the British Empire* (Oxford and New York: Oxford University Press, 2004), pp. 123-53.
Jáuregui Bereciartu, Gurutz. *Ideología y estrategia política de ETA: Análisis de su evolución entre 1959 y 1968* (Madrid: Siglo XXI, 1985).
——. 'Los orígenes ideológicos de ETA' in Antonio Elorza (ed.), *La historia de ETA* (Madrid: Temas de Hoy, 2000), pp. 171-85.
Juaristi, Jon. *El linaje de Aitor* (Madrid: Taurus, 2000).
Juliá Díaz, Santos. 'Anomalía, dolor y fracaso de España' in *Conferencia Anual de la Society for Spanish and Portuguese Historical Studies* (Tucson, 1966), pp. 1-29.
Koller, Christian. 'The Recruitment of Colonial Troops in Africa and Asia and their Deployment in Europe during the First World War', *Immigrants & Minorities*, 26.1-2 (2008), pp. 111-33.
Krutwig, Federico. *Vasconia* (Buenos Aires: Norbait, 1963).
Lang, Stephanie. 'Más allá del Ebro, ¿Los salvajes? La "España Africana" como impulso del regeneracionismo catalán hacia 1900', in Christian von Tschilschke and Jan-Henrik Witthaus (eds), *El otro colonialismo: España y África, entre imaginación e historia* (Frankfurt am Main: Iberoamericana - Vervuert, 2017), pp. 105-30.
Larronde, Jean-Claude. *El nacionalismo vasco: su origen y su ideología en la obra de Sabino Arana-Goiri* (San Sebastián: Txertoa, 1977).
Lecours, André. *Basque Nationalism and the Spanish State* (Reno: University of Nevada Press, 2007).
Leinaweaver, Jessaca. 'Transatlantic Unity on Display: the "White Legend" and the "Pact of Silence" in Madrid's Museum of the Americas', *History and Anthropology*, 28.1 (2017), pp. 39-57.

Levinger, Matthew and Paula Franklin Lytle. 'Myths and Mobilisation: the Triadic Structure of Nationalism', *Nations and Nationalism*, 7.2 (2001), pp. 175–95.

Lindner, Thomas K. *A City Against Empire: Transnational Anti-Imperialism in Mexico City, 1920–30* (Liverpool: Liverpool University Press, 2023).

Lorenzo Espinosa, José María. *Gudari. Una pasión útil. Eli Gallastegi (1892–1974)* (Tafalla: Txalaparta, 1992).

——. 'Influencia del nacionalismo irlandés en el nacionalismo vasco, 1916–1936', in XI Congreso de Estudios Vascos, *Nuevas formulaciones culturales: Euskal Herria y Europa* (Donostia: Eusko Ikaskuntza, 1992), pp. 239–47.

Loureiro, Angel. 'Spanish Nationalism and the Ghost of Empire', *Journal of Spanish Cultural Studies*, 4.1 (2003), pp. 65–76.

Louro, Michele L. *Comrades Against Imperialism: Nehru, India, and Interwar Internationalism* (Cambridge: Cambridge University Press, 2018).

Louro, Michele, Carolien Stolte, Heather Streets-Salter and Sana Tannoury-Karam. 'The League Against Imperialism: Lives and Afterlives', in Louro, Stolte, Streets-Salter and Tannoury-Karam (eds), *The League Against Imperialism: Lives and Afterlives* (Leiden: Leiden University Press, 2020), pp. 17–51.

MacClancy, Jeremy. *Expressing Identities in the Basque Arena* (Suffolk: Boydell & Brewer, 2007).

McCreanor, Kyle. 'Ireland and the Basque Country: Nationalisms in Contact, 1895–1939' (unpublished Master's thesis, Concordia University, 2019).

McGarry, Fearghal. *The Rising: Ireland, Easter 1916* (Oxford: Oxford University Press, 2010).

McPherson, Alan L. 'Anti-Imperialism and the Failure of the League of Nations', in Alan L. McPherson and Yannick Wehrli (eds), *Beyond Geopolitics: New Histories of Latin America at the League of Nations* (Albuquerque: University of New Mexico Press, 2015), pp. 21–32.

Madariaga, María Rosa de. *Marruecos, ese gran desconocido. Breve historia del protectorado español* (Madrid: Alianza Editorial, 2013).

Makalani, Minkah. *In the Cause of Freedom: Radical Black Internationalism from Harlem to London, 1917–1939* (Chapel Hill: University of North Carolina Press, 2011).

Manela, Erez. *The Wilsonian Moment: Self-determination and the International Origins of Anticolonial Nationalism* (Oxford and New York: Oxford University Press, 2007).

Manela, Erez and Heather Streets-Salter (eds). *The Anticolonial Transnational: Imaginaries, Mobilities, and Networks in the Struggle Against Empire* (Cambridge: Cambridge University Press, 2023).

Martín Corrales, Eloy. 'Catalunya i el Marroc: un segle i mig de relació', *L'Avenç*, 256 (2001), pp. 18–26.

Martínez Fiol, David. '1916. Imperialismo, antiimperialismo, "Guerra de les Nacions" y principio de las nacionalidades desde Cataluña: a propósito de "Contra la idea d'Imperi" d'Eugeni Xammar', in Enric Ucelay Da-Cal, Xosé Manoel Núñez Seixas, Arnau Gonzàlez i Vilalta (eds), *Patrias diversas ¿misma lucha? Alianzas transnacionalistas en el mundo de entreguerras (1912–1939)* (Barcelona: Edicions Bellaterra, 2020), pp. 344–63.

Martin-Márquez, Susan. *Disorientations: Spanish Colonialism in Africa and the Performance of Identity* (New Haven: Yale University Press, 2008).

Mees, Ludger. 'El nacionalismo vasco entre 1903 y 1923', *Vasconia: Cuadernos de historia - geografía*, 17 (1990), pp. 115-39.
——. *Nacionalismo vasco, movimiento obrero y cuestión social (1903-1923)* (Bilbao: Fundación Sabino Arana, 1992).
——. 'Tan lejos, tan cerca. El gobierno vasco en Barcelona y las complejas relaciones entre el nacionalismo vasco y el catalán', *Historia Contemporánea*, 37 (2008), pp. 557-91.
——. 'Ethnogenesis in the Pyrenees: The Contentious Making of a National Identity in the Basque Country (1643-2017)', *European History Quarterly*, 48.3 (2018), pp. 462-89.
——. *The Basque Contention: Ethnicity, Politics, Violence* (Abingdon and New York: Routledge, 2020).
Miguélez-Carballeira, Helena. *Galicia, A Sentimental Nation: Gender, Culture and Politics* (Cardiff: University of Wales Press, 2013).
Muro, Diego. *Ethnicity and Violence: The Case of Radical Basque Nationalism* (London: Routledge, 2011).
Neila Hernández, José Luis. '"Entre el palco y la butaca": el apaciguamiento británico y el regeneracionismo internacional de la España de Primo de Rivera', *Pasado y Memoria*, 16 (2017), pp. 47-67.
Núñez Seixas, Xosé Manoel. '¿Protodiplomacia exterior o ilusiones ópticas? El nacionalismo vasco, el contexto internacional y el Congreso de Nacionalidades Europeas (1914-1937)', *Vasconia. Cuadernos de Sección Historia-Geografia*, 23 (1995), pp. 243-75.
——. 'Espías, idealistas e intelectuales: La Union des Nationalités y la política de nacionalidades durante la I Guerra Mundial (1912-1919)', *Espacio, Tiempo y Forma, Serie V, Hº Contemporánea*, 10 (1997), pp. 117-50.
——. '¿Autodeterminación o autonomía cultural? Debates ideológicos en el Congreso de Nacionalidades Europeas (1925-1939)', *Hispania: Revista española de historia*, 58.200 (1998), pp. 1113-51.
——. 'Unholy Alliances? Nationalist Exiles, Minorities and Anti-Fascism in Interwar Europe', *Contemporary European History*, 25.4 (2016), pp. 597-617.
——. 'Ecos de Pascua, mitos rebeldes: El nacionalismo vasco e Irlanda (1890-1939)', *Historia Contemporánea*, 55 (2017), pp. 447-82.
——. '¿Negar o reescribir la Hispanidad? Los nacionalismos subestatales ibéricos y América Latina, 1898-1936', *Historia Mexicana*, 67.1 (2017), pp. 401-58.
——. *Patriotas transnacionales: Ensayos sobre nacionalismos y transferencias culturales en la Europa del siglo XX* (Madrid: Cátedra, 2019).
——. 'Introduction', in Xosé Manoel Núñez Seixas (ed.), *The First World War and the Nationality Question in Europe* (Leiden: Brill, 2020), pp. 1-14.
O'Malley, Kate. '1919, un punto de inflexión antiimperialista: Irlanda, Egipto y la India', in Enric Ucelay-Da Cal, Xosé Manoel Núñez Seixas, Arnau Gonzàlez i Vilalta (eds), *Patrias diversas ¿misma lucha? Alianzas transnacionalistas en el mundo de entreguerras (1912-1939)* (Barcelona: Edicions Bellaterra, 2020), pp. 131-50.
Ortiz, Michael P. 'Spain! Why? Jawaharlal Nehru, Non-Intervention, and the Spanish Civil War', *European History Quarterly*, 49 (2019), pp. 445-66.
Otaegui Arizmendi, Margarita. 'La Triple Alianza de 1923', in Manuel González Portilla, Jordi Maluquer de Motes and Borja de Riquer (eds), *Industrialización*

y nacionalismo: análisis comparativo: Actas del I Coloquio Vasco-Catalán de Historia (Barcelona: Universidad Autónoma de Barcelona, 1985), pp. 431–42.

Pablo, Santiago de. 'El Nacionalismo vasco ante el estado español (1895–1937)', *Studia Historica. Historia Contemporánea*, 18 (2000), pp. 79–93.

——. '¡Grita Libertad! El nacionalismo vasco y la lucha por la independencia de las naciones africanas', *Memoria y civilización*, 15 (2012), pp. 267–84.

Pablo, Santiago de and Ludger Mees. *El péndulo patriótico. Historia del Partido Nacionalista Vasco, 1895–2005* (Barcelona: Crítica, 2005).

Pablo, Santiago de, Ludger Mees and José Antonio Rodríguez Ranz. *El péndulo patriótico. Historia del Partido Nacionalista Vasco*, 2 vols (Barcelona: Crítica, 1999), I.

Phillips, Jr, William D. and Carla Rahn Phillips. *A Concise History of Spain* (Cambridge: Cambridge University Press, 2016).

Pich Mitjana, Josep. 'La Revolución de Julio de 1909', *Hispania*, 75 (2015), pp. 173–206.

Pike, Fredrick B. *Hispanismo, 1898–1936. Spanish Conservatives and Liberals and Their Relations with Spanish America* (Notre Dame: Notre Dame University Press, 1971).

Porte, Pablo la. 'Marruecos y la crisis de la Restauración 1917–1923', *Ayer*, 63 (2006), pp. 53–74.

Prashad, Vijay. *The Darker Nations: A People's History of the Third World* (New York: New Press, 2007).

Pulido Azpíroz, Alejandro. *Neutralidad en pie de guerra. El País Vasco y Navarra ante la Primera Guerra Mundial (1914–1918)* (Madrid: Sílex Universidad-Historia, 2021).

Quiroga, Alejandro. *Making Spaniards: Primo de Rivera and the Nationalization of the Masses, 1923–30* (Basingstoke: Palgrave Macmillan, 2007).

——. *Miguel Primo de Rivera: Dictadura, populismo y nación* (Barcelona: Crítica, 2022).

Rast, M. C. '"Ireland's Sister Nations": Internationalism and Sectarianism in the Irish Struggle for Independence, 1916–22', *Journal of Global History*, 10.3 (2015), pp. 479–501.

Renobales, Eduardo. *Jagi-Jagi: Historia del independentismo radical* (Bilbao: Imprenta Luna, 2010).

Romero, Francisco. 'Spain and the First World War', in Sebastian Balfour and Paul Preston (eds), *Spain and the Great Powers in the Twentieth Century*, pp. 32–53.

Ruiz Descamps, Nicolás. 'La prensa nacionalista en Vizcaya durante la Restauración: el espejo de una comunidad en construcción', *El argonauta español* (online), 5 (2008), https://journals.openedition.org/argonauta/970.

——. 'Juventud vasca de Bilbao durante la Restauración (1902–1923)', *Bidebarrieta*, 24 (2013), pp. 53–62.

——. *Historia de las organizaciones juveniles del nacionalismo vasco (1893–1923)* (Bizkaia: Universidad del País Vasco, 2018).

Said, Edward. *Orientalism* (London: Penguin, 2003).

Sallés, Anna and Enric Ucelay-Da Cal. 'L'analogia falsa. El nacionalisme basc davant de la República Catalana i la Generalitat provisional, abril-juliol del 1931', in Manuel González Portilla, Jordi Maluquer de Motes and Borja de Riquer (eds), *Industrialización y nacionalismo: análisis comparativo: Actas del I Coloquio-Vasco-Catalán de Historia* (Barcelona: Universidad Autónoma de Barcelona, 1985), pp. 443-70.

Saz, Ismael. 'Las herencias intelectuales de la pérdida del imperio americano', *Laboratorio di Storia*, 12 (2016), pp. 1-24.

Smith, Angel. 'Cataluña y la Gran Guerra: De la reforma democrática al conflicto social', *Hispania Nova*, 15 (2017), pp. 472-99.

Smith, Anthony D. *Myths and Memories of the Nation* (Oxford: Oxford University Press, 1999).

Soler Paricio, Pere. 'Ambrose Martin: Nacionalista irlandès. Del quarter d'Estat Català a la defensa del govern d'Euzkadi', *Butlletí de la Societat Catalana d'Estudis Històrics*, XXXII (2021), pp. 91-122.

Solozábal Echavarría, Juan José. *El primer nacionalismo vasco. Industrialismo y conciencia nacional* (Madrid: Tucar, 1975).

Tápiz, José María. 'El Partido Nacionalista Vasco ante la guerra de Abisinia (1935-1936)', *Journal of Inquiry and Research*, 79 (2004), pp. 95-110.

Teicher, Amir. *Social Mendelism: Genetics and the Politics of Race in Germany, 1900-1948* (Cambridge: Cambridge University Press, 2020).

Ucelay-Da Cal, Enric. 'Els enemics dels meus enemics. Les simpaties del nacionalisme català pels «moros»: 1900-1936', *L'Avenç*, 28 (1980), pp. 29-40.

——. 'Política de fuera, política casera: Una valoración de la relación entre nacionalistas catalanes y vascos. 1923-1936', in Manuel Tuñón de Lara (ed.), *Gernika: 50 años después (1937-1987): nacionalismo, república, guerra civil: VI Cursos de Verano en San Sebastián=VI. Udako Ikastaroak Donostian* (San Sebastián: Universidad del País Vasco, 1987), pp. 71-97.

——. 'Cuba y el despertar de los nacionalismos en la España peninsular', *Biblid*, 15 (1997), pp. 151-92.

——. 'La imagen internacional de España en el periodo de entreguerras: reminiscencias, estereotipos, dramatización neorromántica y sus consecuencias historiográficas', *Spagna contemporanea*, 15 (1999), pp. 23-52.

——. *El imperialismo catalán: Prat de la Riba, Cambó, d'Ors y la conquista moral de España* (Barcelona: Edhasa, 2003).

Ugalde Solano, Mercedes. *Mujeres y nacionalismo vasco: génesis y desarrollo de Emakume Abertzale Batza (1906-1936)* (Bilbao: Universidad del País Vasco, 1993).

——. 'Dinámica de género y nacionalismo. La movilización de vascas y catalanas en el primer tercio de siglo', *Ayer*, 17 (1995), pp. 121-53.

Ugalde Zubiri, Alexander. *La acción exterior del nacionalismo vasco, 1890-1939: historia, pensamiento y relaciones internacionales* (Bilbao: Instituto Vasco de Administración Pública, 1996).

——. 'El primer nacionalismo vasco ante la independencia de Cuba', in Alexander Ugalde Zubiri, Félix Julio Alfonso López, Cecilia Arrozarena and Joseba Agirreazkuenaga (eds), *Patria y Libertad: Los vascos y las guerras de independencia de Cuba (1868-1898)* (Tafalla: Txalaparta, 2012), pp. 187-285.

Ugalde Zubiri, Alexander and Enric Ucelay-Da Cal. 'Una alianza en potencia en un contexto más amplio: la mirada distante de los movimientos nacionalistas vasco y catalán (1910-1936)', in Enric Ucelay-Da Cal, Xosé Manoel Núñez Seixas, Arnau Gonzàlez i Vilalta (eds), *Patrias diversas ¿misma lucha? Alianzas transnacionalistas en el mundo de entreguerras (1912-1939)* (Barcelona: Edicions Bellaterra, 2020), pp. 387-415.

Valdaliso, Jesús Mª. 'Spanish Shipowners in the British Mirror: Patterns of Investment, Ownership and Finance in the Bilbao Shipping Industry, 1879-1913', *International Journal of Maritime History*, 5.2 (1993), pp. 1-30.

Velasco de Castro, Rocío. 'España y Marruecos: del desastre de Annual a la dictadura de Primo de Rivera (1921-1930). Introducción', *Hispania Nova. Revista de Historia Contemporánea*, 20 (2021), pp. 661-91.

Vilarós, Teresa M. and Michael Ugarte. 'Cuando África empieza en los Pirineos', *Journal of Spanish Cultural Studies*, 7.3 (2006), pp. 199-205.

Walker, Connor. *Ethnonationalism: The Quest for Understanding* (Princeton: Princeton University Press, 2018).

Watson, Cameron. *Modern Basque History: Eighteenth Century to the Present* (Reno: Center for Basque Studies, 2003).

——. *Basque Nationalism and Political Violence: The Ideological and Intellectual Origins of ETA* (Reno: Center for Basque Studies, 2007).

Wood, Tony. 'Indoamerica against Empire: Radical Transnational Politics in Mexico City, 1925-1929', in Erez Manela and Heather Streets-Salter, *The Anticolonial Transnational: Imaginaries, Mobilities, and Networks in the Struggle Against Empire* (Cambridge: Cambridge University Press, 2023), pp. 64-89.

Zabaltza, Xabier. *Augustin Chaho: Precursor incomprendido (1811-1858)* (Vitoria-Gasteiz: Servicio Central de Publicaciones del Gobierno Vasco, 2011).

Zulaika, Joseba. *Basque Violence: Metaphor and Sacrament* (Reno and Las Vegas: University of Nevada Press, 1988).

——. *Del cromañón al carnaval: los vascos como museo antropológico* (Donostia: Erein, 2000).

Newspapers, Journals, Periodicals

Aberri (1906-1908)
Aberri (1916-1923)
Aberri (daily, 1923)
Aberri New York (1925-1928)
Baserritarra (1897)
Bizkaitarra (1893-1895)
Bizkaitarra (1909-1913)
Bizkaitarra (1916-1919)
El Correo Vasco (1899)
Euskalduna (1896-1909)
Euzkadi (1901)
Euzkadi (daily, 1913-1937)
Jagi-Jagi (1932-1936)
La Patria (1901-1903)
Patria (1903-1906)
Patria Vasca (1928-1932)

Bibliography

Archives Consulted

Archivo del Nacionalismo Vasco, Bilbao

Biblioteca Foral de Bizkaia, Bilbao

Biblioteca Digital:
https://liburutegibiltegi.bizkaia.eus/handle/20.500.11938/2

Euskaltzaindia (Real Academia de la Lengua Vasca), Bilbao

Fundación Sancho el Sabio, Vitoria

Euskal Memoria Digitala:
https://www.euskalmemoriadigitala.eus/handle/10357/1

Koldo Mitxelena Kulturunea, Donostia

Sag150 (online archive containing Sabino Arana's works):
https://www.sabinoaranagoiri.eus/archivo.php

Uranzadi Digital, Hemeroteca de la Diáspora Vasca:
https://urazandidigital.euskaletxeak.eus/index.php#coleccion

Index

Abd el-Krim, Muhamed 115–17, 119–20, 130, 135, 150, 152–53, 158
Aberri (New York) 142, 150, 152, 152n70, 153–57, 177
Aberri (newsletter) 3, 12, 54, 66, 71, 80, 95, 97–98, 100, 105, 109–10, 114n53, 116, 117–18, 120, 121–23, 139, 158–59
Aberri (newspaper) 104, 105, 110–11, 112–13, 114n53, 114n54, 118–21, 123–24, 125–26, 128, 129–30, 132, 138, 147, 158–59
Abyssinian War, the 5, 13, 181, 183–86
Acció Catalana (Catalan Action) 125, 125–26, 150
Acción Nacionalista Vasca (Basque Nationalist Action) 168n6
Adams, Gerry 88
Adul Rabi Arab 122–23
Aguirre, José Antonio 166
Alfonso XIII, King 165
Algeciras Conference (1906) 58, 68n67
Álvarez, Izaskun 33n74
Álvarez-Junco, José 43–44
Arabarra 55
Arana y Goiri, Luis 19, 55, 76, 77, 79, 87, 100, 102
Arana y Goiri, Sabino 1–2, 2–3, 9–10, 42, 161, 167–68
Anglophilia 47
anticolonialism 10, 11, 16–17, 33–42, 50
anti-racist views 32–33
anti-Spanishness 20–22, 31–33, 37–42, 43–50, 50, 65
and benevolent colonialism 46–50

birth 17
Bizkaya por su independencia ('Biscay for its independence') 19–20, 20, 25
call for racial purity 27–28
Carlism 19
concept of independence 20
conversion to nationalism 19–20
Cuba 36–37, 47–49
death 10–11, 24, 51
discurso de Larrazabal (the Larrazábal vow) 20–21
family background 18–19
la evolución españolista (the pro-Spanish evolution) 23, 24, 53
life and work 17–24
and the Melilla War 34–36
Roosevelt telegram 46, 47–49
Salisbury telegram 46–47, 69–70
Aranzadi, Engracio de (alias Kizkitza) 85–87, 91
Arendt, Hannah 1
Aresti, Nerea 69
Arrigorriaga, Battle of 20
Azaña, Manuel 175
Aznar de la Sota, Eduardo 69–70n76
Aznar Zubigaray, Manuel (alias Gudalgai) 82

Balcells, Albert 81
Balfour, Sebastian 24–31, 43, 116
Barranco del Lobo, Disaster of the 59, 61
Baserritarra 22
Belfast 193
Berenguer, Dámaso 165

Bilbao 9, 17, 18, 23, 56, 103, 109, 178, 186, 191
Biscay 19, 20, 25–26
Bizkai Buru Batzar (Supreme Council of Biscay) 21–22
Bizkaitarra (The Biscayan) 21, 22, 54, 55, 60–64, 65–66, 72n87, 79, 87–88, 91–93, 93, 96–97, 99, 100, 114
Bizkaya por su independencia (Biscay for its independence) (Arana) 19–20, 25, 34–35
Black Legend, the 7, 29, 45, 154, 159
Blanco, John 36
Boer War, Second 46–47, 69–70, 73
Bolívar, Simón 161, 191
Broca, Paul 28
Bustinza, Evaristo (alias Kirikiño) 82

Cambó, Francesc 93–94, 95
Cardona, Daniel 139
Carlism 18–19, 21
Carlist Wars 17, 18, 25–26
Casanova, Julián 135
Casas, Fray Bartolomé de las 45
Casas, José Joaquín 160
Casement, Roger 91, 92, 99, 110, 144
Castells, Luis 53
Catalan nationalists 40n107, 124–32, 137, 143, 182
Catalonia 59–60, 63–64, 65, 136, 165
Chaho, Augustin 26
Colombia 160
Comité Pro-Independencia Vasca (Basque Pro-Independence Committee) 139, 150
Comunión Nacionalista Vasca (Basque Nationalist Communion) 75, 76, 77, 77–80, 82–87, 89–91, 93–94, 95, 97, 100, 103, 104, 107, 113, 114, 137–38, 167
III Conference of the Union des Nationalités (Union of the Nationalities) 78
Congress of European Nationalities 180
Connolly, James 90, 110, 172, 175
Connor, Walker 24–25
Conversi, Daniele 7n12, 15n1, 18, 24
Corcuera, Javier 31
Costa, Joaquín 136–37

Cuba 1–2, 3, 22, 23, 27, 33, 36–39, 43, 47–49, 50, 52, 69, 145, 174, 190
Cullen, Niall 71, 98, 143
Cumann na mBan 109
Curzon, Lord 87

Dalmau, Pau 5–6, 115–24, 132n124, 151n64
d'Annunzio, Gabriele 148
Diario Vasco 138
Douglass, William A. 7n12, 16, 30, 31–32

Egypt 108, 112n43, 129
Eibar 166
Ejército de Voluntarios Vascos (Basque Volunteer Army) 139
El Correo Vasco 48
Eleizalde, Luis de (alias Axe) 78, 79, 99, 113
Emakume Abertzale Batza (Association of Nationalist Women) 103–04, 109, 138
English, Richard 93n72
Estat Català (Catalan State) 125–26, 139, 140
Estat Català (newspaper) 129–30
Estella, autonomy statute of 168
Estévez, Xosé 127
ETA (Euskadi Ta Askatasuna) 1, 8–9, 158, 180
Etxebarria, Trifón (alias Etarte) 172, 173, 179
Euskalduna 54, 60, 63, 64–65, 67, 68n67, 69, 71, 72
Euskalerria (society) 20–21, 22
Euskeldun Batzokija 21, 22, 79, 100, 102
Euzkadi 55, 77, 79, 80, 82, 83–87, 89–91, 92, 94, 99, 137, 169, 185
Euzkadi Buru Batzar (National Executive Committee of the PNV) 95
Euzko Deya 91

Fanon, Frantz 32
Federación de Mendigoxales de Bizcaya (Biscayan Federation of Mendigoxales) 169
Fernández Soldevilla, Gaizka 25, 105, 139n18, 170, 187, 188, 189

Index

Ferrer i Guàrdia, Francesc 59
First World War 11, 74, 76, 77, 80–84, 93, 97
France 19n15, 33, 58, 59, 123, 153, 154–55, 185
Franco, Francisco 153, 158, 163
Francoism 9, 180
Fuerismo 21

Gabilondo, Joseba 28
GALEUZCA pact 182
Galicia 12, 37, 102, 115, 126–27, 128n106, 145n36, 182
Galician nationalists 124–32
Gallastegi, Eli (alias Gudari) 91, 102–03, 109, 113–14, 120–21, 125, 130, 131, 136, 138–39, 146, 160, 172n20, 178, 182
Gandhi, Mahatma 144, 177, 178, 188
Garton, Stephen 84
Gaztañaga, Francisco 145
Gestoras, autonomy statute of 168
Getxo 166
Gibraltar 37
Gil Andrés, Carlos 135
Gipuzkoa 17–18
Gizpuzkoarra 55
Gobineau, Arthur de 29
Goebel, Michael 140, 184
Gordejuela, Battle of 20
Granja, José Luis de la 17, 19, 20, 23, 30n62, 33, 79n10, 102n5, 126n100, 128n106
Great Britain 6, 11, 33, 44, 46–47, 58, 69–74, 83–84, 85–87, 88–93, 110, 111–13, 129, 184, 185–86, 195, 196

Hernández Villaescusa, Modesto 62–63
Hidalgo Costilla, Miguel 161
Hispanismo 45, 159–60
Hitler, Adolf 189
Hugo, Victor 40
Humboldt, Wilhelm von 28

Iarocci, Michael P. 29, 44
Iglesias Amorín, Alfonso 57, 115–24
independence struggles, Latin America 158–63

India 8, 60, 84, 85–87, 108, 129, 178, 181, 184n81
International African Friends of Ethiopia 184
International Colonial Exposition, Paris 181
International Committee for the Defence of the Ethiopian People 184
Ireland 8, 60, 98, 128–30, 145, 177–78, 193
   Easter Rising 6, 11, 73–74, 88, 88–93, 110, 196
   home rule 70–73, 76, 85
   nationalism 53, 70–71, 89, 109, 113
   partition 112
   revolutionary period 108–15
Irish Civil War 112, 112–13
Irish Republican Army 98, 109
Irish War for Independence 93, 98–99, 110, 112
Irmandade Nazonalista Galega (Galician Nationalist Brotherhood) 126
Irmandades da Fala (Language Brotherhoods) 125, 126
Italy 101
   Abyssinian War 183–86

Jagi-Jagi (Arise-Arise) 3, 8
   and Abyssinian War 183–86
   aims 167
   anti-capitalist doctrine 172–73
   anticolonial language, anticolonialism 13, 166–67, 174–75, 192
   approaches to race 13, 187–92, 192
   and Arana's ideology 171
   and civil disobedience 177–79, 192
   critique of colonial situation 172–76, 192
   critique of League of Nations 186
   foundation 169
   internationalisation 192
   internationalism 180–86
   and Ireland 177–78
   last issue 180
   references to violence 179, 192
   separation from PNV 169
Jáuregui, Gurutz 8–9

Juliá Díaz, Santos 44n125
Juventud Nacionalista de Bilbao (Bilbao's Nationalist Youth) 104
Juventud Vasca de Bilbao (JVB) (Basque Youth of Bilbao) 56–57, 79, 80, 91, 100, 102, 104, 138

La Gaceta del Norte 82, 89
La Liga de las Naciones Oprimidas 12, 143–49
La Patria 46–47
La Publicitat (The Advert) 125–26
La Renaixença (The Renaissance) 72
Lang, Stephanie 39
Larrañaga, Adolfo de 106
Larronde, Jean-Claude 16–17, 32, 36–37
League Against Imperialism 138–42, 149, 181, 183
League of Nations 5, 12–13, 99, 141, 143, 146, 146–49, 181, 194
  and Abyssinian War 183, 184
  appeals to 149–52
  Comité Pro-Independencia Vasca letter 150–51
  Jagi-Jagi critique of 186
  Madrid meeting 151–52
Lega di Fiume (League of Fiume) 148
Lerroux, Alejandro 81
Levinger, Matthew 25
Liga Antiimperialista de las Américas (Anti-Imperialist League of the Americas) 141
Lindner, Thomas 140, 141n25
Lliga Regionalista (Regionalist League) 93–94, 124, 125, 126
Lorenzo Espinosa, José María 91, 169–70, 178, 187, 189
Lytle, Paula Franklin 25

MacClancy, Jeremy 106
McCreanor, Kyle 98, 143
McGarry, Fearghal 88
Macià, Francesc 125, 139–40, 144, 145, 165–66
MacSwiney, Terence 110, 177, 178
Madariaga, María Rosa de 58n24, 116
Madrid 151–52, 157, 159, 177
Maeztu, Ramiro de 123

Makalani, Minkah 184
Manela, Erez 5, 94, 96, 101, 146
Martí, José 36, 39, 190
Martin, Ambrose Victor 109, 143–44, 182n72
Martin-Márquez, Susan 39–40, 52–53
Maura, Antonio 59
Mees, Ludger 19, 21n23, 51, 53–54, 55, 56, 77, 79, 103, 107
Melilla War 33, 34–36, 37
Mellows, Liam 111n42
Mexico 160–61, 162
Mexico City 140–41
Miguélez-Carballeira, Helena 125
Mina, Francisco Xavier 161
Morocco 3, 37–39, 40, 52, 57–65, 101, 107, 176
  Melilla War 33, 34–36, 37
  Primo de Rivera policy 135, 152–57
  the Rif War 115–24, 130–32, 135, 152–54, 158
Munain, Ángel de 152
Munguía, Battle of 20
Muro, Diego 15, 55
Mussolini, Benito 101, 183

Napartarra 55
Nazi Germany 66n58, 189
Nehru, Jawaharlal 184
New York 140–41, 158
Nicaragua 162
'98 Disaster, the 43–45, 59, 80, 135
Nosaltres Sols 182
Núñez Seixas, Xosé Manoel 4–5, 83, 89, 95, 109n29, 143, 148, 151n65, 160n98

Otaegui, Tomás 160
Otaegui Arizmendi, Margarita 128n106

Pablo, Santiago de 53–54, 77, 103, 107
Pacto de la Libre Alianza (Agreement of the Free Alliance) 139–40
Pacto de Moscú (Moscow Agreement) 140
Padmore, George 184
Paris 140–41, 143, 145, 158, 181
Paris Peace Conference, 1919 98, 101
Partido Nacionalista Vasco's (PNV) (Basque Nationalist Party) 9, 11, 22,

23, 51, 53–57, 68, 71–72, 75, 78, 79n10, 100, 167–70, 171, 180–81, 182, 185
Patria 52n5, 54, 66–68
Patria Vasca (Basque Homeland) 139, 142, 157n86, 158, 159, 160–62, 177n52
Pearse, Patrick 88, 90, 110, 191
Philippine-American War 50
Philippines, the 1–2, 3, 27, 33, 36–37, 43, 49, 50, 52, 145
Phillips, Carla Rahn 165
Phillips, William D. 165
PNV-*Aberri* 12, 80, 100, 102–32, 138, 167
Prashad, Vijay 146, 149
Primo de Rivera, Miguel 8, 9, 12–13, 127, 135–63, 165
Puerto Rico 43
Pulido, Alejandro 83

Quiroga, Alejandro 135, 137

Rast, M. C. 129
Redmond, John 72, 89–90, 90
Renobales, Eduardo 166
Retzius, Anders 28
Rif, the 5, 5–6, 8, 34–36
Rif War, the 12, 115–24, 130–32, 135, 152–54, 158
Rizal, José 36, 191
Romanones, Count of 81
Romero, Francisco 81
Roosevelt, Theodore 23, 46, 47, 48, 49, 159
Ruiz Descamps, Nicolás 56–57, 80, 91n62, 102
Russo-Japanese War 52n5

Said, Edward 39n102
Salisbury, Lord 44, 65, 69–70
Sandino, Augusto 162
Saz, Ismael 43
Second Spanish Republic 136, 165–66, 167, 167–71
Semana Trágica of 1909 57–58, 59–65

Sinn Féin 90, 98, 109
Solidaridad de Obreros Vascos (Basque Workers' Solidarity) 55
Solozábal Echavarría, Juan José 23n23
Sota, Manuel de la (alias Txanka) 178, 179, 187–88, 189
Sota y Llano, Ramón de la 22, 23
Soviet Union 140
Spain 2–3, 7, 11, 17, 22, 26–27, 28–31, 33–42, 43–50, 57–65, 74, 80–84, 97, 101, 115–24, 130–32, 135, 151, 152, 154–57, 174, 175–76, 187–92, 195–96
Spanish Civil War 170, 180, 184n81, 186, 196–97, 197
Spanish-American War 22, 23, 43, 48
Stresemann, Gustav 151–52

Tápiz, José María 137n10, 183
Triple Alliance, the 12, 102, 124–32, 143, 146
Turkey 41–42

Ucelay-Da Cal, Enric 127n106, 156n81
Ugalde Zubiri, Alexander 4–5, 32, 47, 48, 52, 83, 101, 104, 136, 152
Unió Catalanista (Catalanist Union) 126
United States of America 6, 22, 23, 43, 44, 46, 47–50, 147, 156, 162, 183
Uribe-Echevarría, Telesforo 144–46

Valera, Éamon de 110, 145, 182–83n72
Velasco de Castro, Rocío 153
Venezuela 197
Victoria, Queen 87

Watson, Cameron 26n49, 31, 33, 130, 157n91, 180
Wilson, Woodrow 6, 11, 12, 94–96, 99, 101, 111, 146
Wilsonian moment, the 5, 8, 74, 94–96, 149, 164, 194

Zabala, Ángel (alias Kondaño) 24, 54–55

www.ingramcontent.com/pod-product-compliance
Lightning Source LLC
Chambersburg PA
CBHW071408300426
44114CB00016B/2230